Excellence in University

Assessment in higher education is an area of intense current interest, not least due to its central role in student learning processes. *Excellence in University Assessment* is a pioneering text which contributes to the theory and practice of assessment through detailed discussion and analysis of award-winning teaching across multiple disciplines. It provides inspiration and strategies for higher education practitioners to improve their understanding and practice of assessment.

The book uses an innovative model of learning-oriented assessment to analyse the practice of university teachers who have been recipients of teaching awards for excellence. It critically scrutinises their methods in context in order to develop key insights into effective teaching, learning and assessment processes. Pivotal topics include:

- competing priorities in assessment and ways of tackling them;
- the nature of quality assessment task design;
- the student experience of assessment;
- promoting student engagement with feedback.

An indispensable contribution to assessment in higher education, *Excellence in University Assessment* is a valuable guide for university leaders, middle managers, staff developers, teachers and researchers interested in the crucial topic of assessment.

David Carless is Professor of Educational Assessment and Associate Dean (Learning and Teaching) in the Faculty of Education, University of Hong Kong.

Excellence in University Assessment

Learning from award-winning practice

David Carless

Routledge
Taylor & Francis Group

LONDON AND NEW YORK

First published 2015
by Routledge
2 Park Square, Milton Park, Abingdon, Oxon OX14 4RN

and by Routledge
711 Third Avenue, New York, NY 10017

Routledge is an imprint of the Taylor & Francis Group, an informa business

British Library Cataloguing in Publication Data
A catalogue record for this book is available from the British Library

Library of Congress Cataloging in Publication Data
Carless, David.
Excellence in university assessment : learning from award-winning
teaching / David Carless.
    pages cm
Includes bibliographical references and index.
1. College students—Rating of. 2. College teaching—Evaluation.
3. Education, Higher—Evaluation. 4. Educational tests and
measurements. 5. Communication in education. I. Title.
LB2366.C365 2015
378.1'98—dc23
                                                    2014043132

ISBN: 978-1-138-82454-6 (hbk)
ISBN: 978-1-138-82455-3 (pbk)
ISBN: 978-1-315-74062-1 (ebk)

Typeset in Galliard
by Keystroke, Station Road, Codsall, Wolverhampton

MIX
Paper from
responsible sources
FSC
www.fsc.org   FSC® C013056

Printed and bound in Great Britain by
TJ International Ltd, Padstow, Cornwall

To Amy, the love of my life

Contents

PART IV
Reconceptualising feedback and ways forward

Illustrations

Figures

Tables

Boxes

Acknowledgements

I would like to acknowledge the support of the Research Grants Council of Hong Kong for providing a grant (HKU 740812H) from their General Research Fund. My thanks go to the co-investigators, Bruce Macfarlane and Chris Deneen; the award-winning teachers (David Pomfret, Rick Glofcheski, Lung-Sang Chan, Ali Farhoomand and John Lin) who allowed us into their classrooms; and their students who engaged with us. Wang Xiang, Iris played a tremendous role in data collection and provided considerable insight in commenting on various versions of the manuscript.

I am indebted to Dave Boud who annotated a draft of the entire book. He will be pleased to know that his comments really acted as feedback. I would like to thank a number of associates who also commented on various draft chapters: Charles Anderson (Chapter 4); Rick Glofcheski (Chapter 5); Sue Bloxham, Gordon Joughin and Royce Sadler (Chapter 7); Susan Orr (Chapter 9); Margaret Price and Dai Hounsell (Chapter 10). Any remaining shortcomings are, of course, the responsibility of the author.

I would also like to thank my doctoral students who provided research support from their 'postgraduate hours'. Karri Lam acted as my personal assistant during the writing up of the book and made countless valuable contributions.

The Faculty of Education, University of Hong Kong, led by its dean, Steve Andrews, provides a stimulating environment to do research and writing. I would like to thank Bruce Macfarlane again for his collegiality and sage advice: HKU's loss is Southampton's gain.

Finally, many thanks to the Routledge team for their support of the project and their efficient work on the production side of the book.

Last but certainly not least, this work is dedicated to my wonderful wife Amy.

David Carless
Faculty of Education
University of Hong Kong

Part I

Learning and assessment

Introduction
Setting the scene

Assessment is a topic which is hotly debated in both academic circles and in the media. Does examination success equate with high standards? Are we assessing the right kinds of things? Is assessment fair and reliable? Does assessment help students to develop the skills they need for lifelong learning? Does assessment empower or ensnare students and how might they take greater responsibility for their own learning? What kinds of feedback process can effectively inform students about their progress and prompt ongoing improvement? What kinds of assessment task are most promising in supporting student learning? Is there too much time devoted to assessment and not enough to worthwhile non-assessed tasks? Is assessment a symptom of accountability undermining academic freedom? The list of questions could go on and on, such is the extent of issues that arise from assessment.

In this book, I do not intend to address all these issues in detail. Instead, I put forward a vision for assessment in universities in which the major priority is advancing student learning. After all, education should be about student learning and the development of how to learn effectively. So much time and effort are spent on assessment that it needs to be more efficient in enhancing processes and outcomes of learning. Assessment is sometimes seen as a malignant force or an unwanted chore which reinforces the need for us to harness it to promote powerful student learning. An obvious function of assessment is for grading and certification purposes and it is important that this reaches acceptable levels of reliability and fairness. The quest for accurate grades does not, however, overturn my belief that students are best served when they develop meaningful learning from the assessments they undertake.

How I came to be interested in assessment

I first started being responsible for teaching courses on assessment on teacher education programmes in the mid-1990s, partly because my more senior colleagues wished to avoid the topic as they perceived assessment as something painful and difficult. The chore of marking vast amounts of uninspiring student work loomed large in their minds. At around the turn of the century, more attractive aspects of assessment became high profile with the dissemination of work associated with the Assessment Reform Group in the UK and particularly the landmark literature review (Black and Wiliam, 1998) on the potential learning gains arising from well-conducted formative assessment. This work provided strategies for implementation and research evidence from different contexts across levels of education about how assessment could effectively support student learning. It presented a new research-based view of the learning potential of strategies, such as: clear learning intentions and success criteria; questioning and dialogue to engineer productive classroom discussion; peer assessment; self-evaluation; and the development of effective feedback processes. A key point, however, was that practical implementation was difficult. Under the influence of these ideas, I have carried out a variety of funded projects exploring the interplay between student learning and assessment in relation to schooling and higher education.

Working in the context of Hong Kong, where students are defined by summative assessment, impelled me to look at ways in which assessment could support learning even when school tests, examinations and results are dominant (Carless, 2011). In the current work, I explore the potential for learning-oriented assessment at the university level. At the tertiary level, there are some similar and some different considerations impacting on the interplay between assessment and student learning. For example, the greater maturity and competence of students may enable them to carry out richer and more complex assessment tasks. The less frequent contact between staff and students in universities as opposed to schools can reduce opportunities for regular feedback and negotiation of requirements. In both contexts, the dominance of summative assessment through examinations or other end-of-cycle tasks is a factor that captures the hearts and minds of students.

What this book is about

Many books discuss assessment. In recent years, most of them have been edited collections or otherwise developed collaboratively by groups of authors. Very few have been sole-authored, and few report research evidence across multiple disciplines. My aim is to fill this gap by developing a coherent and sustained vision of excellence in assessment and exemplifying it with classroom research evidence from diverse disciplines.

This book is about the relationship between assessment and student learning in undergraduate education, and how tensions between the two might be managed. I present the case for assessment being predominantly focused on the development of productive student learning processes. I call this 'learning-oriented assessment', which I define as assessment which places a primary focus on improving student learning, including summative assessment which stimulates appropriate student engagement. I propose a framework of learning-oriented assessment focusing on three interlocking elements: the kind of assessment tasks which students carry out; how students develop evaluative expertise through gaining a sense of what quality looks like in their discipline; and student engagement with feedback. The aim of the framework is to encapsulate the core elements of a learning-oriented assessment approach and indicate their interrelationships.

At the heart of the book is the interplay between learning-oriented assessment and classroom practice. Accordingly, space is afforded to in-depth discussion of specific assessment tasks, teachers' rationale for them and students' responses; how students react to criteria and make inferences about quality work; and the management of feedback process. The case studies of classroom practice are drawn from my recent research into the practices of teachers who have been recipients of teaching awards at the University of Hong Kong (HKU), a leading international English-medium research university. Their commitment to their students makes award-winning teachers a particularly worthwhile site for research. The analysis and dissemination of the pedagogy of quality teachers has the potential to inform the theory and practice of assessment and exemplify how assessment is implemented across diverse disciplines. A main strength of the book lies in this discussion of assessment in context.

The choice of award-winning teachers as the unit of analysis does not imply that the teacher is at the forefront at the expense of the learner. The student orientation and interpretation is crucial, so a major consideration is to explore students' views of the assessment tasks they were undertaking; how they engaged with quality in the discipline; and how they generated or responded to feedback. A detailed analysis of the important student voice on teaching, learning and assessment practices within specific disciplinary contexts is a feature of the book.

One of the problems in the theory and practice of assessment is the relative lack of coherent scholarship, by which I mean building cumulatively on strands of relevant theory and practice so as to address key issues. Accordingly, further features of the book are reviewing the relevant research base to provide a state-of-the-art treatment of key issues impacting on learning-oriented approaches to assessment; evaluating realistically where we are now; and pointing some ways ahead.

The main aims of the book are summarised as follows:

- to conceptualise and exemplify a framework of learning-oriented assessment through critically analysing the practices of award-winning teachers;
- to contribute to the theory of assessment by providing state-of-the-art litera-ture reviews and analyses of relevant learning-oriented assessment issues;
- to discuss implications for practice of a learning-oriented assessment approach by analysing the interface between assessment and learning contextualised within different disciplines;
- to enable the expression of the important student voice on assessment issues; and
- to present a vision of excellence in assessment.

In short, I seek to put assessment under the microscope, share some good practices from award-winning teachers and bring out some of the complexities of implementing a learning-oriented assessment perspective. Underpinning both the theory of learning-oriented assessment and its practices in classrooms is a quest for change and improvement in the practice of assessment. In the final chapter, I suggest some ways forward for assessment practices and make a number of recommendations on the path towards excellence in assessment.

Learning-oriented assessment

The idea of learning-oriented assessment is that all assessment should support the advancement of student learning. I call this approach learning-oriented assessment. From synthesising and reformulating key literature on assessment for learning in higher education, three interrelated elements are derived and articulated in Figure I.1. The role of the framework is to depict the integration of three key drivers of learning-oriented assessment. It is a simple and uncluttered framework, and hopefully a powerful one. The main argument developed in the book is that it is the interplay of these three elements which impacts significantly on the kind of learning which students derive from assessment processes. As such, these concepts and their implementation in diverse disciplines anchor the volume.

The framework was first developed with colleagues working at the Hong Kong Institute of Education, particularly Gordon Joughin (Carless, Joughin, Liu and associates, 2006; Carless, Joughin and Mok, 2006) and has been updated in the current work. I discuss the revised version of the framework below, drawing on a recent paper (Carless, 2014).

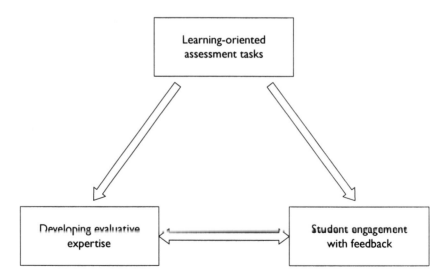

Figure I.1 Learning-oriented assessment framework

The apex of the framework is represented by the assessment tasks which students are carrying out as parts of the courses for their degree programmes. Assessment tasks strongly influence how students direct their effort and what kinds of approaches they favour. Learning-oriented assessment tasks are those which propel student engagement and approaches in productive directions (elaborated in Chapter 2). The two arrows which point from the top to the bottom of Figure I.1 are indicative that the design of the assessment task or tasks impinges on potential prospects for the development of evaluative expertise and engagement with feedback.

Learning-oriented assessment tasks are supported by the interconnected elements, illustrated in Figure I.1 by inverted arrows, of evaluative expertise and engagement with feedback. 'Evaluative expertise' denotes the evolving ability of students to engage with quality and develop their self-evaluative capacities. This is at the heart of student progress because, to improve their learning, students need to know what quality performance looks like.

Feedback processes, in which students engage with and use feedback, are strong drivers for student learning and improvement. Feedback, however, is a difficult issue to manage effectively for a number of reasons, which have been extensively discussed in the literature in recent years (e.g. Evans, 2013). Explicit in the framework is the interconnection between feedback and evaluative expertise. For students to engage effectively with feedback, they need to develop a sense of quality to facilitate the decoding of feedback messages.

Structure of the book

The main argument is that student learning is deeply influenced by the three elements of learning-oriented assessment: the assessment tasks which they undertake; their development of evaluative expertise; and their engagement with feedback processes. I seek to illustrate how these elements play out in different disciplinary contexts. In line with this focus, the book is structured as follows.

In Chapter 1, I discuss key issues which represent competing priorities for assessment and may act as challenges for learning-oriented assessment. Outcomes-based approaches are highlighted as a potential facilitating factor for a focus on student learning outputs.

In Chapter 2, I discuss the underpinnings of the framework for learning-oriented assessment; analyse relevant aspects of student approaches to learning; and discuss the role of student engagement. I explain the rationale for researching award-winning teachers and outline the conduct of the fieldwork for the research on which this book is based.

The main content of the volume follows from the learning-oriented assessment framework. The structure is built around three syntheses of literature (Chapters 3, 7 and 10), which are anchored thematically in relation to the three elements of learning-oriented assessment. The other chapters illustrate how the concepts are operationalised by teachers, and how students experience them (Chapters 4–6, 8–9 and 11).

In Chapter 3, I review and synthesise literature on assessment task design and implementation by analysing different kinds of assessment tasks and discussing their strengths and weaknesses. I set out a framework of assessment task design to promote student cognitive engagement.

Chapters 4, 5 and 6 follow from Chapter 3 in that they discuss examples of assessment task design and implementation contextualised in different disciplines. In Chapter 4, I discuss assignments in History which involve divergent personal responses from students and ways of thinking and practising in the discipline. In Chapter 5, I analyse a Law case, which involved traditional exams as well as a variety of learning-oriented assessment tasks. In Chapter 6, I explore the processes of a group project assignment in Geology; and from a Business case, I discuss group work, oral presentations and the assessment of participation.

Chapters 7, 8 and 9 focus on the development of student evaluative expertise through engagement with quality in the discipline. In Chapter 7, I synthesise the relevant literature to discuss how teachers make judgements about student work. I emphasise the importance of students developing connoisseurship and developing an understanding of quality; I recommend that dialogues around exemplars of student work are a potent means of enhancing student under-standing of criteria and standards; and I discuss some of the practical issues in using exemplars. Then, in Chapter 8, I discuss in the History and Geology cases how students came to understand criteria in relation to their assignments, as well as some of the challenges they experienced. In Chapter 9, I explore an Architecture case which powerfully exemplifies the coherence of learning-oriented assessment in relation to a portfolio assessment task; the development of evaluative expertise through critical reviews in which students publicly present design work to teachers and peers; and dialogic feedback on this work in progress.

Chapters 10 and 11 focus on how feedback processes can be effectively managed. In Chapter 10, I review and synthesise relevant literature; identify key challenges for effective feedback processes; and make the case for a new paradigm of dialogic approaches to feedback. In Chapter 11, I analyse examples of feedback practices from the five case studies and draw out implications.

Chapter 12 articulates some key messages for the three strands of learning-oriented assessment. I explore further competing priorities in assessment and discuss some implications for the management of assessment innovation. I also suggest some areas for further research and summarise a vision of excellence in assessment.

The book aims to be soundly based in research; and, like all good research, carry significant implications for practice. The main implications for practice are summarised at the conclusion of each chapter.

Chapter 1

Competing priorities in assessment

> Assessment is the senior partner in learning and teaching. Get it wrong and the rest collapses.
>
> (Biggs and Tang, 2011, p. 221)

Scope of chapter

In this chapter, I discuss some of the challenges in developing assessment practice and some of the issues with which stakeholders have to grapple in moving assessment forward. A repercussion of the multitude of issues is that assessment faces competing priorities and inevitably involves a certain amount of compromise. Notwithstanding this pragmatic need for compromise, I propose that enhancing student learning should be a primary aim of all assessment. I refer to this orientation as learning-oriented assessment, which is the perspective anchoring the volume. Then I move on to discuss other issues which impact on the assessment landscape and act as facilitating or inhibiting factors for the development of learning-oriented assessment.

The centrality of assessment and the hidden curriculum

Assessment is a critical aspect of undergraduate education because it has a range of powerful impacts on what students and teachers do. A rationale for a focus on assessment and improving assessment is its huge impact on the quality of student learning (Boud and associates, 2010). Assessment tells students what is valued and what they need to achieve to be successful in their studies; it captures their attention and study time, and may act as a spur; its results inform them of their progress, which in turn impacts on how they view themselves as individuals; and, following from these results, it may provide satisfaction or discouragement. Assessment is a major factor in the exclusion and attrition of students, so the cost of unsophisticated practice can be high (Broughan and Jewell, 2012).

Assessment is something that all teachers are involved in because they are required to set assessments and provide grades. It is not like many pedagogic approaches an optional activity but something which is a fundamental aspect of teachers' working lives. This centrality means that assessment is vitally important, but this has a downside: assessment becomes encompassing and there are risks that it may be prioritised more than the learning which should be associated with it. For teachers, assessment can help them understand students' learning progress and it often provides some indication of how successful (or not) their teaching has been. Teachers' assessment practice also comes under scrutiny from internal and external quality assurance or audit bodies, including external examiners. This scrutiny may take up staff time and provoke some nervousness or defensiveness amongst teachers; and inhibit innovative approaches which could be seen as risky.

The centrality of assessment is well recognised in the literature. A possible repercussion of the centrality and ubiquity of assessment is that it dominates teaching and learning in ways that may not be conducive to a good university education, however defined. Learning-oriented assessment represents a possible way forward by focusing all assessment processes on the advancement of student learning. It seeks to take advantage of the observation that assessment is a factor that teachers are able to modify with the highest likelihood of changing student learning (Elton and Laurillard, 1979; Kandlbinder, 2013).

A particular focus of this book is how assessment impacts on the processes of students' learning behaviours. The centrality of assessment in the lives of students is not just a contemporary phenomenon; it was well articulated in studies appearing during the late 1960s and early 1970s, which were influential in showing how assessment impacts on the student university experience. In *The Hidden Curriculum*, Snyder (1971) analysed the experiences of students at a competitive university, MIT (Massachusetts Institute of Technology) in Boston. The hidden curriculum involves academic and socialisation routines which students learn from participation in the institutional community but which are not explicitly stated in the formal curriculum documentation. As Snyder argued, the importance of assessment results and the strategies for obtaining required grades overshadowed some of the higher-order skills expressed as aims of programmes. Students construct their own versions of the hidden curriculum from their perceptions and experiences of assessment, so the outcomes of assessment as lived by students are often unpredictable (Sambell and McDowell, 1998).

The power of grades to influence student behaviours was also a major theme of two other seminal studies of that era: *Making the Grade* (Becker, Geer and Hughes, 1968) and *Up to the Mark* (Miller and Parlett, 1974). I have more to say about these two studies in Chapter 2; suffice it to say here that, from the student perspective, assessment defines the curriculum (Ramsden, 1992). An implication which is at the heart of this book is that well-designed assessment can steer engagement with the curriculum and stimulate student learning in productive directions.

Purposes and tensions in assessment: summative and formative assessment

A fundamental challenge for learning-oriented assessment is that assessment is about several things at once (Ramsden, 2003), which brings tensions and compromises to the fore. As Knight and Yorke (2003, p. 73) put it: 'assessment techniques are often chosen as the least bad way of resolving a number of competing contingencies'. I use this notion of competing contingencies – or competing priorities – to frame this chapter. If assessment was only about supporting student learning or only about grading student performance, it would be much easier to handle effectively. Obviously, the more purposes or functions a single technology needs to meet, the less it can be focused productively on each of these functions. Accordingly, there is a need for balance in assessment: good assessment involves the art of compromise (Carless, 2011).

Purposes of assessment

Although much has been written about the purposes of assessment (Newton, 2007; Yorke, 2008), I believe these can be boiled down to three main functions:

1   to support student learning;
2   to judge the quality of student achievement; and
3   to satisfy the needs or demands of accountability.

Learning-oriented assessment is firmly focused on the first of these but has to account for the other two, as they sometimes act in ways which can be barriers to the learning-oriented assessment perspective.

In a more elaborate treatment of the functions of assessment in higher education, Gibbs (1999) suggests six main functions, with the first four relating to 'supporting student learning', and the fifth and sixth similar to the second and third above. The six main functions of assessment in higher education, according to Gibbs, are:

1   capturing student time and attention;
2   generating appropriate student learning activity;
3   providing timely feedback;
4   helping students internalise standards and quality in the discipline;
5   generating marks or grades; and
6   providing evidence for others (e.g. external examiners) to enable them to judge standards on the course.

Gibbs' formulation captures a number of issues that are relevant to learning-oriented assessment: the role of assessment in capturing student time and effort; the role of assessment tasks in generating appropriate student learning activity;

the issue of timeliness in effective feedback; and the need to support students to understand quality in the discipline. These are explored further in various parts of the book.

Double duty

In his classic paper, Boud (2000) refers to the multiple functions of assessment as 'double duty'. Assessments need to encompass assessment for learning and assessment for certification; they focus on the immediate task and preparing students for lifelong learning; and they have to attend to learning processes and substantive disciplinary content. Hounsell, Xu and Tai (2007, p. 1) sum up neatly aspects of double duty, noting that assessment needs to be 'rigorous but not exclusive, to be authentic yet reliable, to be exacting while also being fair and equitable, to adhere to long-established standards but to reflect and adapt to contemporary needs'.

Recommending shifts in assessment practice are particularly hampered by this realisation that assessments do double duty. The complexity of assessment and its multiple demands make its reform difficult to achieve, but essential to educational progress.

A repercussion of the multiple purposes of assessment is that teachers tend to place emphasis on one more than another based on various factors, such as their own conceptions of teaching, learning and assessment; their own experiences of assessing or being assessed; and the educational context in which they work, including the requirements or conventions of the faculty or institution in which they operate. Institutional and teacher views of assessment impact on such issues as the design of assignments for their course; the kinds of rubrics they provide; and the nature of guidance and feedback. Those instructors with more sophisticated assessment thinking are those who can implement assessment flexibly and for different purposes (Offerdahl and Tomanek, 2011). An implication is that the development of teacher assessment literacy is likely to be a facilitating factor in tackling the dilemmas implicit in double duty.

Summative and formative assessment

One of the most fundamental and vexing double duties of assessment is the need to fulfil summative and formative functions. In essence, summative assessment involves the summing up of achievement at a particular point in time, whereas formative assessment is to do with the formation of student dispositions and actions to enhance ongoing learning. Poorly designed summative assessment may inhibit student learning, whereas the circumstances under which summative assessment tasks carry most potential to promote learning are a central focus of Chapter 3.

There is considerable complexity in the relationship between summative and formative assessment. Many assignments carry potential for both functions when they provide a grade for certification and comments which may be used for ongoing improvement. Summative assessment sometimes, however, risks discouraging students from raising queries, lest the teacher and marker may judge their admission of weakness harshly; instead, students may present themselves as if they understand more than they do – 'faking good', as Gibbs (2006) puts it – in the hope of maximising their grades. Conversely, a formative process in which students received a lot of feedback and support from teachers and peers, and revised their work over time, may be considered less robust as an indicator of individual summative achievement. It begs the question of the extent to which the students could have produced the same performance unaided.

Learning-oriented assessment seeks to circumvent some of the problems in the interplay between summative and formative assessment by focusing both on stimulating productive student learning. Summative assessment can be learning-oriented when, for example, it encourages deep rather than surface approaches to learning and when it promotes a high level of cognitive engagement consistently over the duration of a course. Summative assessment is likely to be learning-oriented when it focuses not merely on reproducing previous knowledge but identifying and engaging with real-life problems in the discipline. The processes of working towards well-designed summative assessment can also afford opportunities for formative assessment strategies, such as peer feedback, student self-evaluation and interactive teacher feedback (Carless, 2014).

Quality assurance and assessment

Quality assurance generally focuses on the outcomes of summative assessment. Often there is emphasis on distributions of grades, reliability of grades and the resolution of plagiarism cases or other instances of student malpractice. Written statements for quality assurance purposes in programme documents send a message to staff that what matter in assessment are summative tasks which count towards degree classifications (Jessop, McNab and Gubby, 2012). These authors bemoan the threat to formative assessment which is implicit in emphasis on summative assessment, reinforcing the challenges of double duty discussed above. The value of formative assessment is often undermined by its invisibility in QA processes (Jessop, El Hakim and Gibbs, 2014).

Reports published by the Quality Assurance Agency for Higher Education in England (QAA) 'typically make more recommendations linked to assessment than to any other area' (QAA, 2009, p. 3): for example, they recommend developmental activities aimed at improving the robustness and consistency of assessment and classification practices within and across institutions. This is consistent with a focus on measuring student achievement accurately as central to the quality assurance aspects of assessment. When they focus mainly on measuring, some forms of quality assurance can come to inhibit the development of assessment practices which promote productive student learning. Quality assurance and associated accountability also often imply a lack of trust in academic staff.

There are also political dimensions to quality assurance. Based partly on neo-liberal ideologies is the need to monitor value for money or added value and the roles of assessment and quality assurance as gate-keepers of standards. The notion of standards is often a political issue which emanates from aspects of assessment as an ideological tool. Decisions about apparently technical matters are often influenced by political and ideological considerations (Gipps, 1999). These political undercurrents and the unpopularity of some forms of quality assurance often seem to contribute to making assessment a relatively unpopular topic for many university teachers.

A current explicit focus of quality assurance on student learning outcomes carries positive implications for learning-oriented assessment and I turn to outcomes-based approaches next.

Learning outcomes and their assessment

Outcomes-based approaches to learning and assessment have garnered quite a lot of attention over the last twenty years or so, in relation to both schooling and higher education. In recent years, learning outcomes have been a key aspect of the Bologna process in developing equivalence in the standards and quality of European qualifications (Sin, 2013) and their globalised reach is evidenced by the OECD agenda of Assessing Higher Education Learning Outcomes. A focus on learning outcomes is predicated on a shift from educational inputs to outputs in the form of direct or indirect evidence of student achievement as a measure of quality university education. Assessment is central in that the products of assessment tasks are a major means of identifying what students have learnt and achieved.

Emphases on learning outcomes are important components of evaluations of the quality of teaching and of programmes, and they assist in evaluating the effectiveness of teaching. In this sense, outcomes-based approaches carry appeal for governments or quality assurance agencies that want evidence that the expenditure in higher education is leading to the kind of workforce which can fuel economic growth. Learning outcomes can be used as a framework to evaluate the effectiveness of higher education by examining what students have learnt by the time they graduate. This represents a tension: there is a risk of learning outcomes mutating from a useful educational tool to a bureaucratic burden (Hussey and Smith, 2008).

Outcomes-based approaches to student learning often focus on different levels. The first is at the module level and its relationship with programme-level outcomes, addressing how a specific module contributes to the wider aims of a programme (see, for example, Hughes (2013), who shows the integration of outcomes at task, module and programme levels). A second level relates to the wider outcomes which university education seeks to develop: the graduate attributes or the kind of generic dispositions which students should develop through their studies going beyond disciplinary knowledge. A challenge for the development of these kinds of graduate attributes is the wide variation in academics' understandings and commitments (Barrie, 2006). Another issue relates to emergent or unintended outcomes (e.g. Hussey and Smith, 2003) in that the most powerful kinds of learning outcomes are often those which go beyond what was originally anticipated. Higher education assessment and its outcomes need to prepare students to cope with the unknown as reflexive lifelong learners (Boud, 2014).

Outcomes-based approaches align well with the three components of learning-oriented assessment. Productive intended and emergent learning outcomes can be encouraged through complex, open-ended tasks which involve students in using a range of skills in developing relevant learning processes and products. The articulation of clear learning outcomes has the potential to support students in understanding what they are trying to achieve and the nature of good performance. The richness of the assessment tasks highlights the need for effective feedback processes which support students in developing complex learning. At their best, outcomes-based approaches are focused on enhancing the quality of student learning and are congruent with learning-oriented assessment.

Previewing learning-oriented assessment

In this section, I preview the three interlocking components of my model of learning-oriented assessment: task design; using quality criteria to develop student evaluative expertise; and student engagement with feedback. The first element of this model is mainly controlled by the teacher in terms of their selection and positioning of assessment tasks; the second and third are facilitated by interaction between teachers and students. Managing assessment is a complex issue which needs an integrated and contextualised approach (Price, Carroll, O'Donovan and Rust, 2011). There is often a failure to see assessment holistically, and one of the contributions of the learning-oriented assessment is to view it in a coherent, soundly conceptualised way.

Assessment task design

Following from the earlier discussion of how assessment defines the curriculum and drives students' learning behaviours, the assessment tasks which students undertake are a key learning issue. Assessment task design is critical because it is one of the most important drivers of how students arrange their study time. Assessment tasks and their implementation form the apex of the model of learning-oriented assessment and are the focus of Chapter 3. Here, I raise a few introductory questions and issues to be explored in more detail later in the volume:

- What kinds of assessment should teachers provide for their students?
- What are the key principles and practices in task design?
- What forms of assessment are most effective at stimulating student cognitive engagement?

- Should teachers use tried and tested methods, such as examinations and essays, or are there more meaningful alternative ways of assessing students?
- To what extent can mobile technologies and technology-facilitated interaction support engaging assessment task design?
- To what extent should assessments be related to real-life applications of the discipline (what is sometimes referred to as 'authentic assessment')?
- Should tasks be mainly individual to facilitate the award of a fair grade or is there a case for a judicious use of group assignments which can evaluate generic skills, such as teamwork?
- What kinds of task design manage the challenge of double duty well?

Another set of issues relate to the number and timing of assignments. Neither a one-off end-of-module examination or essay, nor the setting of too many small, atomised tasks is ideal. The former may lead to concentration of student work at the end of the module and may not create sufficient opportunities for dialogue and feedback, whilst the latter may lead to fragmented learning and assessment overload. Examples of coherent sequences of assessment tasks are analysed in Chapters 4 and 5.

Developing student evaluative expertise

A further set of key issues relates to the potential of assessment criteria as a means to support student engagement with quality in the discipline and the development of evaluative expertise. Assessment criteria or rubrics can be useful in clarifying intended learning outcomes, stating clearly what teachers are looking for, and as such they bring some transparency to assessment processes. Merely disseminating lists of criteria is, however, generally limited in supporting student understanding of quality and standards. When student engagement with criteria is facilitated through activities such as peer review, self-evaluation and the analysis of samples of students' work, there is potential for positive impacts on their learning. This is particularly the case when students are able to develop a sense of what quality looks like in their particular discipline because, without this sense of quality, it is difficult for students to make progress or understand the feedback they receive. This topic is treated in detail in Chapter 7, with some preliminary questions raised here:

- How are terms such as 'criteria', 'standards' and 'rubrics' defined and how are understandings of them developed?
- What are the main strategies to prompt students to engage with criteria and how can they be supported to develop a notion of quality in the discipline?
- To what extent is it desirable for students to contribute their own ideas to the development of assessment criteria?
- To what extent can technology and learning management systems (LMSs) be utilised to enhance student engagement with criteria and quality?

- What are the key issues in using exemplars of student work in supporting students to understand criteria and the nature of quality work in the discipline?

Criteria also play a key role in informing teachers' judgements about the quality of student work through the marking process. Accordingly, another set of questions relates to the use of criteria in relation to marking:

- What form should a marking scheme take and how detailed should it be?
- What are the advantages and disadvantages of holistic marking schemes as opposed to analytic ones?
- To what extent are teachers' judgements of student work based on hidden criteria, such as prior experience or knowledge of the student?

Examples of how the teachers in the study tried to support students in understanding criteria and the nature of quality in the discipline are discussed in Chapters 8 and 9.

The feedback conundrum

The development of effective feedback processes is a topic that is on the agendas of many stakeholders in higher education in view of institutional surveys in various jurisdictions which indicate that students find the effectiveness of feedback one of the least satisfactory aspects of their university experience. Feedback is at the same time an important driver of student improvement and something which is difficult to carry out effectively. Students often have negative perceptions of the feedback they receive from their teachers in terms of its quantity, usefulness, timeliness and/or comprehensibility, and most crucially find it hard to act on the feedback that they do receive. Academics face a feedback conundrum: how to develop effective feedback processes within the constraints of time and resources. The theory and practice of feedback are covered in detail in Chapter 10, with some key issues and questions previewed here:

- What are the main facilitating and inhibiting factors for effective feedback processes?
- Under what circumstances is feedback most useful for students?
- What are the advantages and disadvantages of different modes of feedback, and how might technology be utilised to enhance feedback processes?
- How can student involvement in feedback through peer feedback or self-evaluation be promoted and implemented?
- How can the challenge of timing of feedback be managed?
- To what extent is it feasible to re-engineer feedback so that it can become more dialogic?

- Most critically of all, how can teachers promote student uptake of feedback?

Examples of the feedback and marking practices of award-winning teachers are discussed in Chapter 11.

Key issues in assessment

Now I discuss other issues that the literature suggests are key challenges for effective assessment. These need to be discussed and possibly confronted before a case for learning-oriented assessment can convincingly be made. They influence, to a greater or lesser extent, some of the assessment decisions teachers make and related student responses. I introduce them here, then, in the final chapter, return to them in the light of the case studies and make some suggestions about how competing priorities can be resolved.

Fairness

A key principle in assessment is that it should be fair, but this notion can be interpreted in different ways. From a conventional psychometric perspective, fairness could mean that all candidates are treated exactly the same way so that they have equal opportunities to demonstrate their ability. This conception of fairness also relates to the grading of work, so that students receive reasonable grades which reflect their performance and not other extraneous factors. More contemporary perspectives emphasise that a fair assessment involves providing all students with an opportunity to show their best performance. In such a view, students with impairments would be justified in receiving different treatment (Stowell, 2004).

Students' perceptions of fairness of assessment are paramount. From a student point of view, fairness denotes assessment which: provides a valid appraisal of meaningful and worthwhile learning; relates to authentic tasks; represents reasonable demands; rewards effort, breadth and depth in learning; involves clear expectations and criteria; and includes feedback on progress (Sambell, McDowell and Brown, 1997).

The most in-depth recent account of fairness is Flint and Johnson's (2011) analysis of student concerns about the fairness of assessment in an Australian university. A key factor impinging on students' perceptions of fair assessment was the opportunity to demonstrate what they could do. The analysis also carries implications for the three elements of learning-oriented assessment. First, in relation to task design, Flint and Johnson found that examinations and group work are viewed by students as the most problematic and potentially unfair forms of assessment tasks. Students tended to feel that exams were unfair because they were not a good indicator of capability; and they mainly viewed group work as being at odds with the competitive and individualistic way in which they were held accountable. Second, students felt frustrated when they did not understand teachers' expectations or what criteria and standards would be used to judge the quality of their work. Fairness was also interpreted in terms of consistency of teachers' application of criteria: for example, the extent to which recommended word guidelines for assignments were adhered to; consistency in the granting of extensions; and all students being graded on the set criteria rather than any personal impressions they may have made. Third, when students receive little or no feedback on a task, they invariably think that it is unfair, even if they obtain a good grade. As students have made an effort to produce an assignment, they expect that effort to be reciprocated by the marker. Without comments about *why* a grade has been awarded, students are likely to query its fairness (Flint and Johnson, 2011).

Openness in assessment is a major means of enhancing perceptions of fairness in assessment. It involves dialogue with students in supporting them to understand various issues, including the rationale for assessment tasks; unpacking the criteria on which they will be assessed and how academic judgements are made; and clarifying the multiple purposes of feedback and how these can support their development of appropriate learning outcomes.

Cheating and plagiarism

Park (2003) concludes that cheating and plagiarism are already common (and becoming more so) and that students often rationalise their cheating behaviour and downplay the gravity of plagiarism by themselves and their peers. A study of a thousand scripts from a university in New Zealand found that around 25 per cent of assignments involved plagiarism and around 10 per cent of these were classified as severe cases (Walker, 2010). Concerns about plagiarism have led to widespread use of software, such as Turnitin, to help students to self-monitor and staff to identify plagiarism, although Youmans (2011) found that the type of assessment task was a more significant factor affecting the likelihood of plagiarism than the presence of plagiarism-detection software.

A fundamental issue is why students cheat. Students state that one of their reasons for cheating is alienation from the assessment system, and they perceive cheating as excusable when units are of marginal importance, taught badly, or assessed in a way that invites cheating, such as un-engaging task design requiring merely the reiteration of well-established concepts rather than original thought (Ashworth, Bannister and Thorne, 1997).

It is common for there to be different perceptions between staff and students as to what constitutes cheating or the gravity of a particular act. A repercussion is that teachers are on the front line of attempts to curb or overlook plagiarism, with the result that there is considerable inconsistency in approaches (Glendinning, 2014). Student awareness of plagiarism seems to have developed in response to widespread institutional campaigns, and recent research at an Australian university found that students showed a high degree of accuracy in identifying behaviours associated with plagiarism (Gullifer and Tyson, 2014).

It seems likely that student malpractice is more common in large classes (cheating thrives on anonymity) and when there are generic assessments which change little from year to year. The classroom atmosphere and teacher example can play important roles in reducing student malpractice, for example when a positive stance of intellectual curiosity, honesty and academic integrity is adopted (Glendinning, 2014). The kind of engaging assessment tasks illustrated in Chapters 4 and 5 are likely to act in ways which discourage cheating or plagiarism. Assessment task design to discourage plagiarism can involve students working towards divergent rather than convergent goals, through the use of individualised negotiated assignments, or assignments which draw on personal experience and require evidence of it (McDowell and Brown, 2001). Post-assignment mini-vivas (e.g. Carless, 2002) can also be conducted to verify that work undertaken is the student's own. These could all be sites for productive feedback conversations.

Assessment across disciplines

A feature of this book is exploring assessment practices in various disciplines. A factor influencing the prospects for learning-oriented assessment is the impact of the discipline on teachers' practices. There are, for example, disciplinary modes of teaching which are inextricably linked with preparing individuals for a particular profession: what Shulman (2005) terms 'signature pedagogies'.

Characterising disciplines in broad terms can be a useful way of charting issues and differences, and below I provide a summary of the main epistemological features of disciplinary categories, drawing on Biglan (1973), Becher (1989) and Neumann, Parry and Becher (2002). Although, obviously, there are risks of oversimplification in typologies of this kind, they can provide a starting point for more fine-grained discussion of disciplinary similarities and differences.

- Hard pure knowledge (e.g. Physics, Mathematics, Geology) is generally atomistic, concerned with universals and has a quantitative emphasis.
- Hard applied knowledge (e.g. Engineering, Medicine) involves application of theoretical ideas in professional contexts and is often geared towards products and techniques.
- Soft pure disciplines (e.g. History, Sociology) are mainly holistic, concerned with particulars and have a qualitative basis.
- Soft applied disciplines (e.g. Architecture, Business, Education, Law) aim to develop protocols and procedures and are often concerned with enhancement of professional practice.

Sometimes assessment practices in various disciplines can have historical or cultural antecedents and may not be easily justifiable to a critical outside observer. There seems to be some consensus that assessment practice in the soft disciplines is more developed or less unsophisticated than in the hard disciplines. The obstinacy of norm-referenced influences on grading in hard pure disciplines, for example, may be accounted for by the somewhat conservative and unsophisticated approach to assessment in these fields (Neumann, Parry and Becher, 2002). A more recent study also found evidence of greater desirable assessment practice from the soft rather than the hard disciplines and among those who were more experienced and female (Norton, Norton and Shannon, 2013).

Teachers' conceptions of assessment

How teachers conceive of assessment, its purposes and roles impacts on the kinds of assessment practices they carry out with their students. A potential barrier to the implementation of learning-oriented assessment would be if, or when, its ethos is not in tune with those of staff. University teachers' conceptions of assessment and the impact of those conceptions on students become important issues.

A key early study of teachers' conceptions of assessment (Samuelowicz and Bain, 2002) researched twenty Australian academics from five different disciplines (Architecture, Chemistry, Nursing, Physiology and Physiotherapy). Assessment orientations ranged on a continuum of six sets of beliefs, from 'reproducing bits of knowledge' (particularly evident in the four Chemistry teachers in the study) to 'transforming conceptions of the discipline or world' (amongst three Architecture teachers). A phenomenographic study of the views of Hong Kong and Swedish lecturers (Watkins, Dahlin and Ekholm, 2005) revealed three main conceptions of assessment. The first viewed assessment as largely separated from teaching and functioning as a measuring device to gauge final learning from a course; the second focused on assessment of basic knowledge before more sophisticated learning could evolve; and the third saw assessment as an integral part of the learning process with students focused on understanding, reflecting, interpreting, analysing and relating.

Whereas the two studies cited in the previous paragraph had a relatively small number of participants from different disciplines, Postareff et al. (2012) focused solely on teachers of Pharmacy, a centre for excellence in teaching at the University of Helsinki. These authors describe assessment practices as being generally conventional; the majority of informants had difficulty adequately describing the main purposes of assessment; and assessment was mainly reproductive in nature. Their results suggest that assessment practices lag behind teaching practices in this particular department.

The general picture emerging from this brief review of a small number of relevant studies is that university teachers' conceptions of assessment remain relatively unsophisticated. This has implications for assessment literacy, to which I turn next.

Assessment literacy

A key to improving the theory and practice of assessment is the development of assessment literacy, which needs to be strengthened for both teachers and students, albeit in different ways and at different levels. With respect to teachers, I view assessment literacy as representing understanding of the principles and practice of effective assessment. In other words, the assessment-literate teacher possesses knowledge about assessment and the ability to implement it effectively in practice. The available evidence reinforces the findings of Postareff et al. (2012) above and suggests modest assessment literacy amongst teachers. James (2003), for example, asserts that assessment is probably one of the least sophisticated aspects of university teaching, and that there is an overemphasis on the sorting and certification role of assessment. A barrier to the development of assessment literacy is that many universities, particularly research-intensive institutions, prioritise research over teaching, and this clearly has implications for the amount of time teachers might devote to developing pedagogy or assessment (Norton et al., 2013).

Students' conceptions of assessment are described as 'primitive' (Maclellan, 2001), in that they understand it mainly in terms of grades and do not attempt to exploit it to improve their learning, largely because of the confusing teacher portrayal of its purposes and practices. Smith et al. (2013) suggest that students need to understand the purposes of assessment, be aware of assessment processes and practise judging their own responses to assessment tasks. Accordingly, they define student assessment literacy as: 'students' understandings of the rules surrounding assessment in their course context, their use of assessment tasks to monitor or further their learning, and their ability to work with the guidelines on standards in their context to produce work of a predictable standard' (Smith et al., 2013, p. 45).

In their substantial, book-length treatment of assessment literacy, Price et al. (2012) suggest that student assessment literacy encompasses: an appreciation of the relationship between assessment and learning; a conceptual understanding of assessment; understanding of the nature and meaning of assessment criteria and standards; skills in self- and peer assessment; familiarity with assessment techniques; and the ability to select and apply appropriate approaches to assessment tasks. One might add to this list an understanding of attribution and plagiarism.

Successful implementation of learning-oriented assessment requires teachers to possess a certain amount of assessment literacy and to develop this amongst their students. I have more to say about assessment literacy and how it might be developed amongst teachers and students in the concluding chapter.

Managing assessment innovation

An aim of the book is to discuss prospects for widespread implementation of learning-oriented assessment and consider some issues in relation to the management of assessment innovation. I consider here some drivers and barriers in relation to assessment change, introduce such issues as trust and risk, and consider potential sites for assessment change.

Drivers and barriers

Hounsell et al. (2007) discuss three catalysts for assessment innovation: remoulding assessment practices to reflect contemporary mass higher education with its large and diverse cohorts of students and attendant pressures on resources; building on widespread interest in exploiting developments in information technology; and a heightened emphasis on developing transferable skills in the form of graduate attributes. This third element also relates to the driver emanating from outcomes-based approaches, with their focus on the learning outputs of assessment.

Drivers at the student level include the goal of enhancing the student experience through strategies, such as democratising assessment, empowering learners and the socialisation of students into their discipline (Falchikov and Thomson, 2008). Sometimes students respond enthusiastically to alternative forms of assessment; at other times they are more wary, particularly if they are unsure of the rationale for a new approach or if they feel it makes achieving a satisfactory grade more difficult. Dialogue with students about an assessment innovation and its potential benefits to them is particularly important.

Obstacles to institutional assessment change include: major disciplinary differences in teaching; isolation of academics from the educational research literature; generally ineffective dissemination, especially across departmental or faculty boundaries; and weak linkages between local innovations and overall strategy developments (Nicol and Draper, 2009). The complexity of universities as organisations with their own histories, sub-cultures, institutional norms and practices is a challenge for any single, isolated attempt to initiate change (Roxa, Martensson and Alveteg, 2011). Few universities have organisational structures in place that enable them to learn from and build on successes in locally developed projects (Nicol and Draper, 2009). A preponderance of small-scale, unsustainable work by enthusiastic innovators may fail to build cumulatively on what others have done and the enthusiasm of these innovators may act as a barrier to sound evaluation.

Trust and risk

It is hard to create an environment where students and teachers engage in risk-taking and innovative teaching, learning and assessment without trusting classroom relationships (Carless, 2009). Approaches to assessment focused on student learning involve a certain amount of calculated risk in that they move teachers away from routine practices (Sambell, McDowell and Montgomery, 2013). There is interplay between risk and trust because perceptions of risk are greater in low-trust environments. Trust impacts on assessment task design in that innovative assessment may be seen as risk-taking, and more conventional modes of assessment may be seen as more advisable (Carless, 2009). If innovative teachers appear to threaten the regime in place then they may feel that they are not supported and trusted by their institution (Sambell et al., 2013).

Lack of trust between students and teachers can also inhibit innovative assessment practice. Students' perceptions of unfairness in some forms of assessment can lead to distrust of their teachers. Lack of student trust in the teacher can provoke: negative reactions to innovative tasks; cynicism about the use of assessment criteria; or hesitancy in engaging with feedback messages. Conversely, the greater the trust that students have in their teacher, the more willing they are to accept more innovative or challenging modes of teaching, learning and assessment. This point may be particularly applicable to award-winning teachers who are likely to be well trusted by their students. Teachers also need to invest faith in students: a confidence that students will involve themselves in productive forms of learning and assessment. More limited learning processes sometimes emanate from teachers' distrust of students when they suspect cheating, plagiarism or other forms of limited engagement.

In short, trust and risk are factors which impact on possibilities for change and development of assessment practices. I return to these concepts in the final chapter when I review the kinds of assessment innovation which might be feasible and worthwhile.

Sites for assessment change

Assessment change could take place at the micro level of the individual, at the meso level of the group, or at the macro level of the institution. Meso-level initiatives are probably the most productive for promoting assessment change (Trowler and Knight, 2002) and more general developments in teaching and learning (Roxa and Martensson, 2009). One of the potentially most productive levers for assessment change lies in leadership at the departmental level. For example, if a head of department is seen to be prioritising the improvement of assessment practice, this could be a powerful facilitator for change. Leadership commitment should preferably involve: strategies that go beyond mere rhetoric; allocation of resources for change; and personal commitment either from the individual middle-manager or through a valued colleague – for example, appointing a key opinion leader as facilitator. Support for this position comes from an analysis of institutional change which suggests that facilitating factors are commitment from senior management and champions of the initiative on the ground (Price, 2013).

Another meso-level grouping lies at the programme level, where different subjects coalesce in preparing students for a particular award. Innovation at the programme level may encourage buy-in from a critical mass of staff and facilitate a coherent, integrated approach. A unified assessment plan has the potential to benefit student learning when there is a logical flow of assessment tasks across the whole programme (Jessop, El Hakim and Gibbs, 2014). A focus at the programme level could also be a means of developing larger-scale integrative or synoptic assessment to counter the problem when conventional aggregation of module assessments offers a fragmented and disjoined experience to students

(Hartley and Whitfield, 2011). The development of effective feedback processes might also be profitably tackled at the programme level (Boud and Molloy, 2013b). Addressing feedback via a meso-level grouping might be helpful in developing a coherent and consistent approach to feedback.

Summary of chapter

In this chapter, I have set out some of the key competing priorities in assessment implicit in the concept of double duty. I have argued for a vision for learning-oriented assessment prioritising the development of productive student learning processes. Some key issues impacting on the prospects for learning-oriented assessment and assessment innovation have also been discussed.

Main implications for practice

* Assessment should focus on developing effective student learning processes.
* Well-designed summative tasks have the potential to stimulate learning-oriented student approaches.

Chapter 2

Researching learning-oriented assessment

> The reason for an explicit focus on improving assessment practice is the huge impact it has on the quality of learning.
>
> (Boud and associates, 2010, p. 1)

Scope of chapter

I begin this chapter by discussing the learning-oriented assessment framework which forms the conceptual anchorage underpinning the book. I then discuss the relationships between assessment, student approaches to learning and student engagement. The main focus is to illustrate how assessment impacts on students' university experiences.

The second half of the chapter explains the aim of the research to analyse the assessment practices of recipients of teaching awards. I explore the nature of schemes to evaluate quality teaching; criteria for teaching excellence; and the rationale for researching award-winning teachers. I also describe the sampling, data collection and data analysis methods used in the research.

Learning-oriented assessment

First, I set out the origins of the term 'learning-oriented assessment' and discuss the three strands which form its basis.

Origins

I coined the term 'learning-oriented assessment' in 2003, in the context of a project in the Hong Kong Institute of Education, to represent an approach to assessment focused on developing productive student learning processes. The idea was to sidestep some of the conceptual and practical challenges surrounding the notion of formative assessment; and perceptions amongst some colleagues that formative assessment was an unwanted extra, or even an irrelevance, in a setting dominated by summative assessment (Carless, 2007b). We sought to promote a way of thinking that might cut across both formative and summative assessment so that all assessment could be learning-oriented. These ideas were illustrated through a sourcebook of learning-oriented assessment practices involving colleagues across disciplines and universities (Carless, Joughin, Liu and associates, 2006).

Next I build on the concepts in Figure I.1, which put forward three key interlocking elements: learning-oriented assessment tasks; the development of student evaluative expertise; and student engagement with feedback processes.

Learning-oriented assessment tasks

A fundamental idea behind learning-oriented assessment is that it does not absolve summative assessment from carrying a strong 'developing learning' emphasis. Summative assessment can be learning oriented when it encourages deep and deters surface approaches to learning, and promotes a high level of cognitive engagement. Following from this, a fundamental aspect of learning-oriented assessment is the assessment task which students are tackling (discussed more fully in Chapter 3). As a preview, I suggest six principles of assessment task design and implementation:

1   promoting deep student approaches to learning and facilitating the development of appropriate learning outcomes;
2   balancing the formative and summative aspects to enable all assessment to be learning-oriented;
3   spreading student effort and intellectual engagement evenly through a module;
4   supporting the development of ways of understanding the nature of quality in the discipline;
5   involving some personal student investment or choice; and
6   facilitating dialogic forms of feedback.

The extent to which an assessment task is learning oriented involves the interplay between an assessment task, teachers' facilitation of it, and students' interpretations and responses. This forms part of the rationale for the investigation of teachers' and students' interpretations of assessment tasks (Chapters 4 and 5).

Evaluative expertise

The essence of this element of the learning-oriented assessment framework, strongly influenced by the work of Royce Sadler, is that a key role of an educator is to develop students' evaluative expertise so that they can discern quality. Evaluative expertise is at the heart of learning because, in order to improve, learners need to know what quality performance involves and entails. Effective student learning is, to a large extent, based on students developing appropriate meta-cognitive behaviours (Biggs, 1999). For students to enhance their understanding of the notion of quality in the discipline, they need to develop their ability to make informed judgements.

The development of evaluative expertise for informed judgement is frequently operationalised through some form of peer review and related development of students' capacities in self-evaluating their work. Boud and Falchikov (2007) discuss how building evaluative capacity involves not only exposure to models but opportunities for practice through five iterative elements: identifying self as active learner; identifying own level of knowledge and related gaps, and moving from what is known to what it is desirable to know; practising assessing and judging; developing judgement skills over time; and embodying reflexivity and commitment. In Chapter 7, I explore related issues further by analysing the nature of judgements and how students engage with quality in the discipline.

Student engagement with feedback

Developing evaluative expertise is strongly interlinked with feedback processes in that it is hard for students to decode and act on feedback messages without some conception of quality. The feedback component of the learning-oriented assessment framework places emphasis on student engagement with feedback as being paramount. Unless students are engaging with and acting on feedback, it is limited in its impact on their learning.

I explore current thinking on feedback in Chapter 10 and here preview some key points: feedback needs to be re-engineered to encourage dialogue; a key role of feedback is to support students in developing their own self-evaluative capacities; it is what the students can do with feedback rather than how the teacher provides it which is crucial; and students need to develop greater awareness of the purposes of feedback as part of their evolving assessment literacy.

Understanding student learning and engagement

The learning-oriented assessment framework seeks to promote student engagement with assessment tasks; the development of their evaluative expertise; and engagement with feedback messages. In order to gauge prospects for such engagement, I draw on ideas about how students approach learning; how they engage (or disengage) with the content and processes of what is taught; and how their experiences of assessment impact on their engagement.

Approaches to learning research

A seminal study of how students went about reading a text (Marton and Säljö, 1976) identified that students exhibit different approaches to tackling a particular task. A deep approach focuses mainly on meaning and understanding, whereas a surface approach prioritises recall and reproduction. These observable approaches were socially constructed and varied from task to task even within an individual student.

In a deep approach, students aim to understand ideas and seek meanings. They have an intrinsic interest in the task and high aspirations. They relate previous knowledge to new knowledge and bring together understandings from their different learning experiences. They search for patterns, meanings and underlying principles. They relate and distinguish evidence and argument. They organise and structure content into a coherent whole.

In a surface approach, students tend to see tasks as externally imposed on them and want to complete them without engaging too deeply with underlying meanings of the task. They do not usually perceive much intrinsic interest in the task and often aspire only to a satisfactory grade. They often focus on factual reproduction or listing points rather than developing an argument and organising knowledge into a coherent whole. They are generally unreflective about their learning.

Analysing the impact of formal assessment on studying generated an additional dimension of a strategic approach where students focused on achieving the highest possible grades (Entwistle and Ramsden, 1983), driven by either achievement motivation or a sense of responsibility (Entwistle, 2009). The main characteristics of a strategic approach (Entwistle, McCune and Walker, 2001) are: effective time management and well-organised study methods; awareness of assessment requirements through analysing previous exam questions or assignments; alertness to cues about criteria or marking schemes; and adapting work to the perceived preferences of lecturers. Students using a strategic approach might sometimes use deep approaches or surface approaches, depending on their perception of what the teachers are looking for in a particular assessment task. Successful students often combine deep and strategic approaches (Entwistle et al., 2001).

For current purposes, I am not seeking to problematise the conceptualisation of approaches to learning research or their continuing relevance in massified higher education, although others have done so (e.g. Haggis, 2003; Howie and Bagnall, 2013). The main issue I am raising is that the management of assessment tasks and students' related perceptions are important factors impacting on students' study approaches. Assessment tasks may encourage deep approaches to learning through the development of integrated knowledge, sophisticated cognitive abilities and lateral, creative or critical thinking skills (Sambell et al., 2013). The kinds of task I discuss in Chapters 4 and 5 encourage students to take positions, present arguments and evidence, and have a stake in what they are doing. Conversely, when students perceive a task as merely focusing on recall and reproduction, they are likely to adopt a surface approach. Pressure of workload is another dimension: students who perceive the workload requirements of a subject to be high and when they are facing a series of deadlines are more likely to adopt a surface approach (Ramsden, 1992). This may depend on various factors, including how engaged students are with a task or how they prioritise it in relation to other commitments. Students might adopt deep approaches when they have sufficient time to work on an assignment in depth, but towards the end of a semester, when multiple deadlines are approaching, they may adopt a surface approach.

The majority of student participants in the current research were of Chinese origin, from either Hong Kong or mainland China. There does not seem to be a clear pattern in the approaches to learning of Chinese students. Leung, Ginns and Kember (2008) found that Hong Kong students scored highly on both deep and surface approach scores, suggesting a greater tendency to use combinations of approaches. Kember and Gow (1990) found that, whereas some of their informants from the Hong Kong Polytechnic University demonstrated a deep approach, others evidenced what they characterised as a 'narrow approach': learning tasks defined by the teacher; understanding focused narrowly on a systematic, step-by-step processing of information; and memorising details relevant to the task. Memorisation is a complex element of Chinese approaches to learning and can often act as a first step towards understanding (Biggs, 1996b). The interplay between memorising and understanding can lead to high levels of achievement amongst Chinese students via various strategies, such as seeking comprehension and then committing to memory; or repeating and memorising as part of a process of developing understanding; or strategic memorisation for an examination after understanding has been developed (Kember, 1996, 2000). The ability to memorise well is obviously useful in assessment tasks, such as tests and examinations, which tend to reward students who have memorised key material (Leung et al., 2008).

There have been some attempts to use assessment task design to influence students' approaches to learning. Inducing a deep approach to learning is difficult in that minor modifications to the learning-assessment environment do not modify students' approaches to learning, according to the results of Gijbels et al. (2009). There seem to be a variety of factors which make it difficult to induce students to adopt deep approaches, including: students' perceptions of assessment tasks and associated workloads (Baeten, Dochy and Struyven, 2008); students' previous learning approaches (Gijbels, Segers and Struyf, 2008); and the impact of the teacher (Baeten et al., 2008). Notwithstanding these challenges, there are prospects for encouraging students to adopt deep learning approaches through the use of authentic tasks and a blend of formative and summative assessment (Dochy et al., 2007).

The approaches to learning which students commonly adopt are also likely to be linked to their engagement with university life and the curriculum, and I turn to this notion of engagement next.

Student engagement

Student engagement is embedded within the learning-oriented assessment framework in that how students engage with tasks, quality criteria and feedback is central to the development of their learning. The more engaged a student is, the more likely they are to adopt deep approaches to learning.

Student engagement is a somewhat amorphous term that permits multiple interpretations; for current purposes, it is defined as being concerned with the extent to which students are involved in activities that higher education research has shown to be linked with high-quality learning outcomes (Krause and Coates, 2008). These include such features as time on task, active learning, quality of student effort, interacting with peers and teachers about substantive matters, high expectations and receiving prompt feedback (Kuh, 2009). Student engagement is a multifaceted concept and the review by Fredricks, Blumenfeld and Paris (2004) is helpful in unpacking three reciprocal dimensions of it. First, the behavioural dimension relates to the time and effort students devote to their studies, and their in-class participation. Second, the cognitive dimension includes construction of knowledge, motivation and investment in learning, and meta-cognitive aspects, such as strategies to plan, monitor and evaluate learning. Third, the emotional dimension relates to how students feel about their studies, such as interest, boredom, happiness, sadness or anxiety, and the emotional attachment they have to their teachers, classmates and learning environment.

Teachers obviously play an important role in promoting student engagement. Bryson and Hand (2007) suggest three levels of concurrent staff action to enhance quality student engagement: productive interactions around intellectual content, including the requirements and expectations of assessment; professionalism in teaching, especially through the development of trusting relationships; and enthusiasm for their subject. Teachers' enthusiasm for their students and their subject is often associated with award-winning teachers.

The power of assessment means that it can engage or alienate. The pressure of completing assignments and assessment tasks mainly owned and controlled by the teacher emphasises the role of power in the assessment process, and teachers need to reconsider how or where they might redistribute power (Mann, 2001). This can include involving students actively through strategies which are illustrated in this volume: flexibility to facilitate some ownership of what they are doing; involvement in feedback dialogues about their work; and engagement in self- and peer assessment to enhance their students' responsibility for their learning.

For some students in the study by Bryson and Hand (2007), the pressure to obtain a good degree (i.e. at least upper second class honours) resulted in a focus on what needed to be done to obtain a grade which fulfilled that purpose. So, for example, students often seemed to be focusing as much on who was going to mark their work as they did on the substantive learning outcomes. This often has a counterproductive effect, and surface approaches to learning are sometimes responses to alienation from the context and process of studying, including feeling a sense of being an outsider in the world of academia (Mann, 2001).

Approaches to learning, student engagement and learning-oriented assessment

The promotion of deep learning approaches and student engagement is congruent with the three principles of learning-oriented assessment. First, productive assessment tasks encourage student cognitive engagement and strategies consistent with a deep approach. Previewing issues I explore further in Chapter 3: personal investment in assignments can encourage student agency (Sambell et al., 2013); authentic assessment has a positive influence on student motivation and engagement (Sambell, McDowell and Brown, 1997); and tasks which involve students in consistent effort across the duration of a course encourage persistent engagement (Gibbs, 2006).

Second, deep approaches to learning are associated with a well-developed awareness of goals and standards required in the subject (Trigwell and Prosser, 1991): that is, there is a correlation between deep approaches and students having an understanding of the nature of quality. The development of student evaluative expertise through involvement in various types of meta-cognitive learning is also likely to be congruent with deep learning approaches (Biggs, 1999). Helping students to understand criteria is a means of supporting them in understanding the nature of quality academic work and is one of the most potent ways of encouraging engagement and reducing the kind of alienation described by Mann (2001).

Third, the kind of feedback literacy (Sutton, 2012) which promotes student engagement with feedback also resonates with deep learning approaches: a search for understanding and high aspirations. As I explore in Chapter 10, one of the challenges for feedback processes is the difficulty of generating student engagement with the feedback they receive. Many students become progressively disengaged with feedback during their university programmes as a result of disappointing feedback experiences (Price, Handley and Millar, 2011). For feedback processes to be effective, they need to encourage students to respond actively in self-evaluating their performance and taking actions to improve their learning.

How students experience assessment and learning

The argument so far has been that assessment and students' perceptions of assessment impact on both their approaches to learning and their engagement. The student experience of assessment is at the heart of this volume. In this section, I review two seminal studies, *Making the Grade* (Becker et al., 1968) and *Up to the Mark* (Miller and Parlett, 1974), which have been influential in telling us about the role of assessment in the student experience; how students think they are going to be assessed; and how they search for clues on the criteria for successful performance. Some of the ideas introduced in these studies have enduring influence in the field, and, as Joughin (2010) argues in his useful critique, they are worth scrutinising carefully. I then discuss some more recent UK evidence of students' experiences of assessment and make some points about affective responses to assessment.

Making the Grade

Becker et al. (1968) studied undergraduate life at the University of Kansas, a residential college in the American Midwest. Their research method involved participant observation: following students from a wide range of disciplines; observing what they did; and interviewing them about their experiences over a two-year period (1959 to 1961). They found that student activity was mainly evident across three broad areas: academic work; the organisational domain – fraternities, sororities and extra-curricular activities; and personal relations, in terms of friendships and dating.

The main significant finding of the study was what the authors called the Grade Point Average (GPA) perspective: an emphasis on grades as the main institutionalised reward system which guides student behaviours; the criteria on which people are judged; and interaction or conflicts in goals between the three domains of student activity noted above. The GPA perspective directs students to undertake those actions which help them to earn grades which they perceive as satisfactory for their own purposes and this varies from student to student and/or between disciplines and/or between social groups or sub-cultures. Some may find only 'good grades' satisfactory for their purposes, whilst others may be satisfied by 'adequate grades'. Students generally deemed failure to obtain good or adequate grades as a sign of immaturity, so this had negative consequences for the organisational domain (e.g. admission to fraternities or sororities) and personal relationships (e.g. less desirable as a dating partner). Grades were therefore used as a basis for judging the personal worth of students.

In turn, students judge their teachers partly in terms of how easy or difficult they make it for them to achieve adequate or good grades in terms of factors including clarity of guidance on what is required for assignments or examinations, and the amount, timing and nature of the work they set. Students perceive that the disparities between what professors say and what they do are frequent enough to merit searching for additional information to supplement their teachers' accounts of the assessment mechanisms. These searches for information include trying to identify which courses are 'easier' or 'harder' in terms of obtaining a high grade; the tastes or prejudices of a particular teacher; and insights from more senior students who may have knowledge of a teacher. Students were also reported as believing that the way a teacher assigns grades depends not only on how well the students learn the material but on the congruence between teachers' views and those expressed in the students' assignments. Students also talked of doing things which would gain favour with the instructor, in addition to academic performance: for example, taking an interest in them, praising them or talking about their course in ways which might garner a favourable impression.

Another student informant commented on the meaning of grades within an overall grading system as follows:

> It says in the catalog . . . that C is a satisfactory grade. Well, do they mean that or don't they? Actually it's the minimum grade here. C is just barely passing. The most satisfactory thing is an A, and next is a B.
>
> (Becker et al., 1968, pp. 59–60)

This brings to mind a potential mismatch between what course documentation states is 'satisfactory' or 'good' or 'excellent', and what teachers and students may regard as meeting those criteria. I return to this issue in Chapter 8 in relation to data from the current study.

Becker et al. also write of conflict within the system, particularly in terms of the relationship between learning and achievement. For example, some students felt that a deeper engagement with the material could sometimes be a barrier to achieving the required grade. Others spoke of just memorising the required material for the sake of obtaining a desired grade, even when they felt that this was not optimal in terms of the dispositions they believed they should be developing. An inference is that students using deep approaches to learning may not necessarily find them efficient in tackling assessment tasks which encourage recall and reproduction (cf. Scouller, 1998).

In sum, Becker et al. (1968) offer a richly detailed analysis of college life and 'the GPA perspective' is a useful term to sum up the role of grades in influencing student behaviours.

Up to the Mark

The study by Miller and Parlett (1974) was based on detailed, semi-structured interviews at the University of Edinburgh with staff and students in the subjects of Law, History and Physics. On the basis of interviews with thirty final-year Law students, the students were classified into three different kinds: cue-conscious, cue-seekers and cue-deaf. Eleven students were identified as cue-conscious. They saw a need to be perceptive and receptive to cues transmitted by staff: hints about exam topics; aspects of the subject favoured by staff; and the extent to which they were making a good impression on staff. Two quotations from students classified as cue-conscious illustrate aspects of this category: 'There is definitely an exam technique . . . identifying the technique is what you are here to do' (Miller and Parlett, 1974, p. 62); 'The lecturer gets a picture of you and this impression must affect him as he's marking the papers, however impartial he tries to be' (p. 62).

Five students were classified as cue-seekers. These were students who went beyond perceptiveness and receptiveness to cues by actively seeking out staff and probing them about exam questions; identifying characteristics and preferences of oral examiners; and deliberately trying to make a good impression on staff. A student in this category referred extensively to his engagement with the

Table 2.1 Results of Law students

	Degree obtained			
	First	Upper Second	Lower Second or below	Totals
Cue-seekers	3	1	1	5
Cue-conscious	1	6	4	11
Cue-deaf	1	2	11	14
Totals	5	9	16	30

examination game: 'Everybody's looking for hints, but some of us look for it or probe for it, rather than waiting for it to come passively' (p. 60).

The largest group of students comprised the fourteen who were classified as cue-deaf. These students seemed neither perceptive nor active in noticing or seeking out hints, or making an impression on staff. They expressed the view that working hard was the main ingredient for success and they would not dare, for example, to ask teachers about likely exam questions.

When the researchers knew the results of the final examinations, they conducted simple correlations to identify the relationship between these categories and student achievement. Although the data do not provide an entirely consistent picture, the general trend was that cue-seekers were the most successful students and the cue-deaf the least successful (see Table 2.1). Students 'who were cue-conscious tended to get upper seconds and those who were cue-deaf got lower seconds' (p. 55).

The value of the Miller and Parlett study is in illustrating the extent to which students are attuned to the nature of the assessment system, and in introducing the notion of cue-consciousness into the literature. Although this term arises from a single subject in a single university, it seems that the concept resonates with academics' interpretations of their students so it carries generalisable worth.

Recent evidence on students' experiences of assessment

I want to supplement the above seminal accounts of students' experiences of assessment with recent well-documented evidence from the UK. The National Student Survey provides indications on a longitudinal basis of British students' perceptions of their university experience. Assessment and feedback are usually areas where students seem less satisfied than with other aspects, although there has been some improvement in responses to assessment and feedback in recent years (HEFCE, 2014).

A useful review, based on data from institutional surveys undertaken at eleven institutions from 1994 to 2007, brings out students' concerns about issues relating to assessment and feedback (Williams and Kane, 2008). I note three points from this review that are particularly relevant to the focus of this chapter.

First, students made few negative comments on the type of assessment used, from which I infer that they do not perceive major dissatisfaction with assessment task design. Second, they expressed concerns about the promptness of feedback, and the quality and/or usefulness of feedback. Third, when the most significant feedback they received was in the form of mark, this could prompt direct linkages in the students' minds between marks and feedback. I speculate that some dissatisfaction with feedback expressed in these institutions could relate to dissatisfaction with marks; or confusion as to the rationale for the marks. So my interpretation is that when students voice concerns about feedback, they may be referring to something different from what researchers view as feedback. I explore these issues further in Chapter 10.

A promising means of analysing key aspects of the student experience is through the Assessment Experience Questionnaire, which gauges the impact of assessment on the student learning experience (Gibbs and Dunbar-Goddet, 2009) and has been used recently in the 'Transforming the Experience of Students through Assessment' project (Jessop, El Hakim and Gibbs, 2014). Some relevant findings: disciplines and institutions construct distinctive assessment environments linked to traditions, regulations and perceived requirements or 'myths' about what is mandatory; and students tended to believe that teachers mark to implicit and tacit standards rather than apply public written criteria, previewing a point to which I return in Chapter 7. The accumulated evidence shows correlation between quantity and quality of feedback and students' understanding of goals and standards. To my eyes, this provides support for my interlinking of the two strands at the bottom of the learning-oriented assessment framework: evaluative expertise and engagement with feedback.

Affective responses to assessment

Emotional responses are very much a part of the student experience. Common reported feelings include enjoyment of learning, hope, pride and relief as well as anxiety, anger, boredom and shame (Pekrun et al., 2002); or extreme poles of euphoria and trauma (Cramp et al., 2012). Positive emotions encourage self-regulation and flexible strategies, related to deep approaches to learning, whereas negative emotions prompt external regulation (e.g. over-reliance on teacher guidance) and limited strategies, associated with surface approaches to learning (Pekrun et al., 2002). Students' often perceive that assessment relates to their personal identity, and this can exacerbate feelings of disappointment, a sense of failure, anxiety and suspiciousness about the fairness of grading practices (Crossman, 2007). The complexity of emotional response is also evident: positive emotions are not always beneficial (e.g. if they reduce immediate motivation); and negative emotions are not always harmful (e.g. if they induce strong coping motivation) (Pekrun et al., 2002).

The affective response to assessment particularly relates to the elements of the learning-oriented assessment framework focused on assessment task design and feedback. Some forms of assessment task, such as those that require public performance, may be more nerve-racking than those that can be done privately. Working against the clock, such as in examinations, may also accentuate student stress and anxiety, particularly if there is a 100 per cent weighting for the examination. Affective threats are exacerbated when teachers do not exhibit awareness or sensitivity to students' potentially negative emotional reactions to assessment feedback (Carless, 2006). This is not to advocate indiscriminate or too much praise: comments which focus a student on the self, rather than improving their work, are often counterproductive (Kluger and DeNisi, 1996).

Assessment emotions are a function of both judgements and how these judgements are made (Falchikov and Boud, 2007). Teachers' dual roles of both assisting and passing judgement on the student are bound up with the issue of power and authority. Power differentials increase the potential of judgements to invoke emotional responses within students (Higgins, Hartley and Skelton, 2001). Unequal power relationships impinge on the relational aspects of feedback. Emotional responses to assessment are a function of the relationships between expectations and learner dispositions; and relationships between learners and their teachers (Falchikov and Boud, 2007). This relational aspect is often manifested through trust or distrust. To build trust, interlocutors listen to and empathise with others; seeking to understand is one of the most important trust builders because it communicates that you value the other person (Costa and Kallick, 1995). Trusting virtues, such as empathy, tact and a genuine willingness to listen, are ways in which positive assessment messages can flourish and more critical ones are softened (Carless, 2013b).

How students manage their responses to assessment and feedback is a key consideration and this relates to both their own personal characteristics and the strategies of their teachers. When learners view feedback as a mechanism to support their ongoing learning, defensiveness is reduced; and an associated strategy of developing effective student self-evaluation can reduce emotional impacts of assessment and feedback (Molloy, Borrell-Carrio and Epstein, 2013).

Teaching awards: setting the scene

Now I change focus from the student to the teacher. The current research explores the relationship between assessment and student learning through analysing the practices of university teachers who have received awards in official recognition of their excellence. Such teachers are likely to provide engaging approaches which may support a positive student learning experience. In this section, I explain my rationale for researching award-winning teachers, outline the specific criteria for awards at HKU, and introduce some relevant aspects of literature on award-winning teaching.

The origins of awards for teaching lie in attempts to mitigate, to some extent, the dominance of research in universities. By rewarding teaching, the intention is to raise its status as a highly valued aspect of university work. Teaching excellence is a contested, value-laden concept, with four main conceptions of teaching quality (Skelton, 2005): a traditional emphasis on lecturing about disciplinary knowledge; a focus on the interpersonal nature of teaching and learning encounters, drawing principally on theories of humanistic and cognitive psychology; a more performative focus on procedures, policies and strategies for implementation; or a more critical approach, which Skelton favours, involving participatory, potentially emancipatory, dialogue.

How might teaching excellence schemes contribute to pedagogical developments? There seems to be a consensus that teaching excellence is generally not disseminated particularly effectively (Gibbs, 2008; Skelton, 2005). Without significant dissemination of awardees' expertise, teaching awards are unlikely to promote participation in professional pedagogic activities and research related to teaching; they may become little more than institutional competitions or personal celebrations that have minimal impact beyond the level of the individual teacher (Halse et al., 2007). A contribution of the current volume is the dissemination and analysis of the practices of award-winning teachers within particular disciplinary contexts.

Rationale for researching award-winning teachers

My rationale for sampling award-winning teachers is that they may exemplify one or more of the following: high-quality teaching and learning practice; student-centred teaching or teaching strategies that are attractive to students; and innovative or provocative practices. A critical perspective would suggest that they are likely to generate practices worthy of close scrutiny. In relation to assessment, award-winning teachers may or may not evidence good practice. A rationale for choosing these teachers is that I was more likely to find good, or potentially good, assessment practice amongst these than amongst other groups of teachers who might be sampled. They may implement practices congruent with, additional to, or different from the proposed learning-oriented assessment framework, and this forms part of the investigation.

An additional pragmatic consideration is that award-winning teachers may be well motivated to participate in studies of their pedagogy because of the recognition that their teaching has attracted. This is an important factor when envisaging a research approach involving multiple classroom observations, as per the current study.

Criteria for excellence in teaching

What does the literature say which might speak to the kind of criteria used in award-winning teaching schemes? Based on the relatively few studies (e.g. Bain, 2004; Dunkin and Precians, 1992), Kember (2007) infers that there are generally commonly agreed characteristics of effective teaching which do not differ greatly across disciplines or cultural contexts. Research into award-winning teachers is generally conducted inductively (Skelton, 2005): an educational researcher explores beliefs and practices of award-winning teachers and makes inferences about the kinds of behaviours which seem salient. For example, drawing on written data collected from 708 nominees for Australian teaching excellence awards and interviews with 44 of these, Ballantyne, Bain and Packer (1999) identified a number of characteristics of quality teaching: a love for one's discipline and the desire to share it with others; creating and maintaining student interest; caring for students and valuing their perspectives; making learning possible through interaction; and fostering students' generic skills. A love for one's discipline is part of the enthusiasm which promotes student engagement. A risk, however, is if this leads to a content-driven form of pedagogy focused on the sharing of wisdom: what Prosser and Trigwell (1999) refer to as an 'information transfer teaching focus'.

In a review of teaching award schemes, Gibbs (2008) notes with some scepticism a wide range of conceptions of teaching excellence, including: exhibiting certain teaching behaviours skilfully; facilitating quality student learning; engaging in the scholarship of teaching; exploiting benefits from disciplinary research; nurturing students as individuals; creating effective learning environments; innovating in teaching; leadership in teaching; and supporting others in the development of teaching.

The scheme at HKU, in which the teachers featured in this book had been successful, has evolved from one focused on good individual classroom practice to a wider conception of quality. The stated criteria require: evidence of excellence in teaching and engagement with students and their learning; evidence of excellence in curriculum design, curriculum renewal and innovation; and excellence in the leadership and scholarship of teaching (Prosser, 2013b). This conception involves not only good teaching but wider involvement in curriculum development and innovation, and some forms of leadership in teaching.

Prosser, who was directly involved in the development of criteria for the awards at HKU and the selection of winners, describes some of the processes informing applicants and decision-makers for the scheme (Prosser, 2013a). He relates the criteria for teaching excellence to his research into teaching and learning in higher education (e.g. Prosser and Trigwell, 1999). Award-winning teachers

- set clear goals and support students in understanding intended learning outcomes;
- use a variety of teaching methods to enhance learning for understanding;
- use a variety of assessment methods to monitor and promote student learning;
- reflect on their own knowledge of students and their learning progress, and how to improve their learning; and
- draw on a wide range of evidence regarding success in promoting student learning.

(Prosser, 2013a)

Prosser asserts that these characteristics show that the emphasis of the awards has changed from a focus on what the teacher does to an emphasis on students and developing their conceptions of learning and the subject. He calls this approach a 'conceptual change student-focused' approach (Prosser and Trigwell, 1999), which he associates with high-quality teaching and the ability to transcend contextual challenges, such as large class size. In sum, it seems that the criteria for teaching awards at HKU are both well conceived and supported by relevant research into teaching and learning.

The research processes

The journey of my research into award-winning teachers and the genesis of the current book began in 2008/9, when I carried out a project on the enhancement of feedback processes (Carless et al., 2011). The main component of this research comprised semi-structured interviews about their feedback practices with ten award-winning teachers from different faculties at HKU. One of the participants, Ali, from the Faculty of Business, reported some particularly provocative and stimulating practices. I was interested in learning more about how these practices were implemented, so carried out a follow-up case study of dialogic feedback in his classes (Carless, 2013a). These two interconnected studies convinced me of the value of researching award-winning teachers and became the prototype for the larger, externally funded research project reported in this book.

The research involves interpretive case studies of the classes of five award-winning teachers, and groups of students attending their classes. Case studies are a powerful research strategy for probing in-depth how and why factors in classroom practice. My partner in the research was Wang Xiang, Iris: a recent doctoral graduate specialising in observational and interview research methods. Wang participated with me in the classroom observations and carried out many of the student interviews. In the course of the book, I often use the plural personal pronoun 'we' to denote the research collaboration between the two of us.

The research questions guiding the study are grouped around the three elements of the learning-oriented assessment framework. In relation to task design and implementation:

- How is assessment designed and managed?
- How do students interpret and respond to the assessment tasks they are undertaking?

In relation to the development of student evaluative expertise:

- What kinds of classroom activities involve students in developing an understanding of the nature of quality work in the discipline?
- How do students understand criteria and perceive activities which support them in developing their evaluative expertise?

With respect to student engagement with feedback:

- How is feedback generated by students and teachers in relation to the assessment tasks and classroom activities?
- To what extent, and how, do students seem to be engaging with feedback processes?

Sampling

There is some evidence (Norton et al., 2013) that there are more sophisticated – or perhaps less unsophisticated – assessment practices in 'soft' rather than 'hard' disciplines. Accordingly, I focused the sampling mainly on cases of teachers in the humanities and social sciences: Architecture, Business, History and Law. However, I also wished to include a case from one of the hard disciplines: I chose Geology, based in the Faculty of Science. This sampling was to some extent dependent on the characteristics and availability of award-winners at the university. Award-winning teachers at the university seem to be positively disposed to being researched: all five invited teachers agreed to participate, and each of them identified a suitable undergraduate class to form the focus for data collection. They also all granted permission for their real names to be used:

- David Pomfret, History;
- Rick Glofcheski, Law;
- Lung-Sang Chan, Geology;
- Ali Farhoomand, Business; and
- John Lin, Architecture.

By an unfortunate coincidence, all of these teachers are male. Whilst male entrants and winners of the award-winning teacher schemes at HKU are in the majority, there have been a number of female winners. I had planned to include one of the latter (from the Faculty of Nursing) in my sample, not least because of her specialism in portfolio assessment (see the interview data in Chapter 10), but regrettably she was not undertaking any undergraduate teaching at the time of data collection.

Data collection

The study was ethnographically oriented in that I observed classes regularly and endeavoured to understand the cultures of the courses as they unfolded. I particularly sought to understand how students experienced teaching, learning and assessment in the selected modules, so I sat beside them and joined in activities where appropriate. Classroom observations were a major means of data collection and enabled me to understand what was going on and relate understandings to the three components of the learning-oriented assessment framework. These observations focused on selected undergraduate classes taught by the five informants. The scheduling of classes had some variation: in Geology, History and Law they were of two hours' duration; in Business they were three hours in length; and in Architecture studio activities were open-ended and did not follow a conventional time schedule. Six to ten sessions per teacher were observed, totalling thirty-nine sessions observed amongst the five teachers, which equated to around ninety-two hours of classroom observations. I participated in more than half of these observations, whilst Wang was present in all of them. We both collected detailed field notes to: describe relevant facets of the classroom processes; develop provisional insights on the research questions; and identify salient issues which we would follow up through interviews.

The other main means of data collection comprised semi-structured interviews. I carried out a series of interviews with each teacher. The first, at the outset of the study, sought mainly to contextualise the teaching situation; understand each teacher's rationale for the chosen assessment tasks; determine how, if at all, they developed students' conceptions of quality in the discipline; and assess how they approached feedback processes. The second interview principally explored issues arising from the classroom observations and provided the teachers with an opportunity to comment on selected issues from our interviews with students. Further interaction evolved in relation to ongoing data analysis to shed light on ambiguous issues, and to verify or disprove emerging insights. Some of the teacher participants also provided access to their teaching portfolios, which provided further evidence of their perspectives.

How students perceive and experience assessment is a central focus of the research. Students from each of the observed classes were interviewed to understand their perceptions of classroom processes, assessment tasks, engagement with criteria and feedback. During our observations, Wang and I interacted with a range of students and invited a sample of them to participate in the study, based on our perceptions of their potential willingness to be involved. In this sense, the selection of student interviewees was largely opportunistic. The purposes and the procedures for ethical data collection were explained and most of those we asked agreed to participate. We interviewed a range of students of different dispositions and abilities. It is likely that, overall, the students who spoke to us were towards the higher motivation/achievement end of a continuum, if only because we were less likely to encounter disaffected students who did not attend classes regularly.

The students were generally interviewed face to face, some more than once, and some also supplemented their responses via email. We mostly interviewed them individually, or sometimes in pairs. The number of students interviewed per discipline was:

- Geology – six;
- History – twelve;

- Architecture – eleven;
- Business – eight; and
- Law – fourteen.

In general, the fewer the number of participants in a subject, the more in-depth was the interviewing. I carried out some of these interviews, but the majority were conducted by Wang. All of the student interviewees have been given pseudonyms or are unnamed.

Data analysis

A basic technique I use in all my research is that data analysis should, at least to some extent, proceed concurrently with data collection. This is so that insights from early phases can inform later stages of data collection. The general approach I adopt is inductive analysis to generate insights emerging from raw data; apply them to the research focus; and examine similarities and differences between cases to develop concepts or ideas. More specifically, I see the main steps in qualitative data analysis as an iterative process involving: coding of interview transcripts and classroom observation data; data reduction; categorising codes into themes or motifs; drawing inferences from data; verifying or disconfirming inferences; displaying data and building up a narrative; and relating insights to relevant literature.

The trustworthiness of the analysis was enhanced by various measures recommended in the qualitative research literature: prolonged engagement in the field through detailed classroom observations and interviews with participants; triangulation between different data tools and data sets; member checking and respondent validation through inviting the teachers to respond critically to my provisional interpretations; and critical discussions with Wang, my co-researcher, presenting her with drafts and then making revisions or reflecting further on the basis of her comments. My focus in the following chapters of this book obviously reflects my own selection and interpretation of what I observed and heard. I try to provide sufficiently 'thick descriptions' for the reader to form their own viewpoint on the teaching, learning and assessment processes.

Summary of chapter

In this chapter, I have set out the underpinnings of a framework for learning-oriented assessment and related it to literature on approaches to learning, student engagement and how students experience assessment. I have discussed the rationale for researching award-winning teachers and the key criteria on which they are evaluated. Finally, I have explained the conduct of the research.

Main implications for practice

- Assessment should be designed to encourage deep approaches to student learning.
- Assessment needs to stimulate student engagement.
- Students' emotional engagement with assessment and feedback needs to be taken into account.
- Award-winning teachers potentially utilise engaging teaching, learning and assessment practices.

Part II

Designing and implementing assessment tasks

Chapter 3

Promoting student engagement with assessment tasks

Perhaps the most important single dimension of assessment is the complexity of intellectual operations required to perform the assessment task.

(Miller and Parlett, 1974, p. 27)

Scope of chapter

This chapter is about assessment task design and implementation. In the first half of the chapter, I analyse various common assessment formats and draw out their respective strengths and weaknesses. In the second half, I discuss various principles of productive assessment task design. By synthesising relevant literature, I propose some key features of learning-oriented assessment tasks.

Review of selected assessment methods

First, I review some of the major methods of assessing students; draw out potentials and challenges in their implementation; and discuss the kind of student learning they are likely to generate. I define assessment tasks as the assignments which students need to complete as part of the courses which make up their degree programmes. Assessment methods refer to the types of tasks which students are undertaking. It is worth reiterating that it is not the assessment method per se which is the key consideration, but its impact on students and how they perceive it; how it is implemented in practice; and the extent to which it serves to promote student engagement and appropriate learning outcomes.

A point worth making before I discuss different modes of assessment is that all assessments have strengths and weaknesses. So, for example, it is common to critique group assessment on the grounds of difficulty in assessing individual outcomes fairly; and, clearly, assessing participation rigorously and reliably is a challenge. Yet, more conventional modes of assessment also have their limitations: examinations tend to reward those who are good at memorisation, whilst essays favour facility in written communication. The position taken in learning-oriented assessment is to prioritise assessment modes and related implementation which have the most potential to promote student learning.

Assessment tasks are part of a wider network of influences, including: the nature of the curriculum and the discipline; teachers' beliefs and aims; the educational and institutional context; relationships between classroom participants; students' attitudes and motivations towards the module being studied; and the extent to which students are focused on grades and/or mastery of relevant content or skills. The student response is critical. As Boud (1995, p. 40) puts it: 'an assessment strategy is effective only in so far as it communicates appropriately with the student'.

There are also institutional factors impacting on choice of assessment method; and related perceptions which may or may not accord with reality. So, for example, a departmental ethos may be that examinations are favoured or frowned upon, but the precise historical or real justification for that stance may be unknown. Teachers generally do not have the same freedom to choose assessment methods as they have in deciding their own teaching approaches (Entwistle and Karagiannopoulou, 2014). Choice of assessment method can involve a complex interplay between what has gone on before, contextual issues, the nature of the discipline, and staff (and student) preferences.

The assessment methods reviewed below – examinations, written assignments, group assessment, oral presentations, the grading of student participation and portfolio-based writing – are both common and occurred in the case studies. I discuss them further in light of the cases in Chapter 12.

Examinations

Examinations remain a common feature of assessment in higher education, particularly, though not exclusively, in the hard sciences and in Law. For instance, examinations were used in the Geology case (Chapter 6) and in the Law case (Chapter 5), but not in the other cases.

The limitations of examinations have long been acknowledged: the restricted writing time and need to cram information into short-term memory seem to favour certain students, such as fast writers; and there is rapid loss of recall after exams (Knight and Yorke, 2003). By their time-constricted nature, examinations tend to impede thoughtful planning, drafting, re-drafting and self-evaluation, so students are unlikely to produce their best performance under such conditions and may not be modelling good writing practices. The reliability of scoring of essay examinations is problematic and grades appear highly dependent on language and organisational components of writing (Brown, 2010). Examination success is often not congruent with deep conceptual understanding (Entwistle and Entwistle, 1992), mainly because exams tend to assess lower-order outcomes which are relatively easy to assess, rather than more complex outcomes. Examinations also tend to concentrate student effort at the end of the semester, rather than encouraging consistent effort throughout the course.

A recent review by Richardson (2014) concludes that students prefer to be assessed by coursework alone or a mix of coursework and exams, rather than just by exams. There is also evidence that students achieve higher marks on coursework than in examinations (Bridges et al., 2002), with increases in assessed coursework over the last two decades contributing to grade inflation. The student reaction to examinations is often mixed: they are criticised for being artificial, misleading or unfair but at the same time accepted because of their familiarity and because they usually represent less work than more complex assignments (McDowell and Sambell, 1999).

A well-designed examination may mitigate some of the problems outlined above. The process of preparing for essay examinations can prompt some students to adopt deep approaches to revision in developing a synoptic view of a field of study, particularly where conceptual understanding is required by the examination questions (Entwistle and Entwistle, 2003; Macdonald, 2002). There are also less conventional forms of examination, such as open-book exams or take-home exams, which may preserve some of the supposed rigour of examinations whilst reducing some of the limitations of the typical three-hour race against the clock. A recent – and apparently popular – innovation is for students to write their examination answers on computers (but without access to the internet) (Mogey et al., 2012). Finally, examinations reassure teachers that the answers have been written, unaided, by the candidate, and Scouller (1998) claims that this is a compelling reason for many teachers in higher education to continue to assess by examination.

Written assignments

Extended pieces of writing were a common means of assessment in the cases; these included reports (Business, Geology) and individual projects (History, Law). The ability to write well is both necessary to demonstrate ability to work with module content and an important learning outcome in itself (Torrance, Thomas and Robinson, 2000). Extended pieces of writing involve students in a number of competencies: locating, evaluating and synthesising information, analysing, thinking critically, communicating through a written language, and using referencing conventions (Knight and Yorke, 2003). Essays can, however, lack an audience which goes beyond the teacher, and students may see them as routines in which they access and summarise information. At worst, students may feel that some essays have little to do with communicating ideas, making connections or developing a stance (Sambell et al., 2013). This implies a need to contextualise written assignments in relation to disciplinary problems or issues.

A seminal study of History students' perceptions of essay writing (Hounsell, 1984) identified three qualitatively distinct conceptions of essays:

- argument – an ordered presentation of an argument involving data used as evidence, organisation and interpretation;
- viewpoint – the ordered presentation of a viewpoint, sharing some similarity with the argument conception but with data as evidence being sparse or indistinct; and

- arrangement – an ordered presentation of essentially discrete thoughts with a concomitant lack of integration.

For students who are more oriented towards Hounsell's first position, essays have the potential to encourage deep approaches to learning in that they involve students integrating knowledge and understanding, creating structure, displaying insight and presenting a coherent argument (Brown, 1997). For students who are more oriented to the third position, there is a more reproductive or surface approach to developing the essay. This also may lead to a 'rules of the game' approach in which students adopt certain tactics when producing coursework essays in the hope that these will help them to achieve better marks (Norton, Dickins and McLaughlin Cook, 1996). Examples of such tactics include: choosing the easiest essay title to maximise the chance of a high mark and using numerous or up-to-date references to boost a scholarly impression. It is highly unlikely that teachers will advise students to adopt these strategies, but the latter nevertheless believe that they may lead to high marks (Norton et al., 2001).

When asked to explain what they understood by higher-order skills, such as 'synthesis' or 'critical evaluation', more than half of the students in a Faculty of Education class were unable to provide an adequate definition of the latter, but those who were able to do so tended to produce better essays (Campbell, Smith and Brooker, 1998). Critical evaluation involves 'not only the synthesis of different theoretical perspectives and research evidence, but going beyond these to weigh evidence, evaluate the logical coherence of arguments and develop a position based on integrated evidence from a variety of sources' (Campbell et al., 1998, p. 459). My related inference is that modelling critical evaluation for students and supporting them to develop their understanding of it might be a useful way to enhance their writing skills. An analogous position is taken by Wingate (2012) in relation to students' (and teachers') lack of understanding of how 'argument' is realised in disciplinary writing.

Group assessment

I review the literature on group assessment in some detail because it is both a common assessment mode and often viewed as difficult to implement successfully or unpopular with students. This section also lays the groundwork for the discussion in Chapter 6 of the processes of a group project in the Geology case.

Rationale

The main rationales for group work are the educational one of promoting teamwork skills and the pragmatic one of reducing teacher marking. I concentrate mainly on the first of these, although the second may have contributed to my inference that group assessment seems to be more popular amongst teachers than it is amongst students. A powerful rationale for group projects is made by Boud (2000) in arguing that the more complex learning is, the less likely it is that it will be accomplished in isolation from others. Group work contains an authentic, real-life aspect in that working in groups is an essential aspect of the future workplace (Davies, 2009). Collaboration with fellow students, rather than working in isolation, can also promote student engagement as it opens up the possibilities for discussion, new ideas and varying approaches (McDowell and Sambell, 1999). Following from these points, group work may encourage deep approaches to learning when students are compelled to justify their own positions and engage with classmates' different perspectives.

Ideally, group work should develop positive interdependence in that the group as an entity accomplishes more than a single individual working independently. These are referred to as 'additive tasks', where inputs from each member on parts of a topic add something and the sum forms a composite whole (Davies, 2009). In practice, though, the way group assessment is often implemented does not seem to involve all group members working productively in additive tasks, and I explore related challenges next.

Main challenges for group work

A central and much-discussed problem concerns free-riding, when a student makes a minimal contribution to the group effort whilst obtaining a grade which exceeds the quality of their input. Free-riding is often treated synonymously with social loafing, although Davies (2009) distinguishes them by defining the former as obtaining reward for no effort, whereas the latter involves a reduction in effort due to lack of recognition or a lack of identification in the group: the larger the group, the greater the risk of variable member motivation and related social loafing (Kerr, 1983). Social loafers are often not unwilling to contribute, but they are denied the opportunity by their more competent teammates. A corollary to the role of a social loafer is that of the 'diligent isolate' (Pieterse and Thompson, 2010) – a group member who works alone to complete their task, and those of other members, in order to 'save the project'.

A related phenomenon is that of the sucker effect (Kerr, 1983): if there is a group member who appears to be free-riding on one's efforts, one should reduce one's own efforts rather than become a sucker. The sucker effect is the cause of procrastination in many group activities (Davies, 2009) because students may hope that someone else will do the bulk of the work. Of course, if all group members hold that position, little will be done until the deadline is imminent. Procrastination may also relate to poor time management. This can be exacerbated when group members experience difficulties in finding the time to meet up – a particular challenge for part-time students and those with family responsibilities or casual jobs. One solution is to provide time for students to work together in their groups during the regular class schedule, and this also provides opportunities for teachers to monitor progress and provide feedback.

Some members may be reluctant to participate in or uncommitted to the group or the subject (Davies, 2009). More able students tend to become frustrated with the inability of some team members to contribute in accordance with their expectations (Pieterse and Thompson, 2010). Students may not tackle group work together, instead dividing up the tasks and doing them individually (Brown and McIlroy, 2011). In such scenarios, much of the value of group work is undermined and students may have negative feelings about the group process itself.

Student perspectives on assessed group projects

How do students feel about being assessed on group work? First-year accounting students at the University of Brighton mainly reported positive responses in that their group project was seen as developing a range of useful skills, including working with others in a group, carrying out research, analysing data and action planning (Bourner, Hughes and Bourner, 2001). Students of Business who viewed group assessment positively saw group processes as useful for future employment and experienced fruitful group dynamics (Volet and Mansfield, 2006).

Overall, however, the literature seems to indicate that group assessment attracts a good deal of negative sentiment from students. It is hard to gauge the extent to which reported problems reflect: a weakness of assessing group projects per se; how they were implemented by a particular teacher in a specific setting; or other contextual factors, such as student motivation or relationships between particular groups of students. I highlighted the issue of fairness in Chapter 1, and concerns about it are a central concern in relation to group assessment (Flint and Johnson, 2011; Orr, 2010a). Students often express worries that assessed group work may negatively impact on their overall grades (Pauli et al., 2008). Another major challenge for group assessment lies in students' lack of practice in working cooperatively and their limited understanding of its processes.

Four main interrelated challenges occurring in student group work involve: lack of group commitment or motivation to participate fully in the task; disorganisation in completing the task, exacerbated by logistical difficulties in terms of meeting and engaging with the task; group divisions due to interactional, communicative and organisational problems; and interpersonal conflicts (Pauli et al., 2008). Students who viewed group assignments negatively desired more teacher involvement to support group processes and experienced difficulties with group communication and differing attitudes (Volet and Mansfield, 2006).

Brown and McIlroy (2011) asked eighty-seven students in a Master of Science occupational therapy programme whether they preferred to complete their major research project as an individual or as a member of a group: 68.9 per cent preferred to do it as an individual, whereas only 26.4 per cent preferred to carry it out in a group (a small percentage expressed no preference). The main reasons for preferring individual work related to issues of time management, avoidance

of i.   control over the quality of the final product
and t.   negative experiences of group work influence
students   rence for future group collaboration (Pauli et al.,
2008; Vol.   a, 2006).

Given the   of the current research, it is worth pointing out that
Confucian-heri. e students are generally well disposed towards working, but
not necessarily towards being assessed, in groups. When students have been
acculturated to value communal goals, they should find it easier to form a
coherent and committed team than those of a more individualistic nature
(Kember, 2000). 'Spontaneous collaborative learning' (Tang, 1993) refers to the
habit of Chinese students initiating peer support groups to carry out academic
work together. Students collaborating in this way tend to achieve better outcomes
and exhibit deeper approaches than those who study individually. Conflicts over
grading and individual or group contribution can form a barrier to this natural
willingness to work in groups. In an interview study of twenty-two Business
undergraduate Asian students in a New Zealand tertiary institution (Li and
Campbell, 2008), the students expressed dislike of group assignments where all
members shared the same marks regardless of the contribution they had made,
viewing this as penalising bright and hard-working students and rewarding less
diligent ones.

Group processes and leadership

Central to positive experiences in a group project are the management of its
processes and related leadership. A group project involves both a process of
carrying out the project and a final product, which usually takes the form of a
written report and/or a related oral presentation. The quality of the group
product may be less important than the learning process that created it (Gibbs
and Simpson, 2004). Students perceive that a focus on outcomes can be unfair as
it fails to differentiate between group members who contribute positively, as
opposed to those who are free-riders or have a negative influence on the group
(Bryan, 2006).

An important part of the process of a group project is the management and
coordination of the group members. The emergence of a group leader may arise
naturally from reasoned interaction among the members or may be decided in a
random way, whereas failure to appoint a leader may be a disadvantage. When a
group leader emerges or is assigned early in the process, students perceived it
easier to complete the project successfully (Payne et al., 2006). Some students
volunteer to take on the leadership role in an attempt to gain some control over
the assessment process and ensure a good assignment mark, but group leaders do
not generally have much authority to pressurise classmates whose performance is
hindering the group (Li and Campbell, 2008). A study of Engineering students
at an American university suggested that group leaders were often those with
most prior experience of group work; and, in extreme cases, the group leader

ended up undertaking most of the tasks for the group (Colbeck, Campbell and Bjorklund, 2000). In this way, a group leader can become a victim of free-riding by doing more than their share of the work.

There is also some discussion in the literature of the composition of groups, although no clear path emerges. Homogeneous groups in respect of academic skills and goals may be preferable in that they permit members to be challenged in accordance with their abilities (Pieterse and Thompson, 2010), but in order to be able to learn from each other, students need to bring different types of knowledge and expertise to the group (Davies, 2009).

Awarding grades for group projects

A key issue in group projects is whether students should be awarded an overall project grade, with all members receiving the same grade, or whether they should also be awarded individual grades and, if so, how these should be calculated. The main rationale for awarding, or having the option of, an individual grade is to discourage free-riding. A major means of monitoring student contribution to the group is through some form of peer evaluation (e.g. Cheng and Warren, 2000; Jin, 2012). It seems reasonable to infer that students are in the best position to judge the quantity and quality of input to the work of the group, and involving students in peer evaluation is also a useful generic skill for them to practise and hone. Students perceive that group projects are fairer if they have the opportunity to provide the marker with confidential information on the contribution of each group member (Flint and Johnson, 2011). For example, students can assess the percentage contribution of their group members, with the total adding up to 100 per cent. By aggregating the scores of all group members, teachers can gauge perceptions of respective contributions and marks can be adjusted accordingly. Whether to include a self-assessment of one's own contribution is a further consideration.

A well-implemented example of peer evaluation of group contribution is described by Brooks and Ammons (2003) in relation to an undergraduate Business course with 330 students. The students completed anonymous peer evaluations of group members four times at monthly intervals on the basis of specific evaluation criteria, such as attitude, contribution and attention to meeting deadlines. A feature is the use of early evaluations, which seem useful, particularly with respect to their potential for early identification of possible problems. However, it seems somewhat time-consuming to produce four peer evaluations every semester, so perhaps two (one at the mid-point and one at the end) would be more advisable.

Another common strategy is to award a mark for individual contribution in addition to an overall mark for a group. For example, for a written report, students may indicate the aspect for which they were mainly responsible and they could be given a mark for that. Similarly, student contributions to a group presentation could be assessed individually. In such scenarios, the overall student grade for the project could comprise a weighted balance between the group grade and the individual contribution.

A useful recent example of a strategy for group assessment involving both individual and group grades is described by Swaray (2012). The group and individual assessment was arranged as follows:

1 A presentation delivered by a randomly selected member of the group, counting for 35 per cent of the group mark.
2 A report, counting for 30 per cent of the group mark.
3 A short-answer question for each individual member, counting for 20 per cent.
4 A reflective individual piece of writing, counting for 15 per cent.

All group members received the same grade for items 1 and 2, whereas items 3 and 4 were individual components, so the overall grade (which carried a weighting of 25 per cent of the overall course grade) comprised a balance of individual and group performance. Survey results showed that students were generally positive about the project's arrangements and perceived that these were effective in reducing free-riding. The main negative finding from the student data was that they expressed a preference for choosing their own group presenter, rather than leaving it to chance.

Overall, the issue of finding some compromise between a group grade and individual grades has been much discussed, perhaps too much. Some scholars (e.g. Falchikov, 2005) have reservations about such methods as they go against the spirit of collaboration and the kind of additive designs discussed by Davies (2009).

Oral presentations

Oral presentations have been increasingly common forms of assessment over the last twenty years or so. They tap into the need for effective communication, which is a valuable generic outcome and perhaps particularly so in the soft-applied disciplines. Oral presentations are features of assessment in the cases in Geology and Business; an option in Labour Law; and a key element of the critical reviews in Architecture. Through their relationship to professional communication skills, they are a relatively authentic mode of assessment (Doherty et al., 2011). Oral communication develops a public voice, helps students form their pedagogical identities, and has an authenticity that writing cannot possess (Barnett, 2007a). Oral assessment is also more resistant to plagiarism than written assessment (Joughin, 1998).

When an oral presentation is conceived as a position to be argued, it can facilitate a powerful student learning experience, with students perceiving it as more demanding than written assignments, more personal and leading to better learning outcomes (Joughin, 2007). Oral modes of presentation can enable a better picture of the extent of student understanding and have the advantage of allowing students to reveal their thinking processes (Maclellan, 2004b). The kind of thinking which is emerging can arise from related opportunities for classroom dialogue through peer assessment or peer feedback. In fact, given that the audience of an oral presentation is usually a group of classmates and a single teacher, a valid assessment of the presentation should take into account its degree of success in communicating to fellow students (Magin and Helmore, 2001). The presence of an audience for oral presentations is related to them being 'on-display assignments' (Hounsell, 2003, p. 75), in which student work or performance is openly visible to students rather than being of a private nature, as in most written assignments. Such modes of assessment allow students to acquaint themselves with one another's work and can prompt them to reflect on and self-evaluate both their own ways of working and what they and their peers have achieved.

There is evidence that assessed oral presentations can induce considerable anxiety amongst students (Huxham, Campbell and Westwood, 2012; Joughin, 1998). The performative nature of the oral presentation may inhibit the 'freedom to learn' of introverted students (Macfarlane, 2015). Oral presentations may also be difficult to assess and moderate reliably; and as they are often carried out in groups, they may lead to similar challenges to those for group assessment.

Grading student participation

The grading of student participation is not really an assessment method, but it is worth exploring because it is common in practice (Rocca, 2010), and it was a significant element in the History and Business cases explored in Chapters 4 and 6.

There has been a certain amount of relatively sporadic attention to this aspect over the last thirty years (e.g. Armstrong and Boud, 1983; Rogers, 2013). Assessment scholars generally advise against grading class participation (Bean and Peterson, 1998). At first sight, this seems reasonable in that awarding a reliable grade for something as amorphous as student participation is a considerable challenge. I devote space to it here because my analysis of the cases prompts me to consider whether the assessment of participation might be profitably rehabilitated. I return to this issue in Chapter 12, where I make some recommendations.

Classroom participation

The assessment of class participation differs from other assessment methods in that it is not separated in time and place from normal classroom processes (Armstrong and Boud, 1983) and it forms an integral part of teaching and learning. When students are tuned in to the demands of assessment, they may involve themselves most in activities which are assessed, so rewarding participation may make sense. There is, however, anecdotal evidence that the grading of student participation is a site for dubious practice, such as awarding grades for attendance which is clearly unrelated to quality participation. In a learning-oriented assessment approach, a key issue relates to the extent to which grading student participation may potentially stimulate student learning. I thus wish to consider the rationale, advantages and disadvantages of assessing student participation and consider some ways in which it could be carried out productively.

If an important objective is to facilitate the development of spoken communication, then this should be assessed; assessing participation can provide students with an incentive to prepare and participate in class discussion; it balances the preponderance of written work in assessment; and it provides multiple opportunities for students to perform in comparison with the more one-off nature of some common assessment tasks (Armstrong and Boud, 1983). Grading class participation can send positive signals to students about the kind of involvement in learning that is valued by teachers, such as active learning and the ability to contribute to communication within a discipline (Bean and Peterson, 1998). It is congruent with constructivist learning principles in terms of active learning and student construction of new understandings (Lai, 2012). It is also possible that the current generation of students may be less tolerant of sitting quietly and listening, and may expect or demand a more interactive classroom learning experience. When classes are large, participation can reduce some of the alienation or disengagement noted in Chapter 2, but it may be difficult to manage.

Assessing participation has its challenges. Teachers do not usually provide explicit instruction on student development of participation (Jacobs and Chase, 1992), so some lack of alignment between teaching and assessment may occur. The processes place a strain on the teacher if he or she has to teach, facilitate and assess participation at the same time (Armstrong and Boud, 1983). The extent of classroom participation often depends on students' personalities and may include cultural differences (Jacobs and Chase, 1992). The immediacy of verbal classroom interaction is not always conducive to thoughtful, measured arguments and may be particularly challenging for students from certain cultures (Chiu, 2009). Participation can also seem to privilege oral forms of engagement in comparison with equally valid 'non-performative' forms of participation, such as active listening or note-taking (Macfarlane, 2015). Classroom atmosphere is important for developing student confidence in participation through positive early experiences; use of wait time; and allowing students preparation time prior to speaking (Rocca, 2010).

There are concerns about reliability and bias due to favouritism or prejudice (Armstrong and Boud, 1983). These are exacerbated by the challenge of record-keeping in relation to participation, including whether notes are taken during class; afterwards on a selective basis, such as every other week; or whether the teacher relies mainly on memory at the end of the course. The lack of records makes it difficult for a grade to be reviewed for quality assurance purposes or in the event of a student appeal. The challenge of record-keeping can be mitigated by involving other parties in the assessment: students may be profitably used in peer-assessing contributions; or if there is a teaching assistant in the class, they could take regular notes on participation.

A further key issue relates to judgement and criteria for participation. The judgement of participation is subjective and a participation grade could be used as a 'fudge factor' to upgrade a worthy student or downgrade an unpleasant one (Jacobs and Chase, 1992). The teacher is faced with the issue of judging frequency of participation as opposed to the extent of worthwhile substantive contribution. In addition, students do not generally receive much indication of how they are achieving on class participation, which can make the final grade seem somewhat arbitrary (Bean and Peterson, 1998). A mid-semester assessment of participation can encourage increased participation throughout the semester (Dancer and Kamvounias, 2005). Student involvement in development of criteria for assessing class participation is encouraged because it is likely to strengthen acceptance for teacher judgement and is also a valuable learning experience in itself (Lyons, 1989).

Building on and synthesising lists of criteria for assessing participation (Armstrong and Boud, 1983; Bean and Petersen, 1998; Dancer and Kamvounias, 2005), in Box 3.1 I suggest four main parameters for assessing participation.

Box 3.1 Key parameters of assessing participation

- Preparation for class, e.g. through prior reading or self-study.
- Contribution in plenary and small group discussions.
- Quality of argumentation and appropriate use of evidence.
- Quality of expression, including relevance, clarity and conciseness.

Online participation

An alternative to assessing verbal classroom participation is the assessment of contributions through online means, such as participation in discussion mediated through an LMS or via Facebook. When a classroom participation grade involves both face-to-face and online participation it respects different student personalities and cultures in that verbal and written contributions can be balanced, and students learn to participate in the disciplinary community through different means.

A course blog or discussion forum provides opportunities for participants to interact online in relation to various topics relevant to module content. Blogs permit immediate and targeted feedback on contributions, and through their chronological nature they can also facilitate the identification of development over time (Benson and Brack, 2010). Through blogs, a teacher can create an environment in which students feel themselves to be important elements of a classroom community in which their needs and opinions are recognised and addressed. Based on a case study of his own practice, Churchill (2009) demon-strated that benefits of blogs include: reading contributions of others; receiving comments and previewing tasks of others; and engaging with feedback received in relation to these. A key issue is to provide motivation or incentive for students to participate in blogging. In Churchill's study, encouragement for students to blog included: regular learning tasks which required students to present outcomes in their blogs; blogs being an assessment requirement; and regular blogging by the teacher. When the teacher both participates in and grades student contributions to a blog, this can, however, generate a heavy teacher workload.

A recent example of online participation involved an online assignment with a 15 per cent weighting in which students carried out peer discussion analysing set readings on critical thinking (Lai, 2012). The marking criteria focused on similar aspects to those presented in Box 3.1, with the addition of a criterion focused on how students built on the ideas and contributions of others; this emphasises the cumulative nature of online discussions. The marking criteria also contained an aspect which penalised students whose first post was within two to three days of the deadline, thus encouraging steady effort on the task.

Portfolio-based writing

Under the category of portfolio-based writing, I bring together ideas on portfolios and e-portfolios which share in common the strategy of building up work over time in a cumulative and integrated way. A major attraction of these forms of assessment is their potential to marry summative and formative assessment, which is one of the aims of learning-oriented assessment. They can be assessed summatively to provide a grade and can be arranged to encourage formative elements, such as peer review, self-reflection and dialogic feedback on work in progress.

Portfolios

Klenowski (2010) summarises the main features of a portfolio as follows: a collection of student work; selecting items for inclusion; active student engagement in the portfolio assessment process in terms of self-assessment; and reflection on the process of learning through the portfolio. A further element is signposting of the portfolio to guide the reader through it (Baume, 2001).

One of the attractions of portfolios is that they are integrated tasks. By facili-tating the collection of evidence over time and incorporating peer feedback and reflective thinking, the portfolio is primed to stimulate desirable learning outcomes. A further advantage of the portfolio is that it can be used to represent claims of achievement in authentic tasks and settings (Klenowski, 2002).

A portfolio represents a student selection of material; accordingly, each student has more investment in it and may develop more personal pride in it (Baume, 2001). Selection can, however, also represent a challenge. Students tend to collect a wide array of materials and often have difficulty in focusing the evidence they have accumulated. This may be a particular problem for less capable students and can lead to the submission of an unwieldy portfolio which does not clearly show reflection and cumulativeness. Clear guidelines and reflective discussion of exemplars can ameliorate such challenges.

Portfolios represent many of the features of learning-oriented assessment tasks: students work at them over time; student choice is enabled; there is a relationship with real-world tasks; and the portfolio facilitates constructive alignment. Whilst portfolios can represent difficulties for students in coming to terms with what is required, there is evidence (e.g. Tiwari and Tang, 2003) that over time students become accustomed to what needs to be done. Portfolios also present challenges for establishing reliable grading practices, but there are strategies to minimise these concerns (see Johnston, 2004; Smith and Tillema, 2008). Key elements include clear and transparent marking schemes, training for assessors, and robust methods of moderation.

E-portfolios

E-portfolios, also known as electronic portfolios or digital portfolios, involve collections of work similar to the paper portfolio discussed above with the additional use of technologically developed artefacts. E-portfolios are a means of developing learning trajectories through a range of evidence, such as text, audio, narration and digital video (Finger and Jamieson-Proctor, 2009). Technology provides additional options, for example through the use of hyperlinks, for student communication of their identity and the depth of their learning processes (Cambridge, 2010). E-portfolios can also be useful for documenting authentic contextualised learning in work-based learning placements and for personal development planning, including lifelong learning aspects facilitated by their portability beyond graduation (Stefani, Mason and Pegler, 2007). Some universities have taken initiatives in developing e-portfolios at an institutional level as records of achievement.

By capturing contemporary enthusiasm for social networking, e-portfolios have the potential to become more attractive than traditional forms of assessment (Cambridge, 2010), and thereby respond to student diversity by catering for different student capacities and learning strategies (Stefani et al., 2007). A further potential strength of e-portfolios lies in the possibility of assessing complex learning outcomes as an aspect, for example, of a capstone or integrated experience.

It is probably fair to say that there has been more enthusiasm for than critical scrutiny of the use of e-portfolios (Cummings and Maddux, 2010). In terms of the challenges in introducing e-portfolios, they require students and staff to engage in a number of ways: to understand the portfolio genre; use the technology which facilitates the process; compose and respond to texts; and judge standards for assessing the process (Cambridge, 2010).

The issue of student and staff workload in relation to e-portfolios is complex. If implemented efficiently, there may be workload savings in relation to a traditional portfolio, but this is not a given. Trevitt, Macduff and Steed (2014) suggest that e-portfolios imply a redistribution of workload towards coaching rather than assessing. The development of an e-portfolio may increase staff and student workload, especially for those unfamiliar with the relevant tools (Gulbahar and Tinmaz, 2006). E-portfolios are often cumbersome and time-consuming for teachers to mark and difficult to moderate grades. The key is the selection process of students curating what is to be presented in the portfolio. A variation is for the e-portfolio to be a compulsory stepping-stone to another assessed task, such as an oral presentation or a reflective piece of writing summarising main learning outcomes from the development of the e-portfolio.

Quality assessment task design

Having discussed specific methods of assessment, I now examine more general characteristics of assessment task design. I review various relevant works from the literature on the nature of assessment design with the aim of developing a conception of what quality assessment tasks might look like.

Traditional psychometric considerations suggest that an assessment needs to be valid (assessing what it claims to be assessing) and reliable (producing a consistent score). Contemporary conceptions of validity in line with the work of Messick (1994) emphasise the meaning, relevance and utility of assessment results; the value implications of these results as a basis for action; and the social consequences of their use. This notion of consequential validity includes the intended and unintended consequences of assessment and their possible impact on teaching and learning. Reliability includes consistency of grading of a single tutor across student work and inter-rater reliability when there are more than one teachers of a course. The concept of reliability also intersects with the notion of fairness highlighted in Chapter 1.

A useful framework for evaluating assessment quality is proposed by Baartman and colleagues (2007). They propose ten features of quality competence-based assessment:

- *Authenticity*: the extent of resemblance to the future workplace.
- *Cognitive complexity*: the need for higher cognitive skills.
- *Fairness*: equal opportunities for students to demonstrate competence.
- *Meaningfulness*: value and links to personal interests.
- *Directness* of interpretation of assessment results.
- *Transparency* of requirements and criteria.
- *Educational consequences* in relation to learning and instruction.

- *Reproducibility of decisions:* relates to the generalisability of assessment judgements.
- *Comparability:* consistency of judgement.
- *Costs and efficiency:* relate to the practicality of assessment.

An important issue which their framework sidesteps is the notion of constructive alignment (Biggs, 1996a, 1999) of curriculum objectives, constructivist learning activities, assessment tasks and intended learning outcomes. A major aspect of this formulation is to circumvent the problem when assessment does not match higher-order intentions of the curriculum and may prompt lower-order student learning. Rarely addressed is the extent to which this alignment needs to be married with constructivist teaching and learning methods or whether alignment without constructivism is also acceptable or recommended. Constructive alignment falls within a technical perspective on assessment and may fail to account adequately for over-reliance on the codification of knowledge, and underestimate the constraints that teachers face (James, 2014). A further critique suggests that the geometric connotations of alignment as a metaphor can be taken to imply a single 'line of sight' between a given learning outcome, a particular teaching and learning strategy and method of assessment when various configurations of teaching and assessment might actually be appropriate for a given learning outcome (McCune and Hounsell, 2005).

Assessment tasks supporting student learning

In his book *Being a Teacher in Higher Education*, Knight (2002a) has a particularly useful chapter titled 'Learning tasks'. Some key points: tasks are at the centre of student learning, so the deeper the sought learning, the more complex the tasks need to be; students may resist ambiguous, open-ended and non-routine tasks; good tasks provide opportunities for fresh learning, give practice and foster meta-cognition; there is a strong case for ensuring that some tasks involve students working in groups; and quality teaching involves being a skilful facilitator of tasks which also demands some bravery in putting students at the centre of learning.

An important contribution to thinking about the relationship between assessment and student learning arose from an extensive review and synthesis of literature which developed eleven conditions under which assessment supports student learning (Gibbs and Simpson, 2004; Gibbs, 2006). The first three of these relate to task design; the fourth relates to clear and high expectations for students; and the remaining seven are all concerned with feedback. Despite the importance of feedback, this represents a rather lopsided approach. Of most relevance to this chapter are the first three conditions, discussed below.

Assessed tasks capture student study time and effort

This condition relates to the time on task principle in terms of the amount of study time generated by assessment tasks for a module. Well-designed assessment tasks are likely to encourage students to devote extensive study time outside regular class meetings.

Assessment tasks distribute student effort evenly across topics and weeks

This condition concerns the consistency of effort students are required to produce across a module and across topics. It addresses the risk that most student effort may be focused towards the end of a module, prior to a final exam or in developing a single end-of-course written assignment, such as an essay. It relates also to the breadth of curriculum coverage. Or, to put it another way, teachers should strive to avoid summative assessment tasks which allow students to be highly selective about the elements of the syllabus which they actually study and the particular components of the course to which they devote time (Gibbs and Dunbar-Goddet, 2007).

Assessment tasks engage students in productive learning activity

This condition relates to the kind of study activity stimulated by an assessment task: the extent to which the assessment encourages the student to take deep or surface approaches to learning and also the quality of student engagement with the task (Gibbs, 2006). Is there congruence between maximising the grade and productive learning, or is it possible that students can achieve a high grade without engaging deeply with learning material? The Gibbs framework has little to say on the relationship between assessment tasks and real life, and I turn to that notion next.

WTP and authentic assessment

The valuable notion of ways of thinking and practising (WTP) in the subject denotes the richness, depth and breadth of what students might learn through engagement with a specific subject area: for example, exploring particular forms of discourse, values or ways of acting which are regarded as central to mastery of a discipline (McCune and Hounsell, 2005). WTP also encompasses a developing understanding of the conventions of academic communication within the discipline and the relevant professional community (Anderson and Hounsell, 2007). A major means of facilitating the development of WTP is by assessment tasks focused on real-life problems and issues contextualised within specific disciplinary situations. Such tasks are generally popular with students and support them to develop as participants in a disciplinary community and engage with methods of enquiry which are valued in particular academic disciplines (Sambell et al., 2013).

This relationship between assessment and real life brings me to what is variously termed: authentic assessment (Gulikers, Bastiaens and Kirschner, 2004; Wiggins, 1993); the assessment of authentic achievement (Cumming and Maxwell, 1999;

Maclellan 2004a); or assessing real-world issues or problems (Sambell et al., 2013). The essence of authenticity is the relation of an assessment task to real-life ways in which knowledge or skills are used in the discipline into which a student is being inducted. Gulikers et al. (2004) define authentic assessment as requiring students to demonstrate the same kind of competencies or combinations of knowledge, skills and attitudes that they need to apply in the criterion situation in professional life. These authors also found that authenticity is subjective and what teachers see as authentic may not be congruent with students' perceptions (Gulikers, Bastiaens, Kirschner and Kester, 2006).

To my mind, the term 'contextualised assessment' might also be used to emphasise the idea of assessment relating to some form of naturally occurring context. Authentic assessment in workplace contexts often occurs in soft-applied disciplines, such as Education or Nursing, and increasingly in most profession-based disciplines. Maclellan (2004a) suggests that assessment of authentic achievement can be demonstrated through elaborated written communication about disciplinary concepts, involving analysis, higher-order thinking, synthesis and evaluation. Authentic achievement could also be demonstrated through various forms of oral or multi-modal communication.

Integration in overall assessment design

Much of what I have discussed so far in this chapter relates to the characteristics of individual tasks. An important further issue relates to how assessment tasks in combination can promote the kind of cumulative learning outcomes which are sought. This could involve developing sequences of tasks which progressively build student capacity to tackle more complex problems (Molloy and Boud, 2013).

In a recent vision of 'assessment futures', Boud and associates (2010) propose that assessment tasks should be integrated into curriculum planning at its earliest stages, provide evidence of integrated learning through larger-scale tasks which enable students to demonstrate integrated learning, and promote engagement by assessment tasks which are designed in an interlinked, constructive, organised and coherent sequence. The latter seems to be a particular challenge which merits consideration. Approaching task design from a programme-wide perspective might represent a way forward. Programme initiatives have the potential to benefit student development through mapping assessment to create connections, sequences and a cumulative flow of assessment tasks across the whole programme (Jessop et al., 2014). The design of tasks can permit some overlap and revisiting of key learning outcomes to form an iterative and nested task design (Molloy and Boud, 2013).

Variety and choice

By injecting elements of choice into assessment, students are able to pursue topics in which they have a personal interest (Sambell et al., 2013). Choice provides students with a perception of control in terms of shaping their work to their own individual priorities (Bevitt, 2014). This may enable some matching of task demands to student capabilities, which may be a useful design consideration (Lizzio and Wilson, 2013). Choice can give students a greater sense of ownership in the work and avoid the de-motivating perception that they are simply going through routine tasks which have been done by many students previously (McDowell and Sambell, 1999). Students are particularly sensitive to a task's motivational potential (Lizzio and Wilson, 2013). Choice also seems to be an important factor for international or widening participation students so they can have suitable opportunities to demonstrate their best performance (Bevitt, 2014). Without choice, students may see tasks as imposed on them, which, as I noted in Chapter 2, often leads to surface approaches to learning. Optimal learning is more likely to be achieved when assessment is discussed with students rather than set for them (Lizzio and Wilson, 2013). Summative assessment needs to give space to individuality in which students' educational being can flourish and they can develop their own authentic voice (Barnett, 2007b).

It would seem natural that some variety in assessment formats would be useful in encouraging students to demonstrate varied understandings, showcase different skills and produce a range of learning outcomes. Variety may also encourage student motivation in that it avoids the repetitiveness of doing similar tasks repeatedly. Exposure to a variety of assessment tasks may not, however, be universally beneficial for students. Limiting the variety of forms of assessment can reduce student confusion as to criteria and expected outcomes, and through repeated cycles of performance can help students to develop awareness of requirements and improve with practice (Gibbs and Dunbar-Goddet, 2007). Some students are better served by becoming familiar with the processes of a smaller number of tasks. A wide range of different task types also makes it difficult for students to apply latent learning from feedback on earlier assessed work (Bevitt, 2014). Possible concerns about unfamiliar assignments may also contribute to students sometimes having mixed feelings about innovative assessment.

Summary of quality assessment tasks

To sum up the story so far, quality learning-oriented assessment:

- involves alignment between objectives, content, assessment and desired outcomes;
- promotes student engagement and deep approaches to learning;
- mirrors real-world applications of the subject matter by involving students as participants in the disciplinary community;
- develops student meta-cognition by engaging with criteria, standards and exemplars;
- involves variety through a judicious mix of individual and collaborative, oral and written tasks;

- contains an element of student choice and personal investment;
- stimulates and encourages sustained involvement and effort over time; and
- facilitates forms of dialogic interaction or feedback.

Summary of chapter

In this chapter, I have analysed the main assessment tasks used in higher education and have explored key elements of quality assessment. This review prepares the ground for the following two chapters, which analyse assessment tasks in the disciplines of History and Law.

Main implications for practice

- Assessment tasks should be designed to encourage progress towards desired learning outcomes.
- Mirroring real-life uses of the discipline generally enhances student motivation.
- Assessment should develop student ownership through choice and personal engagement.
- Sequences of assessment should involve sustained effort and intellectual engagement.
- Assessment tasks need to be organised in a coherent, integrated and cumulative way.

Chapter 4

Assessment task design in History

> Being a good teacher is very much about being a good designer of tasks.
>
> (Knight, 2002a, p. 124)

Scope of chapter

In this chapter, I focus on assessment task design and implementation in the subject of History. The discussion fits into the overall framework of the book by analysing learning-oriented assessment tasks in context. The History case involves a suite of integrated tasks comprising a field-trip assignment, two different modes of assessing participation, and an individual project.

Setting the scene

David Pomfret is an associate professor in the Department of History, Faculty of Arts, Hong Kong University. He has a sustained record of teaching excellence since joining the university in 2001, receiving an Outstanding Teaching Award at the University Level in 2010 and across the whole of Hong Kong in 2012. He is also a well-respected researcher and was the winner of an Outstanding Young Researcher Award for 2006/7. He is a historian of youth and his scholarly interest in the changing nature of youth has contributed to his reimagining of the History curriculum and the learning process. One aspect of his teaching that is particularly admired is his use of technology to enliven the learning process through videos, movie extracts, stills, graphs and text within his classes.

The module and its assessment

Making History is a first-year foundation course taken by around 110 students from a variety of disciplines, including Arts, Business, Education, Law and others. The module focuses on the varied ways in which the past is present in contemporary lives, critical engagement with representations of the past, and the importance of thinking historically. The intended learning outcomes are that students should be able to engage critically with representations of the past, analyse and use evidence to construct historical accounts, critically interpret interconnections between past and present, and reflect upon and critically consider the value of historical awareness.

It is a relatively new course and I observed its second iteration. The module comprises twelve interactive lectures, each two hours in length, taught by David and eight one-hour tutorials managed by a teaching assistant, Connie (pseudonym). The assessment for the course involves three main elements, summarised in Box 4.1: the first task involves fieldwork, the final task is a project, and students are continually assessed on their participation.

Box 4.1 Assessment design in History

- Fieldwork report (museum visit or scavenger hunt) (30 per cent)
- Participation (30 per cent):
  - weekly 'one-sentence response' (15 per cent)
  - tutorial participation (15 per cent)
- Individual project (40 per cent):
  - draft (10 per cent)
  - final submission (30 per cent)

Teacher rationale for the assessment design

I asked David about his approach to assessment design:

> I am trying to get away from the orthodoxy of the essay and provide other ways of communicating and arguing, so students can showcase their ability to master discourses of history; see the past is alive and being re-shaped; see themselves as historians; and understand that history can be pertinent to their own lives . . . In the assignments I want the students to express their own ideas relevant to their own lives.
>
> (Carless, 2014, p. 7)

David wants to provide different assessment tasks to essays, which could easily become a repetitive format over a four-year programme. Instead, his goal is 'to excite students about history' through the form of tasks which encourage them to experience what it is to be a historian. The ideas about relating history to real life and seeing themselves as historians resonate with the notions of authenticity and WTP discussed in the previous chapter.

I also asked David to suggest some principles of assessment task design and he responded as follows:

> Diversity would be one key word. It is important to assess students in ways which provide them opportunities to indicate how much they understood;

the extent they are able to master higher-level cognitive analysis in various ways. I think the speed and quality of the feedback is as important as the design of the assessment.

My interpretation of 'diversity' involves different ways of students demonstrating learning outcomes, in this case showcasing their ability to master higher-order thinking and analysis. Open-ended tasks are often the most effective in developing these kinds of diverse outcomes. I also found it pertinent that David considered feedback as an element of task design, and I return to this issue in Chapters 10 and 12, specifically in relation to Table 12.2.

One of the further themes I noticed from the assessment task design was that of choice: students could select their own topics for the project and between the options of a museum trip or a scavenger hunt assignment. David explained:

> I try to encourage a sense that they have a stake in what they are doing, a way of getting them to put themselves into the picture. I provide choice because I want students to feel that they are exploring something that energises them and they can invest more of themselves in a particular assignment. I want them to have an opportunity to achieve something beyond what I can present to them, an engaging exercise in which their own voice is prominent.

David seems to see a link between choice and student engagement. He believes that students will invest more of themselves in a particular task if they have the power to choose, for example by selecting a topic that has some kind of meaning for them.

David also talked about how he saw the relationships between the different assessment tasks so that they came together to form a coherent whole:

> Quite similar skills are being assessed in the different assessment tasks. I use the assessments to enhance their ability to achieve the learning outcomes. I hope they see the connections, for example, between unmasking the historical narratives within the museum space and ways in which the past has been manipulated within discourses of nationhood in Hong Kong. There is a connection, but I don't know whether it is clear to them.

I return to this important aspect of integration and coherence in task design in the 'Implications' section at the end of this chapter.

Analysis of the assessment tasks

I now describe and analyse the three assessment elements of the course: fieldwork report, assessed participation and project. I place particular emphasis on the 'one-sentence response' participation task because it is an innovative assessment task which might merit consideration and adaptation for other disciplines.

Fieldwork report

The fieldwork report is worth 30 per cent of the final grade for the module. It should be no more than 1000 words if submitted in written form, such as essay, wiki or website, and no more than five minutes if submitted in a technology-enhanced format, such as video or podcast. The overarching aim of the report is to provide an opportunity for students to reflect upon the relevance of historical awareness and representations of the past to their own lives and the life histories of family members, classmates and contemporaries. Students are offered two choices: museum visit (to a local museum of their own choice) or scavenger hunt. Both options are intended to address the following key issues: the interconnections between representations of the past and present that are evident in the context of the museum or scavenger hunt; a critical approach to the historical 'artefacts' examined; and a critical engagement with how the past is represented and/or an analysis of the value and uses of history today.

Students are presented with focus questions to guide the museum visit. These include: the museum's mission or purpose; its strengths and weaknesses; how it reflects Hong Kong's historical and current political status; how it deals with controversial topics and events; how space is used; and how various points of view are expressed.

The scavenger hunt is a form of internet-based simulation in which participants visit sites of historical significance in Hong Kong to uncover the past by searching for clues among remnants of the city's historic fabric. Students need to identify historical artefacts using Google Maps; go to the location and find the artefact; answer a multiple-choice question about the artefact which reveals some information about the significance of the place; and unlock a historical document related to the place. Students then need to study this document and answer an open-ended question. There are ten sites for the scavenger hunt and students are asked to visit at least three.

Teacher rationale for fieldwork assessment

David has made the fieldwork report the first assessment task because he views it as the most straightforward exercise. He spoke about the rationale for the fieldwork and its assessment as follows:

> It's important to get them out of the classroom [and] into the context so that they can see ways in which people may look at the past . . . They go into the museum and are asked to critique the space. They are provided with a list of questions as a framework so that they are not passively accepting what there is to see. There may be more than one version of a story and competing discourses; some of the students are attuned to this whereas others are not.
>
> (Carless, 2014, p. 7)

This rationale is well aligned with the stated learning outcome of promoting student ability to engage with representations of the past and ideas of history being contested and socially constructed. As this is the course's first assignment and students are in their first year of university study, the use of guiding questions seems a sensible way of supporting the students.

There is also the second option of the scavenger hunt, which David introduces as follows:

> For the scavenger hunt, the intention is to get them to feel the power of the past in the space in which a historical event actually took place. Usually they see these places but do not think about what they mean in terms of the history of Hong Kong. It's all about seeing the contestation around the past and developing their abilities to critique the use of the past in the present.

In relation to the fieldwork, I infer an emphasis on WTP in that David is providing tasks which relate to what it is to be a historian: involvement in critique, contestation, competing discourses and different ways of thinking about the past. Offering students a choice between two different tasks also reflects David's view that choice and flexibility are important issues in assessment task design.

Student perspectives on fieldwork assessment

Most of the students carried out the assignment which related to the museum trip. There were three main reasons for this. The first was that visiting a museum was more familiar to them than a scavenger hunt, so it provoked less uncertainty. The second was a pragmatic one in relation to the module schedule: the information and content related to the museum visit came earlier in the module, so it seemed more flexible for their schedule to carry out that option. The third – and related reason – was that David seemed to encourage students to choose the museum option because of its potential to avoid a rush towards the end of the semester when many assignments are typically due. Although most of the students did not opt for the scavenger hunt as an assessment task, nearly all of them did participate in it as a learning activity. This is indicative of a high degree of student engagement and that they perceived it as a purposeful activity. Better outcomes are likely to be achieved when students are involved in learning tasks as well as assessment tasks.

In relation to the scavenger hunt, David reported that some students appeared to have little conception of the history of some of the places in Hong Kong with which they were familiar. Others developed interpretations which David found impressive. He reported one student seeing downtown places as involving the 'clustering of sites of power, constructed by the British in order to inflate colonial power'.

Given that few students opted for the scavenger hunt as an assessment task, I focus on the museum visit in what follows. I begin with two students commenting on the field trip and making some comparisons with examinations, the form of assessment with which they had most experience in school:

> Fieldwork is interesting. It's actually more difficult than an examination as you need to think more. I am a bit lazy and I probably wouldn't visit a museum, unless it was a required task. It's good that it gets me to do something meaningful.
>
> I never thought that if we are learning about museums we should visit a real museum. It is more direct than learning in the classroom but it's also time-consuming. Writing a field report is more difficult than examinations as it involves a long process of thinking and a lot of energy. For learning purposes, I prefer writing a field report than taking an exam.

In Chapter 1, I mainly talked about tensions and compromises in assessment from a teacher perspective, whereas here they arise from students' perceptions. These two students see benefits of fieldwork in terms of the thinking processes it generates, but also feel that examinations are more straightforward and less time-consuming.

Joyce was mainly positive about her museum visit:

> I chose to write about my field trip to Sun Yat-Sen Museum because it gave me some strong feelings. I found that once you had really been there, you would have your own feelings about the museum and you would have a lot of things to say. I have gained a lot from this process.

Shan went to the Museum of Tea Ware. She wrote an essay about the visit because she thought this was more straightforward than using a different format, such as a wiki or a podcast. When asked about what she learnt from writing the field report, she replied:

> I realised that there may be hidden messages that a museum conveys to visitors. Through the way artefacts are put together and the use of space, visitors experience history. I learnt that museums are effective means to connect the present with the past. From now on, when I visit another museum, I will pay more attention to the messages conveyed to us.

This seems to be quite a positive reflection on her museum visit and roughly in accordance with the kind of learning outcomes David is seeking to stimulate.

Juliet had more mixed views. She saw benefits in field trips and found them to be interesting, although she did state a preference for learning in the classroom, which she called a 'proper way to learn'. With respect to field trips, she explained, 'You have to depend on yourself and if you are not well organised and well prepared beforehand, you may not learn much.' She also had views on the nature of museums:

A museum is a holder of history and a good tool for a government to have thought control, to educate people and for cultural heritage. We have to see how the museum is run. I went to museums when I was young, but I never got to perceive them from a historian's perspective.

In sum, the fieldwork was a means of developing student participation in history and how it is constructed. The fieldwork carries some resonance with the themes of WTP, authenticity and contextualised learning discussed in Chapter 3 in that students are involved in thinking and communicating in ways analogous to those of historians. A further feature was student independence in choosing when, how and where to conduct their fieldwork, so that an element of choice and flexibility was salient.

Assessed participation

There were two major means of encouraging and assessing student participation: weekly 'one-sentence response' (OSR) tasks (15 per cent of the module assessment) and the assessment of tutorial participation (also worth 15 per cent). Part of David's general rationale was in relation to links he drew between assessment and student learning:

> I've moved towards the position that students would mainly see the relevance of what goes on in the class if it is assessed. I think it is crucial for students to see the relevance of being there in the classroom so I want participation to be assessed and for students to feel they have a stake in what goes on.

To me, this seems a pragmatic and reasonable approach to student motivation in relation to assessment: by capturing student motivation to gain marks, David is involving them in active classroom participation. However, a more critical perspective might view this kind of position as reifying assessment and neglecting valid learning tasks which are not assessed.

Teacher rationale for OSR

OSR is David's own idea and he explained it as follows:

> I want to assess their learning experience during classroom time and provide an incentive for attendance. I am a firm believer in the value of short written exercises. I think it is a great way of honing their communication skills; after all we live in an age of Twitter and students rarely have call to write long research pieces [Carless, 2014, p. 7]. One-sentence responses introduce them to the connections between the subjects which we are discussing and their lives, so they may feel this is something pertinent to themselves.

David originally conceived OSR partly as a convenient way of measuring class attendance (an institutional requirement): he reported attendance rates in excess of 90 per cent. As his experience evolved, however, he realised OSR's potential to encourage student participation in terms of its role in 'putting students' voices' into the classroom and 'contributing their insights'.

The OSR issue upon which students have commented forms a focus in the following lecture. David saw this as 'the basis for me to go away and think about how to present the material as it helps me understand the students and get a sense of who they are'. In the next class, David displays selected student responses and shows some data in the form of pie-charts so that students can compare their responses with those of other classmates and previous cohorts of students on the course. This can raise their awareness of similarities and differences in their views in comparison with those of others. David also believes that in this way, over time, they will build up a 'history' of the course: a link between an activity and the subject itself.

So the main aims of OSR are for students to respond to a historical issue which forms the focus for the next week's lecture, and to inform the teacher's preparation by indicating their views, opinions and previous knowledge. A more generic intended learning outcome is for students to hone their abilities to express opinions in clear written English.

OSR processes

The way OSR works is that in each course lecture, students complete a short hand-written response to an issue (see the samples in Box 4.2) on a small slip of paper. Students can complete this at any point during the session which suits them: for example, some of the punctual students complete it before the lecture starts; others do it during the break; others towards the end of the session. The main features are that the question is not known in advance and students complete their responses during the classroom time. After completion, they place their responses in a collection box. Although the technique is called OSR, students typically write *two* sentences, totalling around twenty words or sometimes a little more – whatever can be conveniently fitted on the slip of paper provided.

Box 4.2 Examples of OSR questions

- Which is more valuable – history in history books or history in the movies?
- What are the essential qualities of a good museum?
- Describe your fondest memory. Explain your choice.
- Is History a science or an art? Explain your answer.
- How might thinking historically help us realise a better future?

There is a correspondence between these short questions and other learning and assessment elements of the course. Some of them relate to the fieldwork; some of them to the project; and they also relate to lecture or tutorial topics. For example, a student might use their initial thinking on an OSR to form a starting point for a project. In these ways, OSR introduces them to the connections between the subjects they are studying and the other assessment components.

Halfway through the course, David provided some general interim feedback and informed the students that he was appreciative of their 'wonderful responses' to the OSR questions. He also reminded them of the importance of attendance and pointed out that failure to submit weekly OSR items would have a negative impact on grades. He informed students that he had identified some student malpractice, such as attending for only a few minutes to submit an OSR, or submitting an OSR for an absent classmate. He warned students against such practices in an advisory rather than a punitive manner by encouraging them to do the right thing rather than threatening them with sanctions for non-compliance. In this way, he presented himself as not being too heavy-handed over assessment. If he had come down hard on the misbehaving students, this might have had negative implications for the kind of classroom atmosphere he was trying to develop.

Student perspectives on OSR

I was unfamiliar with OSR prior to observing it in David's class, so I was particularly interested in how students perceived it. We collected quite a lot of students' perspectives on it and I begin with three of these:

> I quite like it. It is fun and we get to look at others' responses to the same question, so we get to know how others think. It helps broaden the way I think and develop critical thinking.
>
> I think OSR is quite special. It requires you to answer briefly so it really challenges your abilities to express yourself succinctly.
>
> I like it because it involves interaction, not only the monologue of the teacher.

As these responses suggest, students were generally positive about OSR and perceived a variety of benefits: it raises awareness of others' views, develops critical thinking, hones the skill of expressing ideas succinctly and is interactive.

One of the particular teacher intentions behind OSR was to inform David's preparation for the following lecture by identifying relevant student views. Some students commented on this aspect:

> OSR gives us a clue about what we are to learn and talk about in the lectures. These questions help us to think and get an idea of the direction of the lectures.

I've found that the OSR question is always related to the topic of the next lecture. By doing the OSR, I can predict what the next class will be about so it acts as a kind of preparation. The teacher can also use it as a means to collect students' opinions. I think that the teacher needs to know what students think.

This second student was positive about OSR, although she stated that if she had to do it for more than one course then it would be too pervasive and become a burden. She felt that she learnt a lot from carefully composing an answer to a cerebral question, such as 'Is History an art or a science?' For that kind of question she explained that during the ten-minute lecture break she would really go through the ideas in her mind, then compose her response.

Danny revealed some misconceptions about OSR:

Since it is not an assignment, I do not need to consider whether the point gets marks or not, so I can write my answer in a natural way. I think OSR is a way to assess your ideas and the basic knowledge of the topic discussed during the lecture. However, I sometimes feel the question is vague and I feel as if I am answering a question which is outside the topics discussed.

In fact, OSR counts for 15 per cent of the grade but Danny is either unaware of that or has forgotten. Also, it is not intended to assess the student's basic knowledge of the lecture, although at first sight one might think it does; it is meant to raise awareness of the *next* lecture topic.

Another student who was more attuned to the requirements of OSR noted that it was similar to taking attendance, and if you were absent and did not submit a response, you would lose marks: 'Without the OSR, at the end of the course students may be busy with other assignments and skip the last few lectures. So the OSR may encourage them to keep coming.' Another student also picked up on the implications for grading: 'We can actually see from the answers if a student has done some deep thinking. I take it seriously because it will be graded; everything related to GPA is important. Also, it is a good way to take attendance.'

Another student commented on how David follows up on the student OSRs:

The teacher would show some good or representative responses of the students in the following lecture. Also, when he compares the statistics of this year to last year, differences and similarities can be seen, so it helps us to think 'historically'.

This final comment indicates that at least some students had bought into David's discourse around thinking historically. David also reported that some students expressed pride in seeing their responses displayed on the screen and discussed in class.

A considered response on the potential and limits of OSR was provided by Shan:

> OSR is a good way for us to think more deeply about the issues and about our relationship with History. Teachers could understand our views and even be inspired by new ideas we raised. Also, as OSR limits the words written, it is effective in forcing us to express our main ideas. However, it is sometimes difficult to determine if a response is good or bad just based on a few sentences, so I think its grading criteria are not that transparent.

The grade descriptors (presented in full in Chapter 8 when I address the issue of how students engage with criteria) are posted on the LMS, but Shan's comments are reasonable in terms of wondering how grades are awarded. David explained that he gives each answer a mark out of twelve and the ten OSRs are aggregated to a total of 120, which can be divided conveniently by eight to form the OSR grade of 15 per cent. This is a user-friendly way of accumulating marks, although it begs the question of what a mark of seven, eight or nine out of twelve might look like. I think the main point of OSR relates to the engagement and participation it engenders, not its grade allocation or grading methods.

To provide some indication of how students tackled the OSR task, Box 4.3 provides several responses to the question about whether History is an art or a science.

Box 4.3 Sample OSRs

- There is no laboratory for experiments in History. It cannot be scientific because the same set of circumstances may not recur.
- I think History is an art. Art is created by humans while science can only be discovered but not created.
- An art. Although History involves theory and hypothesis, it is an art because it cannot have an exact answer for questions.
- Science consists of hard facts and one interpretation whereas everyone has their own way to interpret historical fact.
- History is not science as we can never revisit the past to verify and records can be false or deliberately modified and manipulated. However, historians can present history in any way they want and this makes History an art.

These OSRs give an indication of the length of the responses and the way in which the students are required to take a position on each topic.

David clearly enjoyed reading the student OSRs, despite the extra weekly workload it imposed. His enthusiasm is apparent in the following quotation:

> One hundred and ten voices are actually telling me something phenomenally interesting about a matter which is pertinent to the topic of discussion in the next lecture. It is incredibly instrumental in terms of understanding the students. I get far more from these short responses than I do from the standard teaching evaluation questionnaires.

So David finds the student OSRs interesting and informative in understanding prior knowledge and experiences of students. He also makes a contrast between end-of-course summative teaching evaluations and teacher-designed modes of interaction within the course. I agree with David that the latter generally provide more useful data to inform the teaching of a course, not least because of the timing *during* the course rather than at its end.

Tutorial participation

The other means of assessing participation is through tutorials, which comprise groups of ten to twelve students. The main aims of the tutorials are to provide opportunities to go more deeply into issues raised in lectures and OSRs, and to carry out activities which relate to the fieldwork or project assignments. There are eight tutorials, with students receiving a letter grade – A, B, C or D – or Fail for each one. The total is then aggregated to form a grade worth 15 per cent.

The basic format of the tutorial is that the students sit in a circle and there is a guided discussion. Towards the end of the tutorial it is common for students to complete some short tasks, such as a poster, a drawing or a written exercise. Students add their names to these pieces of work and they are collected by the tutor. Sometimes they discuss course readings and David stated that there is 'a kind of circularity between lectures and tutorials'.

A feature was the development of links between tutorials and assignments. In relation to the fieldwork assignment, students presented their own alternative versions of the museums, including designs for museums of their own. David sees this activity as involving the students in developing their own narratives of history; seeing contestation around the past; and the interplay between past and present in the forming of personal and national identities. In relation to the project, tutorials further the discussion of what the students are going to produce for their final project and they practise the skills which they need to carry out the project. David sees a connection between the activities and the learning outcomes he seeks to develop.

David recounted a tutorial activity which he believed many students found interesting:

> We set them the challenge of trying to identify the disciplinary conventions of historians in the traditional form of writing, and the ways in which History,

as a primarily written discipline, could be irrigated by other media. They produced what they called 'a history film', using multi-media to create a story about the past while using historians' conventions.

This activity was a way of experimenting with different means of disciplinary expression. It also speaks to the relationship between content and form in History and how teaching, learning and assessment may alert students to the forms of historical expression and their relationship to historical thinking.

The students were generally positive about the tutorials, describing Connie as helpful and encouraging in stimulating their viewpoints. For instance:

> I love the tutorials. The tutor is very inspiring and she makes us become passionate. In some other classes, we don't say much but in these tutorials everyone will say something.
>
> I think the activities during the tutorials were interesting and creative. For example, in the first tutorial, we had to make a drawing of a historical event. I am not sure about the assessment for tutorials, but I think participation is the main criterion to be assessed.

We asked students the extent to which active tutorial participation was derived from the fact that there was a grade for participation. Some believed that the grading participation increased student willingness to contribute, but a majority of those we questioned did not believe this was the case: rather, they participated because they had something to say, because Connie was a good facilitator and because they enjoyed the tutorials.

Juliet enjoyed the tutorials but found them much less demanding than her Law tutorials, for which she needed to do a lot of preparation. She felt that the History tutorials could sometimes be more in-depth and commented on the assessment of tutorial participation and its grading:

> I am not really in favour of assessing tutorial participation. I think university is about opportunities to develop yourself and find things that you are interested in. I don't think in every individual class you should account for participation, which is basically attendance and speaking up . . . The tutorial participation does not play a large part in our final grade; we just know that we need to contribute. As to how it was graded, we do not care too much.

Hearing a Law student say that she did not care too much about grading surprised us a little, so we asked for elaboration: 'We know that Connie is going to do the assessing and we trust her because she is a kind and approachable person.' As I signalled in Chapter 1, trust is an important factor in assessment, and perhaps particularly in relation to the assessment of something unavoidably vague, such as participation. This vagueness begs the question of whether participation should be assessed at all (see Chapter 3). I return to this issue in Chapter 12.

Individual project

The individual project is a 3000-word essay or the equivalent in another medium, such as wiki, video or podcast. It comprises 40 per cent of the overall course mark, and its stated aim is to enhance students' abilities to discover and assess the value of evidence, to make arguments and to communicate effectively. The students go through three stages in developing their project. First, there is a short 'topic brief' where students share what they are planning to do. Second, they submit a first draft, which counts for 10 per cent of the overall course grade. The third component is the final submission, which counts for 30 per cent of the course grade.

In accordance with the principles of choice discussed above, David allows students to do the project in pairs, in which case they need to elaborate the roles of each collaborator. Students can either choose from a list of thirty questions, most of which encapsulate the themes of the weekly lectures, or propose their own topic. Thirty options might seem a lot, but it is in line with David's espoused principle of maximising student choice. Three sample questions are shown in Box 4.4.

Box 4.4 Sample project questions

- What is the relationship between film and history? Can film help us to understand the past better than the written word? Illustrate with reference to your own 'history film' (or storyboard) and explain how it treats primary and secondary materials.
- Design a walking tour of the key sites of Hong Kong identity. Provide a critical analysis of its main monuments, spaces and places, explaining how these places and their pasts have been made meaningful.
- What is the relationship between memory and history? Illustrate your answer with reference to personal memory, collective memory, or both.

Teacher rationale

David explained the rationale behind the project as follows:

> What I am trying to do is excite them about history. In the projects, I get them to generate the materials and then analyse and critique them. This makes it phenomenally interesting and close to their hearts as well . . . What keeps it interesting for me is the variation, students from different faculties, different countries and backgrounds with varied perspectives.

Here, one can sense some of the enthusiasm that David invests in his engagement with the students and their projects. He seems to find it a positive experience to engage with the student work produced in meaningful assignments.

He also referred to how he wanted students to develop their projects over time, which is part of the rationale behind the assessed draft. For the draft, David expects as a minimum a title, a question and a plan for the project; a mode of enquiry; an explanation of how the project will be presented; an indication of the arguments; and a list of references. He stated, 'The aim of the draft project submission is to get students thinking about their final project early and tackle the problem of them working at the last minute.' He feels that this is particularly useful for first-year students as it means they can be guided on a suitable path. He also finds the draft useful in identifying the extent to which students have understood the task or, for example, misinterpreted elements of balance and focus.

Student perspectives on the project

We asked a few students about their projects. Juliet developed her own topic on the popularity of time-travel fiction in Chinese literature. Such novels were very popular with her friends, but she was not convinced of their merit, which was why she wanted to explore the topic. We asked her what she learnt from doing the project:

> I learnt to be independent . . . I have to ask people to complete questionnaires and then I have to make discussion and conclusions. It was challenging and the whole process took two months. I learnt how to improve my academic and research skills.

So Juliet developed her autonomous learning, academic and research skills. Her comment on the process taking two months relates to the point raised by Gibbs (2006) that assessment which supports learning should stimulate time on task and spread student effort evenly during a module. Our wider interactions with her seemed to indicate that she viewed the process positively, not least because she obtained an A grade. She also found the project to be a useful site for dialogic feedback with the teacher. (I return to this aspect in Chapter 11.)

Shan and Danny worked together on their project. As mentioned above, although it is an individual project assessment, students may cooperate with a classmate if they wish to do so. Shan discussed his collaboration with Danny:

> Our topic is to design a walking tour in Hong Kong. We elaborate on the history and value of the various sites we have chosen and explain why these particular sites are selected. We learnt that a walking tour could effectively convey certain messages to the people who undertake it.

Here, Shan reveals a developing awareness of how history can project meanings and implications to participants.

Danny elaborated on his work with Shan:

> We tried to link our walking tour with Hong Kong's core values, such as hard-working and compassionate. We made some contrasts between past and current values to investigate why certain kinds of core values have not been maintained nowadays.

Here, Danny shows an awareness of bringing out historical elements in his project by making contrasts between past and current society, and showing links between the past and the present.

Most of the students presented their projects in conventional essay format rather than in a multi-media or other technologically facilitated presentation mode. However, David commented that a few students were always willing to experiment with these more innovative modes and they were often the more able and/or more adventurous members of the class. He explained that he wanted to provide opportunities for students to experiment as he saw risk-taking as an important part of learning.

One of the particular features of the project is that it allows students to respond in an individual way, taking into account their own choice of topic. I return to this issue in the 'Implications' section below.

General student comments on the assessment design

We were able to elicit some general comments on the assessment design for the Making History course. Juliet compared this module with her major subject of Law:

> This course provides students with more chances to get good grades than the assessment in my Law courses, where it is usually just a final examination. In this course, you've got a project essay; you've got the field trip report; you've got tutorials; you've got many chances. The assessment provides flexibility and there is a variety of assessed activities. Overall, it is good.

Clearly, Juliet is favourably disposed to an assessment design of multiple components, rather than a one-off exam. She also seems to appreciate the interplay between the assessment and the activities in the course, as well as the flexibility involved. We then asked her about the relationship between the assessment and learning in the module. Again, her response was positive:

> The assessments motivate you to learn. If you want to get an excellent result, you have to work hard on every task, whether your motivation is good grades or really learning something. And in this course, if you want a high grade, you really need to learn things.

In this quotation, Juliet refers to motivation in relation to the assessment tasks. In the second sentence, she refers to working hard on each of the tasks for the module, which seems to reinforce Gibbs' second principle (see Chapter 3) – it is desirable for assessment to encourage the spread of effort across a module. The third sentence hints that earning good grades and learning something valuable are not always congruent, whereas in this course they seem to be: an aspect of alignment.

Deirdre commented on the module assessment as follows:

> The assessment of this course is quite open and you can have your own ideas. It is flexible because it is not about finding correct answers; History does not have correct answers . . . I feel what I have gained is not knowledge but regeneration of ways of thinking. I can attempt to understand issues from other angles and aspects.

The first features Deirdre mentions are openness and flexibility. Indeed, many students used the term 'flexibility' when discussing the assessment on the course. There seems to be a resonance between flexibility and the notion of providing student choice in assessment tasks. Deirdre also talks about perceived gains in ways of thinking and seeing issues from different angles. This makes me think of the 'conceptual change student-focused' approach (Prosser and Trigwell, 1999; see Chapter 2), where a teacher aims to develop new student ways of thinking about disciplinary issues. Deirdre's experience of the course seems to have stimulated her to revise how she thinks about History; in other words, we might say she is developing WTP in the discipline.

Jiang commented on the difference between the assignments in this course and what she had done in her previous study, and some of the challenges this posed:

> When I studied in high school, the assignments were standardised. The assignments of this course are quite novel for me, requiring field research and independent thinking. It involved a lot of hard work, whereas completing it gave me a great sense of achievement.

Geoff, who did relatively poorly in his assignments, would have preferred the assessment for the course to have been based more on the tutorial tasks. He felt that he learnt more from participation in the tutorials than he did from the written assignments and admitted that he was still unsure about how to write effectively. He also felt there was a lack of congruence between what was covered in the lectures and some of the assignments. So, for Geoff, there seemed to be some dissonance between the content coverage of the course and his chosen project. His comments suggest that he experienced some lack of alignment between module content and assignments. This reinforces a point raised in Chapter 2 that the implementation of assessment tasks is not just about their design but about how students interpret and experience them. David's view is that the concepts and thinking tools of historical analysis are aligned, but this is difficult for all students to discern. A potential downside of student choice can emerge if the choice itself makes it harder for students to draw links with module content. Alignment is not a static element but one that is also, to some extent, dependent on how a particular course is experienced by individual teachers and students.

Overall, the main orientation of student comments indicated that they were responding positively to the assessments and seemed to be developing the intended learning dispositions. I felt that their workload was quite high, although they seemed to accept this without complaint, possibly because they generally found the tasks engaging and interesting. David acknowledged the relatively heavy workload and mentioned that this was one of the reasons why he divided the assessment into a number of relatively small elements and spread them across the course.

Implications

The assessment task design in History evidenced a number of features. First, it was designed to engage students in WTP in the discipline by involving them in discourses around historical issues: how history is presented in a site, such as a museum; the relationship between the past and the present; and how history relates to the students' individual lives. A strong point of the field-trip assignment was that students experienced history in context and started to think about museums from different perspectives: government, museum curators, historians and users. Students also exhibited some developing awareness of discourses, hidden messages and connections between the past and the present.

A second major feature was that students spread their effort evenly across the course because of the four modes of assessment: fieldwork, weekly OSRs, tutorial participation and their projects. This provides evidence in context to support Gibbs' (2006) notion that assessment which supports student learning should promote time on task and effort spread evenly over the duration of a course. David's students were involved in regular intellectual engagement with disciplinary ways of thinking in support of the development of the intended learning outcomes for the course. Undergraduate study of History has traditionally been assessed mainly by essays and examinations (Booth, 2003). More innovative approaches using continuous assessment seem more effective in stimulating regular student engagement. A recent example involving regular short written assignments in relation to tutorial tasks seemed to have a positive impact on the students' learning experiences on a History course (Frost, de Pont and Brailsford, 2012).

Third, assessment design involved a considerable degree of choice and flexibility. Students could choose between two fieldwork options; there was a wide range of choice of topic for the project, including whether to do it as an individual or in a pair; and the final report could be presented in a conventional written format or in a technology-facilitated medium. As I established in Chapter 3, providing student choice enables students to develop some personal investment in an assessment task which is likely to increase intrinsic motivation. For this reason, I suggest it also carries the potential to promote deep approaches to learning in that intrinsic interest in a task correlates with a search for meanings and understandings.

The main strength of the project was that it allowed students to explore in more depth something in which they were interested. This carries powerful implications for student motivation and ownership. Some tensions might arise when the choice of project does not align clearly with the kind of content discussed in lectures. This may represent a problem for the less competent student in that they may not receive the kind of support they need. The nature of 'historical content' is a complex issue in that the study of History at university is not represented by the mastery of a specific body of knowledge but more the scaffolding of particular epistemological orientations.

The most innovative form of assessment in this case was OSR, and the students were almost universally positive about this strategy. It encourages steady class-room attendance and thinking across the entire duration of the course; promotes concise written communication of a point of view; anticipates the next class, so acts as a preview or preparation; and stimulates dialogue by putting students' voices into the classroom environment. Important learning outcomes from OSR were students refining their ability to communicate effectively in writing, and developing their understanding of other viewpoints. It seems particularly useful in a large class as a means of capturing students' opinions. There are, however, some possible drawbacks of OSR. It reduces student autonomy in relation to attendance if students prefer to learn in a more self-directed way. It is difficult to articulate the grading methods convincingly and is challenging to assess reliably, although this is clearly not the main purpose of the activity which is centred on learning rather than grading. And it requires a committed teacher who is willing to embrace its preparation and marking, although this is not excessive. David also reflected on the OSR in relation to his changing conception of it. At first he had imagined it in a slightly coercive way as a means of encouraging students to attend. Later, he began to place more emphasis on its potential to enable him to improve his understanding of the students in his classes.

The assessments were well-designed and meaningful tasks as individual items and also involved elements of coherence and integration. The teacher intended there to be interrelationships between the assessments and envisaged them as requiring parallel skills, such as experiencing historical ways of thinking and drawing comparisons between the past and the present. Some students were able to discern these connections, but others found it difficult to understand how feedback on one task could lead to improved performance in another. The issue of integration is complex and depends on both teachers' task design and related student interpretations. Perhaps a useful strategy is for teachers to devote classroom time to discussion of explicit links between the assignments and the skills that need to be developed. It is always important for the rationale for course design and assessment to be communicated clearly with students.

The tasks were generally open-ended and involved students expressing their own views and experiences. David clearly found their views interesting, even fascinating. So, for him, marking was pleasurable as he learnt more about his students and their backgrounds. From this, I infer that, with the right kind of teacher and the right kind of task, marking can be a positive and informative activity rather than the chore that many academics feel it to be.

Summary of chapter

In this chapter I have explored assessment task design and implementation in a History course which comprised a series of integrated tasks focused on ways of thinking and practising historically.

Main implications for practice

- Assessment should promote contextualised ways of thinking and practising in disciplinary forms.
- Tasks should be designed to provide students with opportunities to demonstrate higher-order learning outcomes.
- Short assessed written tasks can be valuable in promoting student expression of views and facilitating teacher understanding of student viewpoints.
- Multiple tasks spread intellectual engagement evenly over a module.
- Student choice and flexibility can promote student engagement and ownership.
- Timely, quality feedback processes are an important aspect of assessment task design.

Chapter 5

Learning-oriented assessment in Law

> For an examination, you just remember the things you were taught and you go there and kind of vomit it out on the paper.
>
> (Law student)

Scope of chapter

This chapter focuses on assessment task design and implementation in the subject of Law. As in the previous chapter, the analysis fits into the framework for the book by exploring learning-oriented assessment tasks in context. It illustrates different ways in which the teacher promotes assessment for learning and reduces some of the traditional disciplinary dominance of examinations.

Setting the scene

Rick Glofcheski has won a series of internal teaching awards, and in 2011 he was one of two inaugural winners of a major teaching award that spanned all of the universities in Hong Kong. His work on assessment for learning is the main basis of his teaching awards. I have known Rick for nearly a decade, first encountering him when he contributed an entry to a compendium of assessment practices (Glofcheski, 2006). He was promoted to Professor in 2011, when his teaching achievements were particularly commended.

Rick has implemented innovative practices in assessment for more than a decade. These innovations have gone through a process of deliberation and development over the years. Before implementing his assessment innovations fully, he pilots them on an optional and/or non-assessed basis and collects feedback from students. He has also carried out surveys and other data collection to elicit students' views of their approaches to learning and their perspectives on assessment. He adjusts and fine-tunes the assessment and weighting of assessments on an annual basis in relation to student feedback and his own reflections. He has also studied literature on assessment, presented papers at assessment-related conferences and carried out numerous workshops in Hong Kong and internationally on teaching, learning and assessment in Law. In sum, he alone of the five teachers featured in this book can be said to specialise in learning-oriented assessment.

We observed two different modules taught by Rick. Some assessment tasks in these modules were the same, others were different, and I discuss both in what follows.

The modules and their assessment

Rick teaches two modules: Tort Law, a core first-year course for 180 students or more; and Labour Law, a final-year option limited to a small group of sixteen to seventeen students. Two innovative assessment task designs are particularly prominent in Rick's teaching: reflective media diary (RMD) and photo essay. I also discuss how Rick shares samples of student assignments. Other elements of the assessment task designs are described briefly to provide a full picture of how his assessment is organised, but these are not analysed in detail.

Tort Law

The Tort Law course aims to provide a solid grounding in the functions and principles of torts. Its intended learning outcomes include: student ability to explain common litigated torts and their functions; the ability to think critically about legal issues; and student engagement in meaningful legal analysis of tort law issues. It comprises a year-long period of study (September to May) consisting of two elements – Tort 1 and Tort 2 – which are assessed as a single entity. Rick has been teaching this course for more than twenty years and it has been refined gradually over time. The module is taught through weekly lectures delivered by Rick which mainly cover principles and cases of tort law, and weekly tutorials chaired by a team of tutors who lead groups of around a dozen students each. The tutorials involve activities, such as analysing a case which has occurred in Hong Kong and been reported in the press. The assessment tasks and weighting are outlined in Box 5.1.

Labour Law

Labour Law is a single-semester course which focuses mainly on the broad functions and social purposes of labour and employment law in Hong. Its intended student learning outcomes include: identifying and explaining major terms and debates in labour law, and demonstrating a detailed understanding of a chosen labour or employment law topic. The first part of the module is a series of seminars on major topics in labour law; the second comprises student presentations on the topics they are studying in their research essay assignments. Students present the findings of their research for about twenty-five minutes, followed by a discussion of around twenty minutes. Suggested topics for research are posted on the LMS or students may propose one of their own. To facilitate

---

Box 5.1 Assessment in Tort Law

Students are assessed on:

- Final examination consisting of five to six questions, of which students answer three. The questions relate to tort-law-related news reports from local newspapers (60 per cent).
- Option: students may choose to write a research essay which carries 20 per cent weighting, in which case they answer only two exam questions, carrying 40 per cent.
- Coursework in the first semester: a test, counting for 20 per cent; or the test, this time counting for 10 percent, and an assignment (a tutorial problem submission or a photo essay), also counting for 10 per cent.
- Reflective media diary: Part A submission in December; Part B submission in March (20 per cent).

---

the student research, there are two individual tutorials: the first focuses on an overview of the research topic, progress, sources and methodology; in the second, prior to the class presentation, the student outlines a draft of their presentation. The assessment for the course includes the components summarised in Box 5.2.

Box 5.2 Assessment in Labour Law

Students are assessed on:

- A research essay (60 per cent).
- Presentation on research in progress (10 per cent).
- Reflective media diary (10 per cent).
- Labour tribunal visit and report (10 per cent).
- Class participation or a photo essay (the photo-essay grade is counted if it exceeds that for class participation) (10 per cent).

Teacher rationale for assessment task design

Rick views assessment as combining an understanding of how students are progressing (assessment *of* learning) and a learning opportunity in itself (assessment *for* learning). He believes that 'assessment should be strategically designed to elicit the right kind of student learning'. As part of this, there should be some variety of assessment tasks: 'A diversity of learning activities and assessments is necessary for the achievement of diverse outcomes. Tests and examinations alone are not sufficient for this purpose.' The study of Law at university is, however, usually dominated by examinations, and Rick has fought against this disciplinary convention for many years in a quest to diversify assessment and reduce the weight accorded to exams. For him, good assessment has the following characteristics: 'It advances student learning; it is an illuminating experience for students; it is based on authentic materials; it involves some student flexibility and choice; and it has feedback processes which capture students' attention.' I exemplify most of these features here, whilst a major feedback strategy of 'same-day feedback' is discussed in Chapter 11.

The notion of authenticity is central to Rick's thinking about assessment:

> An important aspect of my philosophy is that learning should be socially relevant; the learning and assessment material should be designed to reflect the way that the discipline has meaning in everyday life; and, where possible, learning and assessment should be based on authentic material. Students then have opportunities to develop the skill of making connections between their learning and the events in their own community.

He contrasts the use of authentic materials with a common trend of teachers inventing and devising legal problems. Rick has abandoned this mode because he finds it artificial and inauthentic. An important advantage of using authentic materials is that they have the potential to relate to what graduates will do in their future careers.

A further principle underpinning Rick's assessment practice is that of student choice, as exemplified by giving students the option to reduce the weighting of a particular task, such as the examination in Tort Law, by carrying out an additional task. He explained this as follows:

> Students are given an element of choice in assessment activities, and are able to view examples of the work of past students in order to make an informed choice. Students take ownership of learning when they can choose, and with that ownership they are likely to be more motivated and perform better. They can also play to their strengths in choosing an assignment which best follows from their own particular abilities.

Rick provides exemplars of past work so that students can understand the nature of the tasks and their requirements, and use that understanding to inform their choices. Through choice, they also develop some student ownership, which Rick believes may lead to higher levels of achievement. This seems reasonable: we often perform better when we are doing something in which we have a stake, rather than something that has been imposed on us without negotiation. Rick also believes that choice tends to increase student satisfaction: they are less likely to react negatively to something that they themselves have chosen, as opposed to something that is compulsory or imposed upon them.

Overall, Rick adopts an assessment for learning orientation perspective in which he seeks to diversify assessment rather than rely exclusively on examinations. Authenticity in relation to real-life uses of the discipline and student choice are two of his main principles in assessment task design.

Analysis of assessment tasks

The analysis focuses particularly on two innovative tasks: RMD and photo essay. I also discuss examinations, which are the most common form of assessment for Law students. I make some comments on a labour tribunal visit which mirrors real-life applications of the discipline in ways roughly analogous to what David aimed to do through the museum visit (see Chapter 4), and offer some brief observations about the assessment of classroom participation as a point of comparison with the History and Business cases.

Reflective media diary

RMD is one of Rick's signature assessment tasks. He introduced it in 2009 after consultations with senior Law students. It requires students to identify and analyse a range of events related to torts reported in the print media in Hong Kong on a regular basis, generally a minimum of two and a maximum of four per month. The first stage involves the selection of eight to ten news items; providing a summary of the facts of the case; identifying the potential legal issues; and tracking the subsequent developments. The second stage involves a more in-depth legal analysis of three to four selected cases, including personal observations. In other words, there is a progressive focusing and deepening of analysis during the process. RMD bears some similarities to portfolio-based assignments in that it involves collecting, selecting, editing and analysing material over a period of time.

Rick is at pains to ensure that each RMD involves regular student engagement rather than being put together as the deadline for submission approaches. Students authenticate their diary by indicating clearly the details of the news source; providing the original version or a printed e-version of the report; and emailing it to themselves to provide a dated record so that summaries and observations are contemporaneous with the news item in question. Students who fail to work steadily as per the guidelines are marked down accordingly.

Aspects of Rick's rationale for RMD are as follows:

> Analysing a verbatim news item allows a more complete treatment of legal and policy issues than is possible in conventional Law studies. This socially realistic approach enables students to move away from the habit of short-term reproductive learning, and to develop skills that will be relevant in post-graduation life. It promotes good reading habits around the subject

and because the material is often incomplete or complex, it mimics realistic professional scenarios.

Here we can see the enactment of some of the elements that Rick is trying to promote through assessment: avoiding surface approaches implicit in reproductive learning; developing skills students need in the workplace; and promoting complex, ill-defined outcomes. He also highlights the role of habit development: 'RMD requires regular entries, so [it] creates a habit of independent learning. For life-long learning, the element of habit-formation is vital.' The wide reading in which students are involved means that they are doing more than simply satisfying the assessment requirement.

Rick also raised the important issue of teacher workload:

> The design is deliberately labour-friendly: through the use of a web-based database [WiseNews], a diary can be kept and authenticated without the need for teacher supervision. This is an important aspect of the design with a large class size in which tutors already carry a heavy marking load.

One of Rick's principles is that he does not wish to introduce new assessment practices if they are more labour-intensive than the ones they replace.

Detailed criteria for successful completion of RMD are presented in the course documentation. In short, the criteria for an A grade include: a well-documented, authenticated diary; covers a wide range of tort issues; makes connections between reported events and legal principles; cogent and well-structured analysis; demonstrates deep understanding of legal issues; proper citations of cases; and forward-looking conclusions.

There are some slight differences in how RMD is handled in Tort Law and Labour Law. In the former, there are two submissions – one at the end of the first semester and one during the second semester. For the latter, as the course is shorter, students are required to keep a diary for only six weeks. There was some consensus amongst students that RMD represents quite a heavy workload, so it is more suitable for Tort Law than Labour Law. This is because Tort is a longer course and worth more credits; also, due to its wider coverage, there are likely to be more news items related to Tort Law than Labour Law.

Student perspectives on RMD

Here I draw on the perspectives of students taking the Tort Law course. They were generally positive about RMD and saw a number of benefits of its processes. First, I address the theme of authenticity and real-life uses of the discipline through three representative quotations:

> It's interesting because you read a wide range of news happening in Hong Kong, different kinds of cases that are linked to Tort Law. It is Rick's idea

that students should work on real cases instead of hypothetical ones. He wants students to be exposed to real-world examples, not just a textbook.

I like how the assessment reflected how Tort Law is part of life. A lot of us find that learning from legal textbooks is detached and irrelevant. RMD is effective at linking Law to our daily context.

I appreciate the RMD because it relates Law to events that are actually happening. After I've done RMD, whenever I read a newspaper now, I think that these are Tort Law issues.

Such comments are congruent with Rick's intention for students to read widely and focus on real-life occurrences of legal issues.

Students also noted a relationship between RMD and the Tort Law examinations, exemplified by two short quotations: 'A good thing is that the exam would be in the same format. RMD trains you how to frame an answer and how to get a good score'; 'The final examination was based on newspaper articles and having written the RMD I did not find the questions particularly difficult.' This brings an element of coherence and integration between two separate assessment elements because the skills for RMD parallel those needed in the exam. This is the kind of iterative and nested task design which I noted in Chapter 3 in relation to the work of Molloy and Boud (2013).

Students also frequently referred to the kind of learning which was stimulated by RMD:

RMD is a useful learning process for us to read more newspapers, be more aware of social affairs and train our ability to identify legal issues related to things happening around us. All of these are useful to our future career.

RMD actually records your progress over time. At the beginning, you do not know what Tort Law is so you just randomly pick some cases and write some reflections. In the later stage, when you work on your analysis, you realise that there are different arguments you can make and then you understand that you have really learnt some skills.

For the RMD, I read the newspaper every few days to spot Tort Law-related news. Despite the heavy workload, I find it useful to enhance my legal analytic skills and my interest in Tort Law grew.

For RMD, it makes you really think because most of the facts in the news are not the study of Law; they are just common situations. There is no guided answer, so many issues are unclear and we have to produce our own analysis.

These students reported a variety of learning, thinking and motivational benefits relevant to being a Law student and to their future careers. RMD seems to be effective at promoting engagement over time; encouraging them to reflect on their learning progress; and stimulating a progressive sharpening of legal aware-ness and skills. As the final quotation indicates, it also encourages them to identify and tackle ill-defined problems, which is one of the overarching graduate attributes that HKU seeks to develop.

Students also reported some minor challenges of doing RMD:

> It is time-consuming to do the reading, but as I have the habit of reading the newspapers every day, it is okay.
>
> It may sometimes get a bit frustrating when there are no new suitable legal items to talk about that week, but RMD is generally a beneficial way to learn.
>
> There is a challenge in the word count because there are many arguable issues but it is realistic because in the exam you have limited time, so you can only write six to seven hundred words on each case.

A general trend in the data was that RMD was seen as quite time-consuming. This could be viewed positively, in that it promotes 'time on task' – the first principle of the Gibbs framework, discussed in Chapter 3. Some students, for example, commented that if more than one module required RMD, then there would be severe overload. Others commented on the implications of the timing of the RMD:

> I think the deadline is too early. We still have content in Semester Two that we haven't learnt, but some of us have to write about them. We have to study the textbook by ourselves without any explanation by the lecturer.
>
> We are forced to choose some topics that we haven't learnt, so we need to spend some time studying them.

Whilst these comments are reasonable, my inference is that part of Rick's rationale is to encourage students to carry out independent and proactive learning. It is possible that these goals could be shared more clearly with students.

Overall, the student data presented a positive picture of RMD as a meaningful task which involved a variety of learning and thinking skills, and application of legal principles to real-life events. Reported challenges were mainly in relation to its somewhat time-consuming nature.

Photo essay

Rick first trialled the photo essay on an optional basis several years ago. After positive feedback from students, he recently made it an optional part of the assessment for his courses. The main intended learning outcomes from the photo essay are that students should be able to recognise how tort law connects to the events of ordinary life and provide legal analysis and opinion of naturally occurring situations. The essence of the photo essay is for students to visit a local neighbourhood and identify potential tort law situations, such as a dangerous pedestrian practice, a traffic black spot, or a dangerous construction practice.

Their essay – of around four hundred words – should explain the potential tort situation through a brief legal analysis of the place and the circumstances, citing one or two case authorities, supported by photographs or a sketch.

Rick's rationale for the photo essay is summarised as follows:

> It enables students to identify tort law issues proactively, as opposed to a tutorial problem, where the content is presented and students supply the legal analysis. It helps students experience law in a real-life setting, so there is a deeper experiential basis to the photo essay than other tasks. It can illustrate how law bears on their life and those of others; and students can develop a realisation that tort law issues are ubiquitous in daily life.

One of the significant elements of the photo essay is that the students are generating primary data themselves through their identification and photographing of a tort law issue. It also involves a process of regular effort and reflection in that students replace early photos with later, more effective ones as they become more accustomed to identifying real-life tort law situations.

Rick's grading principles for the photo essay are based on the following elements and weighting:

- creativity/originality – 20 per cent;
- identification of legal issues – 30 per cent;
- application of law to circumstances – 20 per cent;
- relevance of photograph – 20 per cent;
- English-language literacy – 10 per cent.

This seems to be a relatively crude, albeit user-friendly, analytic marking scheme. Rick acknowledges on the LMS that 'there is great potential for creativity. Hence, the description of the photo essay assignment is necessarily abstract and vague.' In our discussions, he also noted that a problem with the photo essay is subjectivity in the marking, particularly if a large number of tutors are involved.

Student perspectives on the photo essay

Some of the students perceived the photo essay as an attractive option:

> In the photo essay you can write any reflection freely without linking in detailed understanding of law, so some students think it is easier.
>
> For the photo essay, there is so much flexibility. I like the idea that I can go around and think, 'This is the tort issue,' and take a picture of it. That was fun for me. From a marker's point of view, it is going to be boring reading a hundred tutorial responses whereas a photo essay is more creative.
>
> We can see around us whether there are tort issues, so it really helps boost the atmosphere of learning about them.

The themes of flexibility and authenticity are also evident in these responses. The comment about thinking of the assignment from the marker's point of view struck me as a variation on the notion of cue-consciousness in terms of producing work that might be attractive to the marker.

One student focused his photo essay on a narrow bicycle track that he had identified. He took two photos of it and wrote down his observations and analysis in relation to tort law. He commented as follows:

> I think the photo essay assignment is creative and fun, because we are not bound by the usual legal analysis. We can think outside the box and write more personal thoughts. The ability to figure out a novel problem gave me a sense of achievement.

So he gained satisfaction from completing the photo essay assignment, and he was even happier when he obtained an A grade for his work.

In the Tort Law course, students can choose between the photo essay and a tutorial problem which involves a 600-word legal analysis of a newspaper item. Two students explained why they chose the tutorial problem:

> I always prepared well for the tutorials so I can save some effort by writing up a tutorial problem. The photo essay is quite an easy task with little space for legal reasoning. I didn't choose it because I want to save time.
>
> The photo essay is a new assessment method which I am not familiar with and there are fewer samples for us to follow. I was reluctant to do it.

The second comment highlights student familiarity with a task and the role of samples in providing guidance. Rick also commented that students tend to prefer familiar formats and pointed out that this can be a barrier to assessment innovation. In her field notes, Wang suggested that unmotivated students may not wish to invest time in trying to understand an optional assessment task. When an innovative assessment is optional and/or counts for only a small amount of weighting, students may not perceive it as worthwhile to commit any time or energy to working out what it entails.

Assessment by examination

The Tort Law examination consists of six questions. Five of these focus on authentic recent news items from local newspapers and one outlines the facts of a recent court judgement. It is a limited form of open-book exam in that students are allowed to consult the set textbook but no other materials. In terms of support, on the LMS Rick posts a lengthy section of around 2000 words entitled 'Exam Pointers'. This contains ideas and experiences related to exam technique as well as some key points on and examples of tort law. An extract is reproduced in Box 5.3.

Box 5.3 Guidance on answering exam questions based on media reports

1 Read and understand the narrative, and characterise the problem.
2 Identify the legal issues.
3 Provide a coherent analysis of each of the issues with reference to case authority, with some sense of conclusion, even if provisional.
4 The analysis should pay due regard to the ambiguities and subtleties that arise from the facts; any uncertainties in the law; and policy considerations.

Exam practice questions are also posted on the LMS. Once students have had some time to answer them, Rick posts his own suggested answers. This is akin to what I call 'pre-emptive formative assessment' (Carless, 2007a) – teacher actions which attempt to clarify student understandings before misconceptions result in ineffective learning or performance and/or loss of marks in assessed tasks.

Rick believes that examinations carry a number of drawbacks: they promote a knowledge transfer and reproduction mode of education; they have little or no sustainable learning value; and they involve intensive revision in the lead-up to exams rather than a consistent learning effort throughout the year. This form of learning and assessment bears little resemblance to the tasks to be undertaken after graduation. He includes examinations only because his faculty policy requires him to do so, and he tries to minimise their weighting as much as possible. He also attempts to bring in as much authenticity as he can through the use of real-life cases.

Student perspectives on exams

The Law students displayed mixed responses to examinations. Here, I provide no more than a flavour of their perspectives because this issue has already been covered extensively in the literature cited in Chapter 3. I begin with three broadly positive views:

> I think the examination may not be a perfect way to reflect your learning, but I think it is the best way. For assignments, you may copy from each other; for a group project, we cannot distinguish the ability for each student. For exam, you work on your own under the same conditions and time limit, so it is quite fair.
>
> I think the examination could reflect our learning because it is time for you to revise all the things you have learnt. During an examination, you can find out how your ability could be applied and you can realise your level.

> The examination forces us to really understand all the things. If there is no examination, I bet no students will really dig into the book and learn all the things.

More negative or critical views of examinations were also expressed:

> The results of exams are usually not proportional to what you have learnt. There is luck involved and one small mistake can really cost you. Exams are always subject to variations, like your health and how well you slept the night before.
>
> I personally don't like examinations because I don't think that they reflect students' efforts or abilities. Some students, like me, will feel stressed in the examination, so I think our performance would be affected.
>
> I don't like it in some Law courses when students can just memorise two or three topics for the exam and still get a good grade.

A recurring issue in students' opinions of exams is fairness. On the one hand, exams could be considered fair because everyone is treated equally. On the other hand, how fair is it to assess an extended period of study through the artificial mode of three hours of handwritten work? This group of students seemed to be less concerned with the fairness of exams than those cited in Chapter 1 in relation to the study by Flint and Johnson (2011). This may be because students in Hong Kong are acculturated to the idea of examinations in view of the highly examination-oriented modes of primary and secondary schooling which they experience (Carless, 2011).

An important issue is the design of the exam. One student offered a particularly useful analysis:

> Even though generally I don't think examinations are a good method of assessment, for this course it is fine because of the use of real-life examples. It can be difficult to identify the issues, but doing so would be helpful to us as legal practitioners in the future. It is also good because it is open-book; not all courses do that.

In other words, the particular characteristics of a specific examination are more important than whether examinations per se are an effective means of assessment.

Other students commented on the fact that the exam questions focused on real-life rather than hypothetical cases. For example:

> It's more interesting to read a real than a fabricated case. When it is fabricated, you have the pressure in mind that the teacher actually has the answer before he sets the question, but if it is a real-life case, it's up to you to make a logical argument.

Such comments indicate that a well-set examination can develop relationships with authentic uses of the discipline.

About half of the students opted for the exam to count for the full 60 per cent of their final grade, whereas the other half chose to write the research essay, meaning that the exam counted for only 40 per cent, with the essay counting for 20 per cent. Those who opted solely for the examination perceived that, as they had to revise for and sit the exam anyway, they could not justify the time and effort needed to write the essay as well. Several mentioned that this was a purely pragmatic decision and that doing a research essay (or a group project) would have been interesting and valuable. Those who did opt for the research essay did so mainly to reduce the risk of under-performing in the exam.

Tribunal visit

Labour Law students are required to make an independent visit of around two hours to a labour tribunal. They then write a report of around 800 words, in which they describe the experience, the court atmosphere, procedures and the substance of the cases witnessed. The students we interviewed had also visited magistrates' courts and district courts at various stages of their study, sometimes as a group and accompanied by teachers. A key difference between a labour tribunal and these other courts is that participants do not have legal representation in the tribunal.

Students reported that the value of their visits to labour tribunals depended to some extent on how fortunate they were in arriving at a time when there was something interesting or worthwhile to observe. Some informants reported arriving in the middle of a case and finding it difficult to understand the issues. Others were disappointed that the focus was on procedural rather than substantive issues. Some complained that the government officers did not offer them a warm welcome; and they disliked having to request permission to take notes. I feel that resolving such real-life issues is part of the learning experience for students.

Most of the students visited a tribunal only once, but some returned if they felt their first visit did not provide enough information for them to write their report. These kinds of student-controlled tasks can involve students in self-evaluation and additional time on task, bringing additional flexibility into the process. Students referred to the kind of learning experience the tribunal could generate: to experience how law operates in real life and observe processes that cannot be reproduced by book learning; to understand the atmosphere of the court; and to observe the difficulties of claimants or defendants who are not represented by lawyers. I discuss these visits to labour tribunals further in the 'Use of exemplars' section below.

Participation

Participation counted for only 10 per cent of the final grade in the Labour Law course. The interview data suggested that students were generally unsure about what was included in this part of their assessment. To what extent was it participation in discussions? Was attendance part of the grading process? In addition, as 10 per cent is a relatively small weighting, students did not seem to engage with it particularly seriously or worry about it too much. I provide two student quotations to provide a flavour of the responses:

> I always think this kind of assessment is quite mysterious, although I know some professors of other courses really mark down how much participation you have made and tally it at the end of the semester. But I think it is useful to have this kind of classroom participation assessment because you would prepare some readings and try to answer in class. It is not so good, however, if students would only engage in discussion to earn marks. I want to speak up to share ideas, not just for marks.
>
> Class participation means answering and asking questions during class. I am not sure how he is going to assess this part but I think it's quite liberal and it is just a matter of impression-marking.

Overall, the participation grade in Labour Law was rather low key when compared with the wider-reaching treatment of participation in History (Chapter 4) and Business (Chapter 6).

Use of exemplars

To illustrate his expectations of the assessment tasks and indicate to the students what good work looks like, Rick posts exemplars of previous students' work on the LMS for current students' reference. In my view, exemplars are particularly useful and desirable when tasks are innovative and unfamiliar to students. Rick does not, however, devote any time in class to their discussion. When I asked him about this, he explained that he does not want his classes to be too assessment-driven; he wants to focus on law content in the taught sessions. Under those circumstances, some online discussion of the exemplars might have been facilitated.

On the LMS for Tort Law there are: four grade A exam answers; three samples of student RMDs, along with brief teacher annotations; two photos taken by students for their photo essays; four photos taken by Rick himself, accompanied by some legal analysis; and several samples of other assignments, such as tutorial problem answers and marked research essays.

Tort Law students were universally positive about of the provision of these samples of student work. They found them useful in clarifying requirements, and more useful than grade descriptors, which they mainly identified as vague. Some students reported analysing the samples quite carefully and reading them many times, whereas others stated that they looked at them only briefly. Some students used the samples to inform their decisions as to which options to choose, and felt that the more samples there were, the better. One student reported that a handwritten sample exam answer was so 'ugly' that she did not want to read it. Of course, this problem could be overcome by typing up the examination scripts (see Chapter 7; Scoles, Huxham and McArthur, 2013).

We also had some interesting discussions about the exemplars with some of the Labour Law interviewees. One student commented:

> I think the difference between Rick and other tutors is that he provides us examples of assignments. I think the major advantage of having this kind of sample is that you don't have to know multiple ways of presenting the assignment; you just need to know one good way. It is a kind of reference which you don't just copy. If you have ideas which seem better than the example, you use your own ideas; but if you don't, you can imitate its presentation style.

I infer that samples provide reassurance for students in that they show good ways of tackling an assignment. In line with the arguments I develop in Chapter 7, the issue of copying or borrowing from a sample is complex. We discussed this with the Labour Law students, and one who seemed to be quite influenced by the samples commented:

> Rick posted an exemplar of the tribunal report which most of us followed. It served as a useful example of what a good report should be. I looked at his comments, what he wrote in the margins. For the points that he appreciated, I think most of us will include those in our own reports.

Another student echoed some of this but also offered a contrasting view:

> For the labour tribunal report, there is really a risk of us just copying the exemplar. But at the same time, because we know that we have all looked at the exemplar, I think many of us also try to add something more or use our own approach. Actually my approach is totally different from the exemplar.

This student reported that she was rather unsure of her different approach so she emailed Rick, who offered encouragement that her method was just as valid. (Rick has a reputation of being a diligent email correspondent. One of his Tort Law students stated: 'In case of doubt, I would send Rick an email to clarify any confusion. Rick is a very responsible teacher who would reply to every student's email, no matter how busy he is.')

This discussion of the use of exemplars touches on some of the implementation issues which I explore further in Chapter 7. It reinforces the point that students welcome the sharing of exemplars but also speaks to some key issues: exemplars are useful in clarifying expectations and providing a guide or template, but there is a danger that sample work is seen by students as a model, and this can impede their creativity in charting their own individual responses. In some senses, exemplars reduce some of the challenges and complexity of tackling a novel or ill-defined task, and the extent to which this is more or less advantageous is difficult to judge.

Overall student perspectives on the assessment design

I now present some overall student perspectives on assessment task design. A number of students referred to learning aspects and made comparisons with examinations. For example: 'I think the assessments in Tort Law are more learning-oriented than, for example, Contract Law because it is not really about testing your knowledge or performance in an examination hall. Rather, it is about ongoing learning.' Another informant noted the real-life aspect of the assessments, for instance in RMD and the photo essay, in that they motivated or compelled students to produce their own unaided work:

> I like the fact that Rick's assessments cannot be copied. For a lot of assessments, everyone has the same task and there is a lot of copying, not in the sense of plagiarism but students draw a lot of sources or references from friends who got good grades in previous years. I feel this defeats the purpose of learning.

This recalls the discussion in Chapter 1 about avoidance of student malpractice in assessment often being a task design issue.

Themes of choice and continuous effort were also addressed:

> It is good for us to have multiple assessment options, so I can choose the assessment method which suits me. More options mean that you are not forced to do things that you are not good at or don't enjoy doing. Choice also helps us diversify risk, so if we don't do well in one task, we can still have a chance to get a good grade by doing well in others. With assessments throughout the year, we would also put continuous effort into the module, and this enhances our understanding.

Flexibility or choice was a major theme in the students' responses, and I return to this in Chapter 12.

Comparisons with other courses were also made:

> Tort Law is quite different from other Law courses which put a heavy weight on final exams. The assessments allow us to have continuous effort so that we can avoid last-minute preparation for exams. It is a good way of risk allocation. For exams, we may perform badly on the day but for this one we feel more secure as, if we put in more effort, we can obtain a better result. But there is a fairness issue: it may not be fair if the average grade for a coursework task is higher than the average grade for exam questions.

An advantage of choice is that it enables students to diversify risk from a single assessment. This student's comment also brings out the notion of continuous effort whilst also noting the issue of fairness and the point that students usually achieve higher grades for coursework than for examinations (see Bridges et al., 2002).

Another student also mentioned flexibility in relation to weightings:

> Overall, the assessment approach in Tort Law is pretty good because of the flexibility in weightings. I think around 50 to 60 per cent for the final exam is about right because I think if there are too many small assignments added together, then you will think they are insignificant and not want to put much time into it.

Some tensions in allocating and assessing coursework were raised:

> I do think that coursework is good for our learning because you can practice but I don't want to spend too much time doing assessments. It is okay but it is not that good if he tries to put more weight on coursework. We have other jobs and coursework from other modules, so we can't spend a whole day on Tort Law.

I infer that Gibbs' (2006) principles of time on task and even spread of effort across a module are being fulfilled, but there were some student concerns about workload:

> Sometimes I feel there is a bit too much workload. There are quite a lot of elements you have to complete, but for a full-year course it is fine.
>
> The assessment approach is good but the workload is a bit too much. Our learning time is almost completely occupied by this course and we have little time to study other courses. If all the courses adopted the same assessment approach as this one, we would not have time to sleep.

These comments suggest that there might be some tensions between the benefits of time on task and students' understandable desire for a lighter workload.

Turning to the Labour Law informants, they were also broadly positive about the assessment design, although they had even more reservations about workload. I was unable to establish whether this was due to the fact that they were final-year students and so might have been less hard-working and committed because they were nearing the end of their studies.

The following quotation is representative of the positive comments from Labour Law students:

> I think the overall design of the assessment is well balanced in the sense that the percentage given to each assessment is proportionate to the amount of

effort and learning required. I also think that RMD and the labour tribunal visit report require students to be proactive in their learning and to apply what they have learnt in the classroom to real-life events.

The more critical comments tended to focus on weighting as well as workload:

> I would say that, to implement any assessment strategy, an important criterion is proportionality: effort and time proportional to weighting. As this is a final-year research course, I would say that the research essay is of primary importance and the weighting should be higher.

This student thought that RMD was too much work for relatively low weighting; he would prefer to remove the assessment of class participation or photo essay altogether and increase the weighting for RMD accordingly. Another student had similar critiques of the weighting of assignments:

> The labour tribunal [report] and RMD both take 10 per cent, which doesn't make sense. For RMD, you have to spend much more time and effort on it, whereas for the labour tribunal [report] you can finish it within one day. I suggest removing the labour tribunal assignment and increasing RMD to 20 per cent.

I feel that 10 per cent is a rather small allocation for the weighting of any task, and for the strategic student this could represent a certain amount of effort for a small amount of grade. I suggest a principle that no assessment task should be weighted at less than 20 per cent. For a one-semester course, the assessment of two or three assignments seems to be quite a useful strategy as it encourages consistent effort and a variety of tasks. In the Labour Law course, four elements each have 10 per cent weighting (see Box 5.2), which I believe runs the risk of assessment overload or fragmentation. I put this to Rick and he had some sympathy with my position. However, he put forward the counter-argument that if the task is meaningful and stimulates productive learning activity, then it is worth doing even if the mark allocation is low.

Implications

The main motifs in this case are that Rick wants assessment to be a positive learning experience for students, not something that is done solely for certification purposes. He also wants to resist the dominance of examinations by engaging students with a variety of tasks which relate to real-life uses of the discipline and consistent effort.

RMD is one of Rick's signature assessment strategies, and in my view it is a particularly well-conceptualised assessment for learning task. It resonates with McCune and Hounsell's (2005) analysis of WTP in that students are involved in analysing legal occurrences arising in real-life local contexts and mirroring disciplinary ways of operating. RMD has the potential to stimulate deep approaches to learning in that students are encouraged to search for patterns, meanings and underlying principles in the cases they analyse. It develops student reflection and meta-cognition as they sharpen their focus and analysis during the process of developing their diaries. RMD also seemed particularly effective at spreading effort and student engagement over the duration of the course as students regularly accessed media coverage to identify and analyse relevant real-life legal issues. They were also involved in selecting cases from their database; following developments over time; and developing legal analyses. Through these processes, there is a significant amount of student engagement, not all of which is reflected in the final product. In other words, RMD is a rich learning task as well as an assessment task. Its main learning outcomes seemed to be for students to appreciate the relevance of tort law in daily life, and to develop skills in identifying and analysing tort law issues from real-life cases.

The design of the activity as being marker-friendly is also a positive feature of RMD. Versions of RMD could be adapted for use in other soft disciplines which feature regularly in the news, such as Business, Education or Social Work. To broaden horizons, it could include international media reports in addition to the local focus favoured by Rick.

It is worth making some comparisons between RMD and the photo essay. Both of these encourage students to relate book knowledge to real-life situations. In Tort Law RMD is compulsory, whereas the photo essay is optional. I felt that RMD was a stronger and richer task than the photo essay, and when I put this to Rick he concurred. However, he argued that the photo essay was still valuable, particularly in its encouragement of student self-identification of issues for analysis. Moreover, when Wang commented on my interpretations she said that she saw great value in the photo essay as it demands alertness, effort and creativity. Unlike RMD, where information is found in newspapers, photo essay students experience something themselves and use their senses to identify clues to tort law issues in the local environment. This involves a further level of proactive student engagement.

Rick also provides student choice both in relation to tasks and in the weighting applied to them. This exemplifies some of the benefits of choice discussed in Chapter 3 in relation to the motivational benefits arising from some degree of student ownership of tasks. Whereas permitting students to choose topics is common, options in relation to the weighting of assignments is rarely highlighted in the literature. This is a relatively novel aspect and one which brings an additional level of flexibility into the assessment design.

A further feature of Rick's practice is that he strives to provide clear guidance as to what he expects from students. He provides samples of what is required, and students use these to guide their choice of options. In Chapter 7, I advocate the dialogic use of exemplars in which there is classroom discussion to generate debate about the exemplars. In my view, classroom time should be allocated to discuss the strengths and weaknesses of samples; to clarify expectations and criteria; and to debate the pros and cons of different approaches to tasks. It is important for students to understand that there are alternative ways of achieving desired learning outcomes.

It is worth reiterating that the Tort Law course involved a large class of students, yet this was not an insurmountable obstacle to the implementation of a variety of innovative assessment methods. A critical factor was the teacher's determination to overcome the constraints that were inevitably present. Rick's principle that assessment innovation should not increase the teacher's workload is also important and pragmatic, although it should be reiterated that he is diligent and responsive when attending to students' queries and needs.

With respect to the potential scaling up of his innovations to wider groups of colleagues, Rick is a senior and respected colleague in the Faculty of Law. There appears to be no overt resistance to his ideas from his colleagues on the Tort Law course, all of whom seem willing to follow his ideas. On the other hand, there seems to be limited interest or commitment from colleagues to expand his ideas in their own classes. The prevailing attitude seems to be: 'As things are going quite well as they are, why put in extra effort to change them?' This is a major barrier to innovation.

Summary of chapter

This chapter has focused on learning-oriented assessment task design and implementation in the subject of Law. Rick implemented a variety of tasks which were alternatives to the dominant disciplinary focus on examinations. A particular highlight was RMD, which engaged students in identifying and analysing legal issues over extended periods of time.

Readers will have noticed that I have not mentioned Rick's views on feedback in this chapter, nor explained how he incorporates it within the design of his assessment activities. This is because this aspect of his teaching is discussed in depth in Chapter 11.

Main implications for practice

- Assessment tasks should relate to real-life uses of the discipline.
- A useful strategy is to afford students choice of assessment tasks and weighting.
- Assessment tasks should encourage consistent and sustained effort.
- Exemplars are useful in clarifying expectations.

Chapter 6

Group assessment and participation in Geology and Business

If you are doing a group project, do you want to learn or get a good grade? I want a good grade so I choose my classmates carefully so I can team up with the stronger ones.

(Chi, Business student)

Scope of chapter

In this chapter I focus mainly on group assessment and participation. I explore in detail how students carried out their group project in the Geology case. I also analyse those aspects of the Business case that focused on group work, oral presentations and different forms of participation.

Geology case: setting the scene

Lung-Sang Chan is a professor in the Department of Earth Sciences, Faculty of Science, Hong Kong University. Chan was awarded a university teaching fellowship in 2004 and was a winner of a university distinguished teaching award in 2009. His research interests include the tectonics and geology of South China. One of his teaching passions is for experiential learning: taking students on field trips to explore geological features in the Hong Kong environment. He describes this approach as 'problem-based learning in the field'.

The module and its assessment

The module involves an introduction to Geology, mainly taken by first-year students majoring in that subject or in other disciplines. The main intended outcome is for students to understand the earth's structure, its material composition and its internal and external processes. The module was taught by a teaching team of Chan, another professor, a teaching assistant and several Ph.D. students. Around 135 students were enrolled. The module is well established and has been running for a number of years in a roughly similar mode of implementation. The assessment methods are outlined in Box 6.1.

Box 6.1 Assessment methods in Geology

- Two-hour written exam: 50 per cent
- Practical, field reports and quizzes: 20 per cent
- Group project: 30 per cent

I focus on the group project as it represents both a common assessment task and one that presents the various implementation challenges discussed in Chapter 3. Project work also relates to an overarching educational aim of HKU in relation to aspirations for students to communicate effectively in academic, professional and social settings, and to work with others to make constructive contributions. The teacher-provided module documentation gave an overall introduction to the project assignment, the essence of which is summarised in Box 6.2.

Box 6.2 Group project instructions

Students divide themselves into groups of three or four and carry out a project on a topic of their own choice, based on a novel problem related to geology. The report should not exceed 4000 words, and each member of the group is responsible for writing at least one section. The project counts for 30 per cent of course marks, with 20 per cent based on group report and oral presentation, and 10 per cent based on individual write-up. Each group is allowed twelve minutes for their presentation, followed by a two-minute Q and A session.

The criteria for the project are discussed further in Chapter 8. In short, students need to demonstrate some degree of originality in addressing a focused problem related to geology. So the main intended outcome seems to be related to problem-generation and problem-solving in geology, with subsidiary outcomes in relation to developing teamwork and the ability to communicate ideas orally and in writing.

In Chapter 3, I discussed whether students in group projects should be awarded the same overall project grade or individual grades. In this case, the module team used a strategy by which there were marks for both group performance and individual written performance. Chan reported that the individual grading element was added after some free-riding a few years earlier.

Teacher perspectives on assessment task design

Chan reported that his faculty favoured the use of examinations, but he felt it was useful to provide a variety of assessment tasks:

Students have different abilities and some may respond better to different forms of assessment. Many students are accustomed to examinations and respond well to the pressure. Exams are useful as part of the assessment, but not more than 50 per cent of the total. A good exam can, amongst other things, differentiate between students and generate a spread of marks.

I asked him to elaborate on his comments about differentiating between students and a spread of marks, and he commented: 'Although we don't mark in a fully norm-referenced way, we have some norms in mind and overall for this course we usually have about twenty per cent A, and 40 per cent B grades.' So it seems that there is some sense of spreading marks roughly in accordance with a bell-curve distribution. This is not a recommended approach at HKU but it is an honest admission of the residue of norm-referenced assessment and the role of comparison in academic judgements (see also Chapter 7). Assessment practices are influenced by social, structural, historical and disciplinary dimensions (see James, 2014).

Chan felt the group project was valuable principally because it gave students an opportunity to gain experience of working in teams and exposed them to alternative views and different ways of working. Other members of the teaching team felt that the group project, especially the oral presentation part, was the element of the course that students found most challenging. A small adjustment made by the teaching team in the course we observed was to require each group to submit an outline of their project which would receive brief feedback. The purpose of this process was to try to help students to get on the right track, given that previous cohorts had experienced some difficulties in choosing an appropriate focus for their topic or chose a topic which was too broad.

Student management of the group project

Our research tried to determine how students managed the process of working in a group. This is a topic which I have seldom seen discussed in the literature, perhaps because it needs an ethnographically oriented style of data collection, which is relatively uncommon in studies of assessment in higher education. We collected detailed interview data from six students and tried to understand the processes of their projects. Table 6.1 summarises their project topics and majors.

Penny's group

Penny was majoring in Law and chose the course because she wanted to strengthen her GPA and because she had heard that it was not difficult to obtain a high grade in Geology. Her teammates were Wan, Carol and Wing. They explored the topic of 'sixth mass extinction', which was framed by two questions: 'Is the sixth mass extinction approaching?' and 'If so, to what extent is it caused by human activity?'

Table 6.1 Student informants in Geology

Name	Project topic	Major
Penny	Mass extinction	Law
Wan	Mass extinction	Geology
Ming	Weathering processes	Earth and Environmental Science
Tsang	Weathering processes	Earth and Environmental Science
Jackie	Can people live on the moon?	Biology
Fung	Sea-level rise	Risk Management

At the outset of the project, Penny assumed the role of group leader because the other students perceived her as having some seniority and experience, possibly because she was a Law student. Her roles included dividing up and assigning tasks, calling meetings and setting deadlines. She was also quite a confident, articulate and serious student. Wan explained that the whole group first agreed on a definition of 'mass extinction', then each member was responsible for drafting a specific section of the report. There was both individual work in terms of drafting one's own section and teamwork in terms of developing consensus and sharing resources.

Once the draft sections were sent to her, one of the strategies employed by Penny was to encourage peer evaluation. She described the process as follows:

> Because the groupmates are quite passive, I asked them to circulate their sections and make comments. It's a group endeavour and I want them to comment on other people's sections. If something goes wrong with the project, then we all share the burden.

From this comment, I infer that Penny wanted to maximise the contribution from all her team to ensure their active participation, and she wanted the outcome of the project to be a team effort, rather than resting solely on her shoulders.

When asked the extent to which she believed that group members would provide substantive peer feedback, Penny explained that she had also devised a back-up strategy: she would arrange a meeting and further encourage team members to provide peer feedback comments. There were three drafts from the group members, and students raised questions, requested elaboration and suggested minor amendments to phrasing. I found Penny's strategy of promoting peer evaluation to be particularly interesting as it mirrored the kind of role one might expect a teacher to play in developing learner autonomy and responsibility. When asked to explain her enthusiasm for peer evaluation amongst her group members, Penny reported that she wanted to promote democratic responsibility, to maximise the chances of obtaining a high grade, and to share responsibility.

She also talked about her experience in Law, where students often commented on each other's work as part of a process of improvement so as to maximise their opportunities for achieving high grades. She described her editorial role for the mass extinction project as drawing the separate sections together and making some minor revisions, and explained, 'Revisions are focused on the content, not the style of writing, because I think that the professor expects to see different writing styles for each student.' The four students' contributions to the group report are summarised in Box 6.3.

Box 6.3 Structure of project report

- Introduction (Penny)
- Is the sixth mass extinction occurring? (Wan)
- To what extent is the sixth mass extinction caused by human activity? (Carol)
- To what extent is the sixth mass extinction caused by non-human activity? (Wing)
- Conclusion (Penny)

Penny's coordinating role is indicated by the fact that she contributed both the Introduction and the Conclusion. In terms of maximising her grade for the 10 per cent individual contribution to the project, it is unclear whether this contribution fully showcased her leadership of the process. A marker who merely read the Introduction and Conclusion may not have been aware of Penny's total contribution. I return to this issue of process versus product in the 'Implications' section below.

We also asked Wan and Penny about the challenges and benefits of doing group work. Wan talked about the problems of finding resources and scheduling meetings. The main benefits she perceived were learning to see the topic from different perspectives and learning some writing skills from other students. To some extent, her sharing relates to Chan's stated intention that a key rationale for the group project is for students to be exposed to different perspectives.

Penny talked about her overall impression of group projects:

> I personally don't like them because they are slow, inefficient, time-consuming and your group members may not be capable. It's hard to coordinate the meeting dates and discuss things together because everybody is busy, so I prefer to do individual work.

However, she also mentioned some of the benefits of acting as a group leader: 'I learnt how to coordinate and ask the groupmates stimulating questions to make them think. I need to consider their feelings and attend to different voices. It's a good bonding exercise and a way to make friends.' Perhaps Penny benefited less from the process in terms of academic learning because she was the most capable member of the group. She certainly seems to feel that there was an imbalance between what she taught the other members and what she learnt from them. On the other hand, she gained the generic skills of managing and coordinating group work, learnt how to be a caring and efficient leader, and developed her interpersonal skills. This indicates that students may develop a wide range of learning outcomes when participating in a group project.

An overall grade in a project may not always reflect the time and effort invested or the quality of individual contributions. Penny's overall grade on the course was a B, which left her dissatisfied because her original perception that she would be able to score a high grade with relative ease was not really borne out.

Ming and Tsang's group

Ming and Tsang worked with two other classmates on the topic of the utilisation of weather processes to benefit humankind. Tsang explained that they launched a group on Facebook, each student uploaded their own piece of written work, then the group unified these drafts into a final report. Ming commented on the organisation of the group as follows: 'We don't have a group leader because no one has particular expertise on the topic or strong organising abilities. I feel that we are in a mess and a rush. It's better to have a leader to make arrangements.' So it seems that although every member thought it would be desirable to have a leader, no one came forward to take the coordinating role and this was a barrier for the smooth operation of the group.

Ming expressed some positive perceptions about doing group projects because she perceived that it was a good way to make friends, develop interpersonal competence and hone discussion skills. She did, however, echo some of the points made by Wan in terms of difficulties in finding resources and arranging meetings. Consequently, the group often communicated through Facebook. Similarly, Tsang perceived that a major problem in the project was insufficient discussion between the group members. He felt that they were sometimes preoccupied with the logistical issues of when to meet and how to communicate, rather than the substance of the project. He also commented that they were all more accustomed to working individually, so their capacity to work in a group format was relatively poor. In one sense, this related to the teacher rationale for the project. Chan understands that his students do not have much experience of working together, nor with classmates from different backgrounds and with different working styles, so he wants to promote peer collaboration.

We asked Ming and Tsang for their perceptions of group projects as modes of assessment. Both compared them with examinations:

> I prefer a group project to an examination. You need to spend a lot of time preparing for an exam. For a presentation, you don't need to memorise so many things. You just need to search for some materials and present them in an interesting way.
>
> (Tsang)

I have been accustomed to exams. I haven't done projects before and I experienced difficulty expressing myself. I also don't know what to do when there are conflicts among the group members.

(Ming)

Clearly, Ming is comfortable studying for exams and working individually, whereas she feels uneasy about some of the unfamiliar challenges of group work. However, her overall opinion of the latter was far from negative:

I like doing group projects. It's a good way to make friends, develop interpersonal competence, communication and problem-solving skills. I think that what I learnt from doing the project will make a deeper impression on me than the examination does.

So, while group projects seem to provoke uncertainty, they also carry more potential for a deeper learning experience than an examination.

Jackie's group

Jackie's group comprised two first-year students (Jackie herself and Crystal) and two second-year students. Jackie commented that the two older students seemed to be quite busy: 'Sometimes they do not attend the classes so we cannot meet together in the lecture.' In an attempt to counter this problem, the team set up a group in What'sApp, but the second-year students often did not respond, so communication problems arose.

Jackie explained that they worked individually until just one day before the deadline for submitting the project report. At that point, Crystal put the separate parts together to make the complete report. It seemed that Crystal did more work than the other group members, especially the two second-year students. Jackie offered an explanation for this: 'She is quite serious about this project as she is worried about whether we can finish our task on time. The second-year students are busy and we just received their parts on the day of the deadline.'

After submitting the report, the group had to hurry to prepare for their presentation, which was scheduled for two days later. Crystal suggested that each of them should prepare individually for their own part, which would correspond to their section of the report, and they should all submit their slides by 1 a.m. on the day of the presentation. Jackie volunteered to gather together and edit all of the sections into a complete presentation document because she felt that Crystal had already done more than her fair share of the work. However, the second-year students did not submit their slides on time as they were busy with other assignments. Jackie said that she did not worry too much about the grade for the presentation because Crystal was well prepared and the second-year students could simply read from their slides.

This account reveals that Crystal and Jackie did considerably more work than the two second-year students. Although the group did not formally appoint a leader, Crystal assumed this role by assigning the work and setting deadlines. As she was the most serious about the grade and did not have much authority to coordinate the project, she also seemed to do the most work.

Jackie talked about a specific difficulty they encountered during the project: 'Although the teachers require us to provide insights for the project, this is difficult and I think we cannot do so. I have a friend who used materials from secondary school but this did not generate insights.' Here she is revealing a critical self-evaluation of the extent to which insight is being provided, an issue I discuss further in Chapter 8. Her reference to school also implies that students need support to make the transition from secondary to tertiary ways of thinking and studying.

Jackie explained that she did not like to do group projects because she found it difficult to communicate with and reach consensus between the group members. Despite these problems, though, she acknowledged that there were some benefits: she developed a friendship with Crystal; and she appreciated that she could enrich her knowledge and gain experience by working in a group.

Fung's group

Fung's group divided the task into a number of discrete parts, with each member responsible for several of them. They set up a group on Facebook and used it to share documents and for discussions. The latter intensified as the deadlines for the report and presentation approached. Fung commented on his role:

> I play the role of a group leader because I've done the largest proportion of the work. I wrote a lot and I also need to revise what they've written. I made a group work plan at the beginning but they didn't execute it carefully, maybe due to the time constraints.

Fung seems to have emerged as group leader because he contributed much of the work. However, in comparison with Penny, he seemed to have more difficulty in persuading his teammates to cooperate. It is unclear whether this was due to the individual characteristics of his team members or their perceptions of Fung's authority or expertise.

Fung highlighted one group member who had been busy with other matters and had contributed only modestly to the project. This free-rider eventually apologised for his poor contribution and asked Fung to assign him a task. Fung asked him to correct the grammar in the other two students' submissions, which he did, and this provided a degree of resolution of the free rider issue. Fung stated that he was not particularly concerned about fairness or unfairness in terms of each member's contribution; rather, his main concern was that the group should achieve a high mark. Overall, he certainly seemed to have a positive opinion of the project, despite the difficulties he faced with the free-rider: 'I have gained interpersonal skills, writing competence and citation skills. I am willing to do group projects. It can reduce loneliness because you can share feelings with groupmates.'

Summary of student perspectives

Students generally seemed to regard the group project as challenging. They had little experience of this kind of work and found it difficult to collaborate, especially in terms of developing suitable roles for each team member and setting times for meetings. One of the common strategies to tackle these issues was to use technology, but the students were aware of some of the limitations of 'virtual meetings' when trying to develop deep interaction.

From the students' perspectives, the main learning outcomes of working in groups were varied. The acknowledged advantages of participating in a group project included: learning and sharing knowledge and understanding about geology; learning to work in a team and developing interpersonal skills; learning from peers, particularly those with greater experience or complementary skills; developing friendships and getting to know classmates better; and learning in more depth than is usually the case with other forms of assessment, such as examinations.

Teacher views and reflections

When I interviewed Chan at the end of the module, he expressed satisfaction with the students' performance during the group project in terms of effort and outcomes. He felt that the aims of providing students with experience of working in teams and exposing them to different perspectives and ways of working had been largely achieved. However, in terms of areas for improvement and overall appraisal of student performance, he noted:

> A limitation of student performance is that many of them are not particularly strong at developing arguments. Similarly, they are not always confident in expressing their insights and supporting them with evidence. Superior performance was shown when the group was well organised and coordinated with unity and coherence: for example, when rehearsing their oral presentation.

Chan identified three main problems for the students. First, he perceived that they tended to provide information rather than insight, reinforcing one of Jackie's points (see above). He felt that this was a consequence of how they had been taught at school in terms of a mainly reproductive orientation. Second, he stated that students often had difficulty in developing collective insights, rather than simply presenting the individual opinions of group members. He exemplified this point with reference to a group that explored tourism and geological heritage. They failed to reach a consensus, even though consensus is clearly an important aspect of any group project. Third, he noted that students often found it difficult to schedule meetings to discuss the project, another issue which the student data consistently highlighted.

Chan perceived that the award of individual and group grades seemed to be reasonably effective in discouraging free-riding and balancing individual and group accountability. However, he identified a further challenge which the teaching team had yet to tackle: 'A limitation is that a group project like this cannot assess efforts or attitudes. It can only assess the final product.' I discuss this issue of process versus product in the next section.

Implications

The issue of process versus product in a group project seemed particularly salient when we observed Penny and her group. We saw the deep and sustained contribution she made to the group, and soon realised that this could not be fully reflected in her grade. This finding provides support for Bryan (2006), who suggests that an exclusive focus on project outcomes does not account fairly for different student contributions to the process.

Teachers could try to collect evidence to improve their understanding of the processes of group assessment. For example, students could be required to write a short appraisal of the respective contributions of the other team members. A further level of reflection might include analysis of the learning processes which could inform effective engagement with future group assignments.

The way in which Chan organised the group assessment did not involve any interim review of progress. This is a pragmatic and not unreasonable approach, a 'maximum autonomy perspective', as it were: students work in groups with no or minimal input and are left to resolve (or not) any problems through cooperation. More critically, it is probably a general problem in the management of group work that teachers often opt out of providing coaching and support. This represents a missed opportunity in terms of scaffolding student evaluative expertise in relation to the management of group work. Alternatives could involve providing advice to students about how to work in groups or, even better, to interact with them around the issues of productive teamwork. An interim review of group progress could also provide a forum for students to raise and discuss specific challenges, and for teachers to provide feedback. Reflecting on issues at a mid-point and/or requiring some kind of work-in-progress report may also discourage free-riding and procrastination. Teachers and students together could develop some guide-lines for effective group management. For example: appoint a suitable group leader; establish meeting times and schedules; involve all team members in speci-fied roles; work steadily; and rehearse the oral presentation to develop coherence.

Both Crystal and Fung exhibited some of the characteristics of diligent isolates (Pieterse and Thompson, 2010) in that they were willing to do more

High intensity   Medium intensity   Low intensity
Students most committed   Students least committed
to group project   to group project

Figure 6.1 Continuum of intensity of grade-related desire

than others to complete the project, although they still tried to involve teammates as much as they could. From their testimonies, I infer that the student who contributes the most to a group project is probably the one who is most concerned about the overall grade. I denote the strength of student motivation to achieve a high grade as their *intensity of grade-related desire*. The higher the intensity of grade-related desire, the more likely the student is to invest fully in group assessment. Free-riders in group projects are probably at the low-intensity end of the continuum presented in Figure 6.1.

In Chapter 3, I emphasised the value of student choice in assessment, and perhaps this can also be applied to group work so that students can choose to work either individually or in a group. Students with a high intensity of grade-related desire may prefer to work individually, so that their grade is wholly under their own control.

I return to this case in Chapter 8, where I undertake further analysis of how students perceived and engaged with the assessment criteria for the group project.

Business case: setting the scene

Ali Farhoomand is Professor of Innovation and Information Management in the School of Business, Hong Kong University. He has received two faculty teaching awards as well as the University Outstanding Teaching Award in 2008. He specialises in the development and dissemination of business cases, and is the director of the Centre for Asian Business Cases. He is also the creator and executive producer of the popular *Focus Asia Business Leaders* series, aired by BBC World.

We observed and interviewed students taking two of Ali's classes: Creativity and Business Innovation (class size: twenty) and E-business Transformation (class size: thirty). Both of these were elective courses taken by second- and third-year students. I focus mainly on how Ali involves students actively in his classes through various kinds of participatory activity, including discussions, oral presentations and group activities.

This case was the prototype for the current research: I have previously discussed dialogic feedback in relation to oral presentations in Carless (2013a), and aspects of dialogue and trust in Carless (2013b).

Creativity and Business Innovation course

The essence of this course was for students to apply the fundamental principles of creativity, design thinking and innovation in designing new products and services. The main intended learning outcomes are for students to: develop understanding of the nature of knowledge; apply concepts and techniques in dealing with complexity and uncertainty inherent in decision-making; develop creativity in design thinking; and demonstrate effective skills in communicating their thoughts. The type and weighting of assessment are summarised in Box 6.4.

Box 6.4 Assessment methods in Creativity and Business Innovation

- Case, class and blog discussion: 40 per cent
- Individual written case assignment: 30 per cent
- Term project: 30 per cent

The main stated criterion for contribution to case, class and blog discussion is 'to communicate your thoughts effectively', based on the following focus questions: 'Is the communication clear and to the point?', 'Does it follow the flow of the discussion, or is it an isolated comment?' and 'Does it build on what others are saying, involving re-evaluation of analysis and conclusions?'

The individual written case assignment is a conventional task whereby each student submits a written analysis of three assigned cases. The report – of about four to five pages in length – should highlight and analyse the major issues in the case; present a well-thought-out course of action; and suggest a feasible implementation plan.

For the term project, groups of four students work throughout the course to develop a socially innovative idea. This can relate to social corporate responsibility or to an innovation that will improve the lot of an underprivileged group living anywhere in the world. The project outputs are a group oral presentation and a related written report that is submitted one week later.

E-business Transformation course

This course focuses on how networked technologies can provide firms with the necessary infrastructure needed to align their business strategy with IT strategy; manage relationships and partnerships; and adapt to emerging global issues, such as outsourcing and off-shoring. The intended learning outcomes are for students to be able to work in teams effectively, write effective business reports, and make compelling presentations in relation to complexity theories, management processes and global issues surrounding transformation.

Assessment for the course is similar in structure to that for Creativity and Business Innovation, with minor amendments: there is no assessed blog for the course and case presentation is weighted separately. The tasks and weighting are summarised in Box 6.5.

Box 6.5 Assessment methods in E-business Transformation

- Class contribution: 30 per cent
- Case presentation: 20 per cent
- Written case analyses: 20 per cent
- Design project: 30 per cent

Ali's views on teaching, learning and assessment

Ali wants students to learn how to think out of the box and move away from forms of learning focused on memorisation to deeper levels of reflection and understanding. He believes that students need to unlearn the bad habits that they have accumulated in secondary schooling and learn how to think more deeply and critically. Part of this process involves reflection and self-evaluation: 'Self-assessment is a big part of learning. I think every course should encourage the students to assess the quality of other students' work so that they develop an understanding of the meaning of quality.' From this, I infer a strong relationship between Ali's philosophy and the component of the learning-oriented assessment framework that students need to develop self-evaluative expertise. Peer review is a major means of operationalising this aim.

Ali's assessment task design aims to provide alternative forms of assessment to examinations for one simple reason: 'I don't believe in exams because it is wasteful if students spend time memorising things that can easily be found any time on the internet. We should move away from memorisation to focusing on how to think and how to learn.'

One particularly interesting aspect of his courses is the significant amount of weighting he gives to participation:

> Participation constitutes 30–40 per cent of the grade for my courses, so it is a large part of the assessment. Students need to be interactive in the class and also be prepared for the class through the reading and thinking they have done beforehand.

So there is an emphasis on both activity during class and preparation before it. My interpretation is that the emphasis on participation is in line with Ali's teaching and learning approach, which puts students at the centre of the learning process and encourages them to develop their thinking and communication skills.

Our observations indicated that students were very actively involved in the classroom learning process. They were expected and required to participate in dialogue, extended questioning and discussion, and to engage in formal and informal oral presentations. A particular feature of Ali's practice is this emphasis on oral presentations, both as a formal assessment technique which counts towards grades and as briefer informal sharing. Part of the rationale for the use of oral presentations is that clear and effective presentations are important to achieving success in the field of business. In other words, oral presentations are a part of WTP in the discipline.

Ali talked about the importance of what and how students present, including the use of videos and dramas. He arranges cash prizes for the group which is voted most popular by the other students, which made the course fun and competitive. Competitiveness is something Ali emphasises as an element of the business world. Students gave peer feedback to each other and 'tried to shoot the other groups down with tough questions'.

Given his emphasis on participation, I asked Ali how this was evaluated:

> Attendance is different to contribution. Showing up is necessary but you need to make an effective contribution. Students are expected to 'demonstrate effective skills in communicating their thoughts'. So class participation is based on effectiveness of communication, not the quantity of contribution.

Exactly how he evaluated the effectiveness of communication was unclear, but our observations revealed positive atmospheres in his classes, and the quality of student engagement was extremely impressive.

Ali also wished to promote dialogue outside class. One of the strategies was technology-facilitated interaction through the use of a course blog:

> In the Creativity course, the blog is there for discussion. I post some articles on controversial issues, which is a good way to start discussion. The students also post articles. It is effective because it makes them think and gives them a sense of sequence as they can build on each other's arguments.

It was graded holistically on the extent to which students were effective in communicating their thoughts.

Overall, Ali believed that:

> Assessment methods should focus on gauging students' understanding of the subject matter. That can be done if students are engaged cognitively and physically in the learning process through continuous assessment. Assessment design should measure whether the new material has been synthesised and integrated into the students' overall knowledge base, although perhaps this is idealistic.

His use of terms such as 'understanding', 'cognitive engagement', 'synthesis' and 'interpretation' is indicative of aspirations for higher-order learning outcomes evolving from student participation in continuous assessment in his courses. I also infer alignment between his teaching approach and his assessment approach: thinking processes; learning to learn; and de-emphasising transmission and reproduction of knowledge. In short, Ali is attempting to encourage deep approaches to learning.

Student perspectives on participation

The continuous assessment referred to above and the emphasis on participation in Ali's classes were striking aspects of his courses. We asked students for their thoughts on them:

> For his class, it is 30 per cent participation, which is the most I have encountered. At first I was not accustomed to the intensive participation, but I forced myself to speak up and after a few weeks it became normal. Ali asks you to speak a lot because answering his question is not enough. He always asks, 'Why?' and many follow-up questions.

This focus on questioning was corroborated by our classroom observations. In extended dialogues with students, Ali often probed their responses with 'Why?' questions, which prompted them to elaborate upon the thinking processes underlying their comments. The extended questioning could also stimulate student thinking, as exemplified by the following student comments:

> I have developed my critical thinking skills to a higher level in this course. We have to think in-depth because we know there will be follow-up questions. Sometimes it is harsh because his questions are challenging. I tend to dig more deeply now because of his 'Why?' questions.
>
> The course doesn't deliver a lot of business knowledge; it's more about inspiring a way of thinking through questioning and dialogue.
>
> He doesn't have a fixed syllabus and the teaching plan can change at any time. The point of the class is to learn how to learn and learn how to think.

So the learning outcomes are highly focused on critical thinking, learning how to think more deeply and learning how to learn. Our classroom observations also provided evidence that, over time, students were providing deeper, more sustained contributions and honing their skills in communicating their thoughts effectively.

A further positive element of the participation was that there was evidence of student preparation before class. For instance, Cecilia commented:

> I think most classmates are well prepared and alert for this class and that is different to other courses. If you participate more in the class, you learn more. It is not just about the participation grade; it's the learning process.

This is an important point. I infer that participation grades are more about learning processes than assessment. The classroom observations evidenced an atmosphere which was cordial but concentrated, with participation expected and delivered.

I also asked students for their views on precisely how their participation might be graded. They were often uncertain:

> My conception is that the assessment of participation is related to activity; the quantity of participation is probably more important than the content of what you say. But it's kind of ambiguous. Maybe he should give more feedback to the students who are not so active.

So there was some confusion about how the grade for participation was awarded. The student quoted above felt that the degree of activity or the quantity of participation was a factor, whereas Ali claims to be more focused on the *quality* and *effectiveness* of the students' contributions. The point about interim feedback for less active students is also pertinent, and indeed this is recommended in the literature discussed in Chapter 3 (e.g. Dancer and Kamvounias, 2005). I wonder if Ali does not offer explicit interim feedback on participation because it might invite unwelcome student queries about precisely how student participation is recorded and evaluated.

Other students offered opinions about the assessment of participation:

> There is an incentive system to participate. Your grade depends on Ali's perception, so it makes no sense to keep silent in class. The participation grade keeps you concentrated.
>
> I don't really know how Ali assesses participation but I am not too concerned. From the results of previous classes, we know he is not that strict on grades. He gave a lot of As and Bs.

I infer that the main aim of participation grades is to encourage students to invest fully in their classes. As it is difficult to assess participation, teachers are likely to be relatively generous when assessing it, possibly to protect themselves from potential student complaints. Ali stated that he was perceived as 'tough' partly because of some of his challenging comments in class, but he corroborated the view that he awarded a lot of high grades. I felt that the high grades were justified because the students generally performed at a very high level in his classes.

Student views on group work and oral presentations

As part of the classroom dialogue, students were frequently involved in different kinds of group oral presentation. For example, Ali explained that, in the Creativity and Business Innovation course, student groups of four should come up with an idea for a new product, a new service or a new business. They have four weeks to draft a one-page proposal, so the students go through the process of idea generation and feasibility for implementation. After some feedback from Ali, some ideas are rejected as unfeasible, in which case students have a further week to come up with an alternative proposal.

Ali likes to video students when they are doing their oral presentations. Once the presentation is over, he promptly shows a couple of extracts from the video and asks the presenters to reflect on their performance. Students were generally positive about this activity:

> From the video I can see clearly what I have done. He played just one minute of the presentation and it grasped the typical things, so it is helpful. I could clearly see what to improve.
>
> I think his main purpose with the oral presentations is that we should find a way to be convincing. It doesn't matter so much what you wear or your mannerisms, but the essence is to sell an idea.

The videoed oral presentations and the related discussions supported students in developing a conception of quality oral presentations and reflecting on their own performances (see also Carless et al., 2011; Carless, 2013a).

Some students also related their oral presentations to what they learnt from participation in Ali's classes:

> Ali is a good model as a presenter. I learnt from him that if you can address a group of people and impress them, it is good. You need to think fast and be interactive in relation to your audience; present an argument with evidence and logic.

Students seemed to relish working in groups and reported spending a lot of time in collaborative discussions. In preparing their group oral presentations, they were also involved in a lot of dialogue, interaction and peer feedback. Ali mentioned that there were occasionally free-riding issues in groups, and he encouraged students to solve these themselves. Only in an extreme case would he step in to resolve such conflicts.

Cecilia commented:

> I like group work because I can't do everything on my own and my classmates can help me solve problems. I often act as a group leader. I usually allocate

different jobs to different people based on their abilities and strengths. I think group work is more useful than individual work.

She also talked about the benefits of such processes in terms of relationships between participants, and working with a variety of group members. When asked about fairness and equity issues in relation to group assessment, she replied:

I don't think it is unfair if I do more work as group leader. I have better time management and better skills so I should do more. I want to work towards the best result for my team, not just for myself. I feel happy if my teammates get a good grade.

This comment resonates with the views of Fung earlier in this chapter. I infer that Cecilia has a strong intensity of grade-related desires, as does Chi, the student whose comment about choosing his team members carefully to maximise his own grades opens this chapter.

Student views on the course blog

Students had a variety of views on the grading of the blog in the Creativity and Business Innovation course:

Having a grading allocation for it gives some life to the blog. If there is nobody commenting there, it wouldn't be an incentive for others to participate.

I think the intensiveness of the blog discussion increases towards the end of the semester, because blog participation counts for grades.

The oral discussion and critique during the class can be a bit fierce sometimes. So he includes a blog as part of the participation grade to accommodate those students who feel a bit intimidated in class.

The inclusion of the blog in the participation grade clearly promotes student involvement. Without the grading element, there would be a danger that only a small minority of enthusiastic students would engage in it. The third quotation above highlights the important point that it is potentially useful for participation to be afforded both a verbal, in-class element and an out-of-class, written component so as to cater for students' different capacities and personalities.

Students also talked about some benefits accruing from participation in the blog: it was a useful forum for discussion; they were exposed to some interesting articles; and there was an opportunity to interact with students who did not speak up in class. It was also noted that a blog might be particularly useful in a large class, when extended verbal interaction in the classroom is often less feasible. Perceptions of the length and interest of the posted articles seemed to be a factor impacting on involvement in the blog.

There were also student suggestions about how the blog could be improved. A notion which I felt was particularly pertinent was the idea of integrating the blog within the teaching of the class. It was suggested that Ali could sometimes highlight contributions from the blog and comment on them. Teacher participation in the blog is an important factor in encouraging students; providing an incentive for further involvement; and promoting oral discussion or feedback. My impression is that Ali wanted the blog to be student-driven, and workload-friendly for himself.

Ali gave me access to the blog, and I noticed that certain students participated very actively, whereas others were minimally involved. One enthusiastic student even set up a Facebook group in order to continue the discussion once the course was over. Another active participant expressed two main reasons for her involvement: it counts towards the grade; and it is interesting to search for something inspiring. She reported that some students mainly focused on their own contributions – posting a text or an article but seldom commenting on any other students' postings. She was disappointed that when she posted something interesting on the blog and wanted to know others' opinions, she rarely received any interesting feedback.

Overall, the blog encouraged students to engage in issues outside regular lectures; it provided some opportunity for peer feedback, although, as the previous student informant noted, participants often made their own contributions but neglected to comment on the posts of others. The grade allocation for the blog provided some motivation for students to participate: some seemed to involve themselves solely because of this grading aspect, whereas others were less concerned about it and seemed to participate mainly out of interest.

Contrary to the practice reported in Churchill (2009), discussed in Chapter 3, Ali was not active in responding to student contributions to the blog. In my view, this is a justified, pragmatic approach because of the workload implications. If he had done so, however, the blog could have been better integrated into the course and students might have found it more compelling. I return to the issue of workload in assessment innovation in Chapter 12.

Overall student perceptions on assessment task design

Now I present student perceptions of the overall assessment task designs in Ali's two Business modules. Some interviewees compared Ali's approach with exams, which were the dominant approach in the discipline:

> I like the assessment approach because it promotes my critical and analytical thinking skills. I don't want to memorise for an exam; I've spent fifteen years doing that in school. But for students who lack a solid foundation of business knowledge it may be hard for them to learn from the assessment approach.
>
> (Chi)

> I like the assessment approach because I can really learn something. With exams, you memorise and then forget. But what Ali has taught us about thinking will stay in our memory for a long time.
>
> (Cecilia)

> I am more advantaged by exams. I know how to prepare for them and tend to get good grades. For class participation, you can't really prepare. Yet, from his assessment approach, I have the chance to apply theory and knowledge in practical situations, like analysing business cases.
>
> (Han)

The main theme in the students' responses was that the assessment approach promotes sustainable learning, in contrast to the more short-term, reproductive nature of exams. Another student in the Creativity and Business Innovation course commented:

> I think the assessment approach is good and it suits the module content. How do you assess innovation on paper? You can't really do that, so I think that asking students to present innovative projects is the right way to do it. We also get marks for participating in the blogs.

This observation suggests alignment between course content, learning activities and assessment.

Another student concluded:

> The assessment task design inspires thinking. I like writing reports, doing projects and doing the case assignment as that will enable me to learn more than doing exams. By doing a project or report, if I found something interesting, I could spend time digging more deeply into that question.

From this, I infer that assessment which is intrinsically interesting to the student provokes greater engagement, study time and effort, and has greater potential to generate higher-order learning outcomes. This extends Gibbs' principle of spreading effort evenly across a module by adding elements of the kind of engagement which accrues thinking, learning and going deeply into aspects of interest.

Implications

The Business case carries a number of implications for learning-oriented assessment. In relation to assessment task design, there was coherence between interactive learning through various forms of participation, group projects and analysis of business cases. This was facilitated by a high degree of integration between teaching, learning and assessment. There was plenty of evidence that students were using deep approaches to learning focused on understanding and the development of ideas. There was also considerable flexibility and choice, including modes of participation, group project membership and selection of topics. The assessment tasks involved student engagement over time across the duration of the module. There was also a focus on the real-life needs of the discipline in terms of persuasive oral presentations and the analysis of business cases, resonating with the notion of WTP.

The development of evaluative expertise was supported through the classroom dialogues, by which students were prompted to reflect on how to think, learning to learn, and the effectiveness of their communication. A further specific means of developing student self-evaluation was through the videoing and reflective discussions, which aimed to develop students' understandings of the nature of quality business presentations.

Students were prompted to engage with feedback because it was integrated into classroom dialogues, oral presentations and the processes of group projects. Feedback was intertwined effectively with classroom activities, so it took place principally within the module; little post-course feedback was required. This was a time-efficient and effective way of handling feedback processes for maximum impact on students.

The competing priorities which framed Chapter 1 were resolved by focusing on enhancing student learning; the robustness of grading practices appeared somewhat less central. Students were actively involved and they generally achieved high marks, but it was somewhat less clear exactly how Ali arrived at the students' participation grades. Student trust in Ali as their teacher seemed to be a factor in promoting their acceptance – or tolerance – of some of the ambiguities in the grading of participation (Carless, 2013b). In Box 3.1 I suggested some criteria for assessing participation. After observing this case, I feel that there are classroom benefits in encouraging participation, but that the challenge of applying criteria rigorously is hard to resolve in practice. I return to this issue in Chapter 12.

Summary of chapter

In the Geology case, I have discussed group work assessment and analysed how students experienced this form of assessment. Implications include the desirability of valuing process as well as product, and the need for guidance and interim reviews of group progress.

In the Business case, I have noted that Ali focused on a variety of interactive learning activities which promoted dialogue amongst the students. This dialogue was facilitated through assessment task design, which included oral presentations and related group projects, and assessment of class and blog participation.

Main implications for practice

- Group assessment should involve some form of interim review and related guidance.

- Attention should be paid to both the processes and products of group assessment.
- The assessment of group work should generally involve some combination of individual and group assessment.
- The integration of classroom dialogue, teaching, learning and assessment promotes student engagement.
- Assessing participation orally and in writing can be useful in promoting active student engagement.
- There are tensions between the benefits for engagement of assessed participation and the challenges of grading participation systematically and reliably.

Part III

Engaging with quality criteria

Chapter 7

Promoting student engagement with quality

> The possession of evaluative expertise is a necessary (but not sufficient) condition for improvement.
>
> (Sadler, 1989, p. 138)

Scope of chapter

In this chapter, I focus on the means by which students can develop their evaluative expertise through activities which engage them with quality in the discipline. The aims are to unpack how teachers and students use criteria in forming judgements; and how students can be supported to decode criteria. In the first half of the chapter, I focus on synthesising relevant literature on the nature of judgement and the use of criteria. In the second half, a particular focus is on dialogue around exemplars of student work which are a promising way of developing student evaluative expertise. The main argument is that students need to engage with quality and standards in ways that enable them to monitor and improve their own work.

Definitions and setting the scene

Judgements are part of teachers' lives in evaluating student work; they are part of students' lives in terms of judging their work in progress; and they form a core element of life-long learning in that, throughout our lives, we are involved in judgements and decision-making. Criteria are often used to substantiate teachers' largely intuitive judgements or may be deployed in arriving at those judgements. The set criteria for module assignments suggest to students the quality indicators for their performance, although their format, content and language may be difficult for students to access.

A number of issues arise which set the scene for this chapter. When marking, how do teachers arrive at judgements? What does a good marking scheme or rubric look like? How useful are rubrics to students, and how might we promote student engagement with them? What kinds of activities promote student engagement with quality?

Before I go any further I need to define, differentiate between and discuss some key terms: what we mean by criteria and standards; and how they are embodied in rubrics or marking schemes. 'Criterion' can usefully be described as 'a distinguishing property or characteristic of any thing, by which its quality can be judged or estimated, or by which a decision or classification may be made' (Sadler, 1987, p. 194). 'Standards' are 'a definite level of excellence or attainment' (Sadler, 1987, p. 194). So a criterion refers to a property or characteristic of a student response, whereas a standard refers to a particular degree or level of quality (Sadler, 2009b).

Rubrics, also known as 'marking schemes', 'ssessment criteria' or 'grade descriptors', combine criteria and standards in the form of a grid to provide statements of the performance needed to achieve different standards. They can involve either holistic interpretations of criteria in which an overall judgement is made; analytic schemes in which judgements are made in relation to separate individual criteria; or some combination of the two. In analytic grading, in theory the teacher makes distinct qualitative judgements on separate criteria and the aggregate of these judgements is converted into a grade or mark. In practice, teachers often use various combinations of these methods or substitute, knowingly or unwittingly, their own personal criteria to supplement the documented criteria (Wolf, 1995). This is partly because some teacher expectations cannot be fully communicated using criteria (Sadler, 2005, 2013b). This kind of tacit knowledge (Polanyi, 1967) is hard to transfer to learners because of the difficulty in expressing it in words. Only when a student develops tacit knowledge which corresponds broadly with that of the teacher is the student in a position to make sense of the teacher's judgement and its rationale (Sadler, 2010a). Tacit knowledge acquisition can follow from joint participation in evaluative activities, such as constructing and using criteria, and discussion of exemplars of different levels of performance.

Another relevant term is 'subjectivity', which arises when judgements are influenced by one's own sensations, experiences or personal opinions. Subjectivity is usually contrasted with 'objectivity', which is generally taken to mean the ability to judge fairly, without bias, external influence or personal feelings. However, the complex interplay between subjectivity and objectivity in social practice goes beyond the simplistic dualisms implied in these definitions. Shay's work, to which I return later in the chapter, illustrates that academic judgement is both subjectively and objectively constituted, and generally a product of the social situation in which it is enacted. Subjectivity is often used in a pejorative way, but subjective judgements are common in various professions and under suitable circumstances they can be soundly based, consistently trustworthy and congruent with those made by qualified and experienced professionals (Sadler, 2013a). It is probably fair to say that all judgements carry some degree of subjectivity and that a key is to manage that subjectivity in a reasonable way. Such processes may be somewhat akin to how the qualitative researcher manages subjectivity in their data analysis procedures through methods such as triangulation, peer review and rigorous interplay between evidence and argument.

Making judgements

Hager and Butler (1996) contrast two models of educational assessment: a scientific measurement model, mainly in tune with traditional assessment methods; and a judgement model, reflective of shifts towards processes of thinking through modes, such as problem-based learning or portfolio-based performance assessment. This judgement model shares some common ground with learning-oriented assessment in terms of the implication that students should be involved in processes which encourage them to learn how to make increasingly sophisticated judgements for themselves. Judgement models of assessment acknowledge that assessment can involve subjective and context-dependent aspects of knowledge, and includes open problems with divergent responses, some of which have been illustrated in Chapters 4 and 5. Another possibility in the judgemental model is that assessment can become a dialogue between the assessor and the person being assessed, so that the latter can present a case. Rick Glofcheski utilises a variation on this possibility in relation to same-day feedback, discussed in Chapter 11.

The role of judgement is also addressed in various works outside the more restricted purview of educational assessment, and this helps to illustrate some key issues in relation to processes of making judgements. In *Thinking, Fast and Slow*, Daniel Kahneman (2011) discusses the role of decision-making and how judgements are made. He suggests that there are two systems for making judgements: one fast, intuitive and emotional; the other a slower, more deliberative and generally more logical one. I speculate that in the marking of student work, teachers may prioritise one of these over the other, or utilise some combination of the two.

In *Human Judgement*, Donald Laming (2004) explores the principles of how people make real-life decisions. He discusses, amongst other things, the role of bias and the fallibility of many judgements, including the grading of examinations in universities. In a technical sense, bias means the involvement of extraneous information which is actually irrelevant to the judgement, whereas in its more everyday sense it means attending to one's own interest in a matter. One of Laming's inferences is that when someone comes to make a judgement in the everyday world, their point of reference is usually past experience, so judgements involve comparisons of one thing with another (Laming, 2004). He goes on to discuss how these comparisons are basically at an ordinal level: people can accurately say something is louder or softer, better or worse than the focus of comparison, but that is generally the limit of the quality of their judgement. The evidence he accumulates and discusses is a stark reminder of the limitations of human judgement. A related implication is that quests for reliability in assessment judgements face serious and ongoing challenges (Bloxham, 2009; Yorke, 2008). There is more on this issue below as I turn to how teachers make judgements about student work.

How teachers judge work

In order to understand how criteria are used in the making of judgements, I first need to discuss some issues in relation to how teachers mark student work. Judgements in assessment are sometimes seen as technical processes in which: assessment task guidelines are set; assessment criteria are applied; and professional judgements are made and then ratified through some form of moderation or similar quality assurance process. There is plenty of evidence that, in practice, the process of arriving at judgements is a complex one involving a number of issues. How teachers use published criteria or substitute their own to make judgements thus becomes a key issue for consideration.

The research base on marking in higher education is relatively modest. In relation to how teaching staff make judgements, there seems to be a consensus that experienced assessors act in ways which are largely intuitive and they are often not able to articulate the tacit knowledge on which a decision is based (Brooks, 2012; Ecclestone, 2001). For example, the claim to identify an upper-second-class performance accurately is both the articulation of an intuitive judgement without mechanically following a set of criteria, and an implicit claim of expert professional status (Ecclestone, 2001). In a study of the marking process and application of criteria for a final-year dissertation, Hand and Clewes (2000) found tensions between the freedom of academics to apply their own deeply held convictions about the value of student work and the quality controls necessary to operate a modern academic institution with a large number of students. In addition, worthwhile tasks often demand divergent outcomes (James, 2014), so pre-specified criteria may fail to account for the richness of potential student response. The related inference that marking is more complex and intuitive than the application of criteria is consonant with Sadler's position, sketched earlier in this chapter.

Shay's work (2005, 2008) provides compelling evidence of how the processes of making judgements are social practices through which colleagues interact within organisational micro cultures and may be influenced by such factors as personal relationships, values and attitudes. She argues that the assessment of complex tasks is a socially situated interpretive act involving a 'double reading': an iterative movement between the objective and the subjective (Shay, 2005). The latter is inevitable because professional judgement inescapably involves some embodiment of the assessor. Subjective readings also involve pragmatism as teachers are sensitive to the consequences of their assessment for themselves as professionals as well as for their students: particularly an issue in cases of potential student failure. Shay's work also speaks to the role of the discipline, discussed in Chapter 3 in relation to WTP. Shay (2008) suggests that a missing link in the discourses of assessment criteria is a language of description to talk about the valued forms of disciplinary knowledge. A related inference is that rubrics need to avoid overuse of generic vocabulary and focus on discipline-specific quality indicators.

How assessors learn to mark has also attracted some attention in the literature. In a similar way to Shay's conception of marking as a socially constructed act, it seems that learning to mark is predominantly a socialisation process acquired by grading papers in the university workplace. A useful recent study by Bloxham, Boyd and Orr (2011) was based on think-aloud protocols during the marking process from twelve competent and conscientious lecturers in two universities. These markers seemed first to make a judgement and then make reference to the grade descriptors, rather than making explicit reference to the descriptors while marking. In other words, they seem to decide the grade first and only then use the published criteria to justify or support their decision. This finding supports the position outlined above (Brooks, 2012; Ecclestone, 2001) that staff tend to downplay criteria, choose not to use them or use implicit standards of their own which may not closely match those provided to students. Given this evidence and the challenges of reliably assessing complex achievement, it is perhaps unsurprising that the literature reveals a frailty and lack of robustness in summative assessment at the university level (Bloxham and Boyd, 2007; Knight, 2002b; Yorke, 2008).

When marking, teachers may use holistic grading schemes, analytic ones, or (particularly in the hard disciplines) more numerical schemes, such as marks awarded for correctness on objectively assessed items. Holistic grading was in the ascendancy until the 1990s, but since then there has been a steady swing towards analytic grading so as to bring more structure into the grading process and reveal more clearly to students how their grades have been awarded (Sadler, 2009b; James, 2014). In principle, well-designed criteria have potential to increase the consistency of marking. Analytic marking provides greater consistency of judgement, according to Gosling and Moon (2002), although proponents of holistic grading would contest this. Analytic marking schemes provide a framework for which inexperienced assessors can develop expertise and over time they may gain greater confidence and ability in marking holistically (Yorke, 2011). The Bloxham, Boyd and Orr (2011) study of experienced markers found no evidence of them assigning marks to individual elements and then combining these to arrive at a final grade. If this can be generalised, an implication would be that experienced teachers tend to make holistic judgements even when using analytic marking schemes. This follows from a major limitation of analytic grading in that combining the results of individual components does not adequately represent the complex way in which judgements are actually made (Sadler, 2009b).

A further, related issue is that all criteria are not equal, although a grading rubric might lead the undiscerning reader to think that they are. Lists of assessment criteria rarely indicate weightings or the comparative importance of certain qualities in relation to others (Shay, 2008; Woolf, 2004), although they are starting to do so. This is possibly more of a problem for analytic marking schemes than holistic ones in that when making a global judgement, an assessor has probably internalised what they see as more important qualities they are looking for in a piece of work. There are, of course, inevitable inconsistencies in the degree of emphasis that teachers place on a particular aspect. A mundane example would be the format of reference lists. Some markers may wish to see full accuracy of the kind required by the final proof of a journal article; others may just want to feel that students have a general awareness of reference formats, without expecting fine-grained accuracy of aspects such as punctuation details; others may be relatively indifferent to the reference format, focusing instead on more substantive matters in a piece of writing. This lack of perceived consistency can be puzzling to students and emphasises the need for enhanced communication around assessment-related issues.

Moderation and connoisseurship

Teachers in higher education also learn about marking and how their grading compares with that of colleagues through moderation processes. Moderation can take various forms, but generally refers to the promotion of consistent teacher judgements across multiple teachers on a course. Social moderation involves teachers in discussion and debate about their interpretations of the quality of assessed work (Klenowski and Wyatt-Smith, 2014). At best, moderation processes could support the sharing of tacit understandings of quality and standards in healthy communities of practice. At worst, moderation can be an unwelcome quality assurance procedure which may produce nothing more than perfunctory support for the original marker judgement. Bloxham (2009) also argues that there is a risk that time-consuming moderation processes may squander resources for modest impact; for example, she points out that even relatively major changes for a single module assignment grade are unlikely to influence a student's overall degree classification. More positively, processes where staff members interpret criteria and standards of achievement together are likely to be integral to teachers' ability to carry out similar activities with students (Ecclestone, 2001). In other words, moderation has implications for learning-oriented assessment when it promotes teachers' capacities to engage in activities which support student development of evaluative expertise.

Moderation conversations often reveal that teachers are not just assessing a piece of work, but also making inferences and adjustments in relation to the student and their characteristics, such as motivation, complacency or frailty (Orr, 2007). This reinforces a strand in both Becker et al. (1968) and Miller and Parlett (1974) (reviewed in Chapter 2): students believe that it is more than the quality of their work which leads to a judgement being made. They often perceive a hidden curriculum where teachers express certain requirements for assessment tasks but then reward other elements as well (Norton, 2004). For example, a well-known campus athlete reported that he received higher grades than he merited because his teachers were aware that he needed to spend a lot of time on his sporting activities (Becker et al., 1968). More recent evidence confirms the view that stated criteria are only part of the judgement process. Markers bring into play their own concepts and interpretations, which include 'making allowances' or 'compensating' for elements, such as the difficulty of a question or a task, or using other evidence about the student (Wolf, 1995). Furthermore, assessors may be unaware that they are operating in this way. Conflating assessments of the quality of students' work with judgements about their personal attributes risks being counterproductive if we purport to be assessing a student's level of achievement. Grades should represent learners' attained levels of academic achievement, uncontaminated by other characteristics, such as effort, previous performance or attendance (Sadler, 2010b).

When moderation enhances the professionalism of teacher participants, it develops their connoisseurship as judges of quality and standards. Connoisseurship is defined as 'a highly developed form of competence in qualitative appraisal' (Sadler, 2009c, p. 57). The connoisseur possesses a critical appreciation of the qualities of something, whether it is a bottle of wine, a painting or something grounded in a particular academic discipline. A related risk arises if connoisseurship becomes imbued with images of elitism or mystery and might intensify the challenge of student understanding of higher education standards (Orr, 2010b).

For Eisner (1985), connoisseurship is the art of appreciation. Here, 'appreciation' is defined as the awareness and understanding of what one has experienced, and it provides the basis for judgement. In relation to assessment, Eisner's notion of educational connoisseurship is that the complexity of many aspects of assessment or evaluation suggests that it may bear some resemblance to forms of aesthetic appreciation, particularly – but not exclusively – in relation to such disciplines as fine arts. In these disciplines, the critic plays a particular role in developing student connoisseurship, and this has implications for how dialogue is managed (a core theme of Chapter 9, in relation to Architecture).

The processes surrounding the development of connoisseurship merit some consideration. Connoisseurs may form a community which enables them to share tacit understandings and experiences and to debate issues which relate to the development of community viewpoints. Connoisseurship of this kind is underpinned by informed professional judgements located in communities of practice (Orr, 2010b). The potential value of communities of practice for developing understandings about assessment is well recognised. Price (2005) makes a number of relevant points: explicit articulation of assessment standards becomes meaningful only when tacit knowledge, developed within a local community of practice, is effectively shared; module teams could operate in this way but are generally restricted by lack of time, commitment and relevant assessment expertise; lack of feedback to teachers on their marking seems to be a missing link in the process of internalising standards; and ways forward might include marking bees where, team members sit together prior to marking, mark scripts and discuss any issues that arise.

Student engagement and understandings of criteria

In Chapter 1 I introduced the use of criteria as a way of bringing transparency into assessment and the related potential to support students in understanding the nature of quality work. The roles of criteria also loom large in the previous section on judgements with the implication that criteria in themselves are not able to express fully some of the tacit nature of quality, and teacher judgements are more complex and intuitive than the application of criteria. In this section, I focus principally on what students make of criteria and how they use them – or might use them – to monitor their work. One of the most important things a student can learn in becoming assessment literate is how to make judgements about quality, to begin to acquire the kind of connoisseurship alluded to above. Understanding and using criteria are aspects of the development of connoisseurship.

Woolf (2004, p. 479) contends that 'there is widespread agreement among writers on assessment in higher education that the production, publication and discussion of clear assessment criteria are a sine qua non of an effective assessment strategy'. There is certainly potential for assessment criteria to clarify assessment processes and outcomes. Criteria in themselves, however, may be of limited use to students unless they engage with them purposefully or are stimulated to do so by relevant classroom activities. Nuanced understandings of the qualities which are intended to be developed by tasks and assignments, and of the quality of particular pieces of work, are not easily captured in lists of goals, standards and criteria (Torrance, 2012). Gosling and Moon (2002), for example, point out that a criterion like 'critical thinking' is open to multiple interpretations, and novice students may regard it simply as being critical of others. The way higher education is currently organised may also act as a barrier to student understandings of criteria. The traditional model of students writing work for their own tutor and having opportunities to come to understand that tutor's beliefs about criteria is at odds with modular programmes and lower levels of contact between staff and students (Hand and Clewes, 2000).

An initiative at the Business School, Oxford Brookes University in the late 1990s involved the development of an assessment grid aiming to establish common standards and provide related guidance to students (Price and Rust, 1999). Research into its usefulness revealed that students' perceived the criterion-referenced assessment grid to be a 'good idea' but also identified a number of challenges, including: students' difficulties in understanding terminology used in the criterion descriptions; individual students interpreted not only the purpose of the grid but the criteria themselves differently; understandings involved subjectivity and multiple interpretations of criteria and standards; and some focus group participants found the required level of abstraction to link criteria with tasks too demanding and perceived a need for exemplars to illustrate them (O'Donovan, Price and Rust, 2001). This represents a useful summary of the challenges of student understanding and engagement with criteria.

In a small-scale study of assessment criteria in the subjects of Business and History, Woolf (2004) makes a number of relevant points. Criteria assume meaning only when used and there can be striking similarities between grade descriptors for different subjects in that they mainly focus on generic academic and intellectual skills. More specifically, the stated requirements for a successful project in Business or History were found to be essentially the same (Woolf,

2004). An inference is that these descriptors might have been better designed if they were better focused on the particular subject-specific learning outcomes required by the task, rather than using generic statements, such as 'good understanding' or 'very good level of critical analysis'. When criteria appear the same to students, this can act as a barrier to engagement – an element which emerges strongly as a theme in the data discussed in the following chapter.

Under which circumstances are lists of criteria in the form of rubrics likely to have a positive impact on student learning? There is likely to be a positive impact on learning outcomes when rubrics support student self-regulation (Panadero and Jonsson, 2013). Rubrics have the potential to promote learning when they are co-created or negotiated with students; they make the goals and qualities of an assignment transparent; and students use them to guide self- and peer assessment and subsequent revision (Reddy and Andrade, 2010). A recent quasi-experimental study of a second-year Sports Science course analysed the impact on student examination grades of providing and using marking criteria (Payne and Brown, 2011). An experimental group of fifty-four students was given the criteria before the exam and experienced a related workshop during regular class time. During the workshop, the criteria were explained; examples were provided; and practice in grading examination scripts was carried out. The control group, a cohort of thirty-two who had taken the course a year earlier, took the examination without any prior exposure to the marking criteria. The mean examination grades were 55.4 per cent for the experimental group and 36.9 per cent for the control group, suggesting that use of explicit criteria was associated with significantly higher examination grades (Payne and Brown, 2011).

There are also challenges surrounding the productive use of criteria. Sometimes students seem to use criteria in a formulaic way, perceiving that this may help them to gain a satisfactory grade (Norton, 2004). This is a limited form of engagement. Focusing mainly on satisfying the teacher can distract students from a more meaningful goal of searching for and producing quality work. In the context of post-secondary education and training, Torrance (2007) extends this argument in that some uses of criteria can inadvertently limit the student learning experience. He refers to this as 'criteria compliance' (p. 281), whereby explicit criteria, coaching and formative feedback can collude in producing a limited and reductive form of instrumentalism rather than a deeper learning experience. There are tensions between the transparency aspects of clear criteria and the risk that students may end up delivering merely what is asked for rather than using their own creativity and developing outcomes which have the potential to exceed expectations. Torrance (2012) suggests that features of good practice in the deployment of criteria include: clarifying both 'task criteria' (what needs to be done to *accomplish* the task) and 'quality criteria' (what constitutes doing the task *well*); developing student understanding of the contingent nature of criteria and that some can outweigh others; and supporting the development of student meta-cognition and the ability to transfer overarching criteria to other tasks and situations, such as linking conclusions to evidence.

Peer review

A common method of promoting student engagement with criteria is through some form of peer review. By 'peer review' or 'peer feedback', I mean students commenting on the work of their peers with the aim of developing mutual insights into how tasks can be approached or performance improved. This kind of process would often be focused on an assignment in progress. My belief is that it is usually more productive to focus on peer feedback comments, rather than peer assessment using grades, because students often feel uncomfortable about awarding grades to their peers (Liu and Carless, 2006).

The main rationale for peer review is that, through commenting on the work of their peers, students develop sensitivity to features of quality which can be applied to their own work (Nicol and Macfarlane-Dick, 2006). Producing peer feedback is also more cognitively demanding than just receiving it, so constructing feedback comments carries potential to increase student engagement with quality and standards (Nicol, Thomson and Breslin, 2014). The benefits of generating peer-feedback comments need to be communicated to students as the literature provides a number of examples where students felt disappointed by their classmates' failure to commit to the process seriously (e.g. Patton, 2012) or by their failure to produce good-quality comments (e.g. Yucel et al., 2014). A challenge is to create the course conditions of intellectual involvement and trust for students to want to engage with the work of their peers. A method of motivating students to engage seriously with the work of their peers is through awarding marks for the quality of peer-review comments (Bloxham and West, 2004). Another option involves peer-review triads, where students can receive comments from two classmates rather than just one (Ballantyne, Hughes and Mylonas, 2002).

Prior to providing peer feedback, students could also be involved in devising their own assessment criteria. Students are most likely to engage with and understand criteria if they have played some role in generating them (Boud, 1995). Peer assessment generally works well when criteria are jointly determined by staff and students prior to peer review, and when expectations are clear (Dochy, Segers and Sluijsmans, 1999). A simple alternative to student generation of criteria is for students to be involved in putting criteria into their own words (Carless, Joughin, Liu and associates, 2006; Sambell et al., 2013). What is crucial for improved understanding of assessment criteria and standards is repeated practice using assessment criteria through self-evaluation and peer-review exercises, supported by discussion with teachers (Price et al., 2012).

Inferences and implications

One inference from the evidence I have presented is that tutors often do not follow the criteria as embodied in descriptors either precisely or rigidly; rather, they interpret and personalise their use of criteria. There may sometimes be reasonable justification for this in that teachers may revisit descriptors in the light of engaging with student responses, some of which may add to the intended learning outcomes embodied in the criteria. Judgements also involve comparative elements which are largely based on experience and personal perceptions of the relative importance of various elements. These factors may act as barriers for deep student engagement with criteria because they sense that teachers are using somewhat different criteria from the published ones, including personal evaluations of students. Challenges are compounded by criteria being embedded in a discourse that is difficult for students to interpret. Students are likely to need repeated exposure to criteria and practice in using them to appreciate some of their nuances. I am also struck by Woolf's points about sameness or similarities in criteria, as this is a theme in the student data discussed in Chapter 8. If lists of criteria all appear in similar grid forms with recurring terminologies, this may impact negatively on student engagement with them. These challenges are compounded by other factors: teachers' relatively low levels of assessment literacy; rubrics generally not being particularly well designed; and a natural unwillingness of teachers to devote time to the crafting of grade descriptors which they may perceive as a low priority or a quality-assurance chore.

To sum up, the extent to which criteria impact on students' learning is largely dependent on the quality and depth of their engagement with rubrics. I turn next to what I see as the most effective means of prompting students to engage with criteria and the nature of quality: the analysis of exemplars of student work.

The use of exemplars in clarifying criteria

A key inference from the first half of this chapter is that students find it difficult to make sense of, and use, assessment criteria in the form of rubrics or grade descriptors. The argument now to be developed is that dialogue around exemplars of student work in association with criteria is a major means of supporting students to improve their understanding of the nature of quality work and develop their evaluative expertise. I elaborate the rationale for the use of exemplars, synthesise the relevant literature on their use, and discuss issues in relation to classroom implementation.

Exemplars and worked examples

Research into exemplars in assessment in higher education has been developing gradually over the last fifteen years or so. Exemplars have considerable potential to support students in understanding the nature of quality work – a view that has been particularly championed by Royce Sadler. He defines exemplars as 'key examples chosen so as to be typical of designated levels of quality or competence' (Sadler, 1987, p. 200). They are also sometimes referred to as 'samples', 'student samples' or 'worked examples'. These samples are usually assignments from previous cohorts of students, carrying merits of authenticity and ease of collection, although they could be devised by the teacher. Exemplars are often in written format, such as essays or reports, but could also involve such formats as oral presentations, posters, e-portfolios or disciplinary artefacts, including law briefs, art designs and laboratory reports. An advantage of using exemplars from a previous cohort, as opposed to peer assessment or peer feedback, is that it avoids some of the challenging interpersonal or affective issues that can arise when analysing the work of a classmate (Wimshurst and Manning, 2013). First-year students expressed a strong preference for working with exemplars rather than carrying out peer review, mainly because of poor-quality or insufficient peer feedback (Yucel et al., 2014).

Although research into the study of exemplars in higher education is not yet a major field, the use of worked examples has a lengthy history and has included research in such subjects as Mathematics, Physics and Computer Programming. Similarly, working through problems with model answers has a long tradition and is a common pedagogic practice in science subjects, Technology, Engineering and Mathematics. In a study in Biology, for example, Huxham (2007) found that model answers seemed to impact more on achievement than individualised feedback, even though students expressed a preference for the latter.

I draw here on a useful review article (Atkinson et al., 2000) to highlight some relevant points about worked examples. They provide an expert's problem-solving method for the learner to study and emulate, and they make expert thinking visible to students by modelling flexible, creative problem-solving as well as meta-cognitive strategies. Analysing worked examples supports learners to develop knowledge structures representing important, early foundations for understanding and using substantive ideas that are illustrated and emphasised by the instructional examples. The most effective way of structuring a worked example session is to link each example to its target practice problem. The number of examples is constrained by instructional time and problem complexity; two examples seem to be a useful guideline. There is, however, a danger of cognitive overload when students are required to reference and integrate multiple sources of information (Atkinson et al., 2000).

Atkinson et al.'s (2000) review provides some useful pointers: worked examples provide methods for students to emulate; they model problem-solving strategies; and they make expert thinking visible. As I see it, a difference between worked examples and exemplars is that the former are ideal and expert-managed, whereas the latter are usually student samples which may contain a combination of good and weak points. It may be that worked examples are more popular or useful in hard disciplines with more convergent answers, whereas exemplars may be more useful in soft disciplines which encourage more divergent responses to an issue or question.

Rationale for using exemplars

Exemplars have significant practical value because of their concreteness (Sadler, 1987). They convey messages that are hard to share by other means and are particularly useful in illustrating a continuum of quality identifiable in student work (Sadler, 2002). The rationale for the use of exemplars is cogently summarised as follows:

> Students need to be exposed to, and gain experience in making judgements about, a variety of works of different quality. They need planned rather than random exposure to exemplars, and experience in making judgements about quality. They need to create verbalised rationales and accounts of how various works could have been done better. Finally, they need to engage in evaluative conversations with teachers and other students. Together, these three provide the means by which students can develop a concept of quality that is similar in essence to that which the teacher possesses.
>
> (Sadler, 2010a, p. 544)

Discussion around exemplars plays two significant and related roles. The first is exposure: analysing exemplars and drawing implications for one's own work. The second is students making judgements about these works and explaining or justifying these judgements. These involve somewhat different cognitive processes, and the second is more likely to support students in developing evaluative expertise, particularly when they are involved in suggesting how exemplars might be improved.

Exemplars also have the potential to induct students into the learning community of the discipline when they construct knowledge through exploring notions of quality with teachers (Rust, O'Donovan and Price, 2005). Engagement with good exemplars can support students to notice discrepancies between their present proficiency level and the expected one; this can prompt them to self-regulate their work and deploy learning strategies to narrow the gap (Bell, Mladenovic and Price, 2013; Handley and Williams, 2011). A quantitative exploration of assessment literacy in an Australian university (Smith et al., 2013) found that the ability to judge exemplars against criteria and standards stood out as a 'high-leverage' dimension. In other words, work around exemplars is effective at developing skills in making judgements and promising in facilitating student improvement in performance on similar tasks. The intervention took fifty minutes of classroom time and evidenced a positive educational return for a modest pedagogic investment: an important consideration in view of resource limitations and the wide array of pedagogic strategies available to teachers (Smith et al., 2013).

Research on exemplars

Here, I present what I see as key studies of exemplars in chronological order to provide a perspective on how exemplars research has been developing. An early study by Orsmond, Merry and Reiling (2002) involved twenty-two undergraduate Biology students working on an assignment which required the development of a poster. The students were exposed to five sample posters from a previous cohort and used them to inform their development of criteria to be used for peer and self-assessment. When students later constructed their own individual posters, they used the co-constructed criteria to carry out peer and self-evaluation. A number of benefits were revealed, including improved student understanding of marking criteria and enhanced potential to engage with feedback, although there was a danger that being exposed to samples may reduce student creativity. An important point is that exemplars help students understand what to produce but are not necessarily helpful in increasing their ability to produce it (Orsmond et al., 2002).

The key aim of an intervention in the first semester of a Business degree programme was to support students in developing their understanding of assessment criteria (Rust, Price and O'Donovan, 2003). Prior to an optional workshop, student participants marked two sample assignments using the assessment criteria provided. The workshops, of ninety-minute duration, included: student group discussion of their marking of the sample assignments; tutor-led analysis of the samples and criteria; and tutor-provided annotated and marked versions of samples. The main findings were that student participants in the optional workshop achieved better results than non-participants, although it is possible that motivational aspects, influencing whether they joined the workshop, may also have been a factor. The intervention supported the sharing of tacit understandings through the use of exemplars, marking practice and the opportunity for dialogue to complement explanation of the criteria. The authors conclude that emphasis on explicit articulation of assessment criteria and standards is insufficient to develop a shared understanding of 'useful knowledge' between staff and students; rather, socialisation processes, as embedded in the workshop, are necessary for tacit knowledge transfer to occur (Rust et al., 2003).

In a study where 400 students had the opportunity to access online annotated exemplars and could post questions or comments to lecturers and peers on a discussion board, the majority of students found the facility to be useful (Handley and Williams, 2011). To the disappointment of the researchers, though, students did not raise questions for discussion, which prevented much dialogue from emerging explicitly. In a discussion of what makes a good exemplar, Handley and Williams (2011) suggest that constructed and short exemplars designed to convey specific information about archetypal problems or good practices may be more useful than exemplars drawn from complete student work. Constructed examples may be more effective in making key qualities visible to students. This is worth considering, although I feel that using student samples is the most practical option in view of the workload implications of constructed exemplars.

Graham Hendry and colleagues at the University of Sydney have also carried out a series of valuable studies. Hendry, Armstrong and Bromberger (2012) explored the perceptions and performance of first-year Law students who analysed three exemplars (one distinction, one credit and one fail) on a different legal issue from the one for their assignment, then participated in marking and discussing exemplars in class. Exemplars are particularly helpful for first-year students who may be unfamiliar with some of the characteristics of university assignments as they help them to construct understandings of the structure of good-quality written work (Hendry et al., 2012). Data were collected from three teachers who used different implementation strategies. All three started with peer discussion of the exemplars, but the next stage varied: teacher A focused on a teacher-led discussion; teacher B placed emphasis on the weaknesses of the exemplars; and teacher C did not carry out any explanation or follow-up. The students in the class of teacher A, who received a balanced explanation from the teacher about why the exemplars were graded how they were, performed significantly better on their assignment than students in the classes of teachers B and C. Most of the students found it difficult to differentiate between poor or good assignments until they engaged in teacher-led discussion about the rationale for the grades awarded. When students understand why exemplars are graded as strong or weak the exemplars have the potential to provide them with a template to craft their own work on similar assignments (Hendry et al., 2012). The quality of the dialogue between teachers and students seems to be a key factor in mediating students' engagement, helping them to understand how judgements are made and developing ownership of usable insights from exemplars (Bloxham, 2013; Hendry, Bromberger and Armstrong, 2011).

Hendry and Anderson (2013) report the use of essay exemplars in Mathematics Teacher Education. Students found the exemplars useful in prompting reflection on the quality of their own work, and thinking about it in a more critical way or from a 'teacher's perspective'. As a result of engaging in marking and student- and teacher-led discussion of exemplars, students were generally more confident because expectations were clearer. Students also reported that the discussion stimulated engagement when it provided challenges to their ways of thinking about essays.

A study of a first-year Accounting course sought to gauge students' perceptions of the usefulness of supplementary resources comprising grade descriptors, marking criteria and annotated exemplars (Bell et al., 2013). Data came from 119 students, 45 per cent of the cohort. Students generally found the resources useful, particularly in terms of providing guidance on completing their assignment (a reflection task about ethical reasoning) and developing a notion of required standards. A small number of students perceived that exemplars may limit the scope of actual student responses if their assignment is shaped by their reading of the exemplars.

A study of senior students in an undergraduate course in Youth Justice (Wimshurst and Manning, 2013) involved six examples of different levels posted on the course website. These exemplars were case studies of how community agencies contributed to crime prevention, which informed the students' own case-study assignment. Students chose three of the exemplars, read, marked and wrote a commentary of 100–150 words, with 10 per cent of the course assessment weighting allocated to the exercise. A positive finding was that exemplars can offer a broader guide to improvement by providing a sense of the bigger picture of coherence and integration. Students generally made accurate judgements about quality in the exemplars and the seniority of the students was considered to be a facilitating factor in this outcome (Wimshurst and Manning, 2013). This was despite the fact that detailed criteria were not provided. Awarding part of the assessment grade for the analysis of exemplars represents a novel aspect compared with the studies reviewed above. The advantage is that the grade component encourages students to take the activity seriously. The disadvantages are that it is assessing the process of learning which is taking place for a small weighting, and that it might distract students from the main task of carrying out their own case studies.

Through the typing of handwritten examination scripts, Scoles, Huxham and McArthur (2013) enabled a large group of Life Sciences students to review exemplars of student exam performances. Students who accessed the exemplars performed better than those who did not, suggesting that exemplars impact on student academic achievement. The students also perceived these exemplars as a useful component in their repertoire of revision and exam preparation techniques.

A further important finding from research on exemplars is that clarifying the nature of quality work may support students in understanding teacher feedback (Handley and Williams, 2011; Orsmond et al., 2002) because they are developing enhanced understandings of criteria and their application. This is especially important given the relatively high levels of reported dissatisfaction with feedback (see Chapter 10). The relationship between dialogic use of exemplars and student understanding and uptake of feedback merits further exploration.

Implementation issues and challenges

A number of challenges arise in relation to the successful implementation of exemplar use. There is a lack of teacher understanding of the usefulness of exemplars and how they can support students in developing evaluative skills (Thomson, 2013). This may be one of the reasons why their use has not been more commonly reported. There are issues in relation to student permission to use their work as exemplars; a strategy to overcome this might involve some form of blanket institutional statement that student assignments may be reused anonymously for educational purposes. There are also tensions between classroom time devoted to content coverage as opposed to the discussion of exemplars. Teachers who prioritise delivering disciplinary content over facilitating student learning – and, according to Prosser et al. (2005), these are in the majority – are unlikely to assign a high priority to the discussion of exemplars. Proponents of exemplar-based teaching, staff developers and researchers could strive to communicate the case and present the research evidence in favour of exemplar use. The potential gains from exemplars are high, and the investments of time and resources are relatively modest.

A challenge impeding the use of exemplars is that teachers are sometimes reluctant to show examples of student work because students may infer that this represents a standard, model answer which might simply be imitated (Handley and Williams, 2011; Norton, 2004). A counter-argument is to discuss several examples so that students can notice that there are different ways in which work expresses quality (Sadler, 1987). The analysis of two high-quality exemplars which used radically different approaches (Wimshurst and Manning, 2013) illustrates Sadler's position that a given level of quality can be expressed in a number of different ways. The danger remains, however, that exemplars may impede student creativity or novel approaches to a task, and may reduce some of the richness and challenge of an assignment.

Generally, it seems sensible for the exemplar to be analogous, but not identical, to the one that students are attempting. In this way, students engage with criteria and quality, without being exposed to an assignment which could be copied or adapted as their own assessed task. This may not always be easy to arrange, especially if the same task is used repeatedly in a course.

A study in the discipline of Design Education focused on gauging whether exemplars might impede creativity (Hendry and Tomitsch, 2014). Four samples from the previous year were analysed (two high distinction; one credit; and one pass), with there being slight variation in the required task for the cohort studying these exemplars. Concerns about students producing formulaic or stereotypical work as a result of exemplar-based teaching seemed to be unfounded, and the processes actually increased student awareness of the need to produce original and creative designs. A conclusion was that the analysis of exemplars may be particularly well suited to Design Education, where goals and criteria are often hard to articulate.

Some students, particularly those in transitional stages, such as the first year of an undergraduate programme, often find it challenging to appreciate quality and may find it difficult to evaluate exemplars accurately (Hendry et al., 2012; Sambell et al., 2013). This may cause some anxiety or hesitancy amongst teachers and may even lead to doubts about the value of using exemplars. Such implementation challenges could also indicate that students need repeated involvement in analysis of the nature of quality as part of their adaptation to academic literacies. Students need scaffolding and support in evaluating exemplars; it is also important that they link their analysis to the specific grade descriptors (Bell et al., 2013).

For students to make the most of exemplars, teachers may need to develop enhanced skills in facilitating and leading student discussion around exemplars (Hendry et al., 2012). It is the engagement with exemplars, not their use per se, which is critical, and for that reason the quality of the dialogue around them is crucial. Good practice in dialogic use of exemplars might include some combination of the following: student generation, or analysis, of criteria; peer discussion of exemplars; teacher-led eliciting of student views with related commentary; discussion of how the exemplars could be improved; and students taking ownership of insights to use in relation to their own assessed work in progress.

Synthesis of exemplars research

To sum up, there have been a number of useful studies of exemplars from different disciplines and with a variety of modes of implementation. Most studies are small-scale and they are often carried out on a single module or with a single class. In fact, it is fair to say that there have been relatively few authoritative studies of exemplar use in higher education. Some interim conclusions have emerged, however. Exemplars analysed in association with assessment criteria are a potentially powerful means of supporting students to develop increased awareness of dimensions of quality work. There is plenty of evidence that students are positive about exposure to exemplars: they help them understand expectations and the nature of quality, and they allow them to see what good work looks like.

There is less of a consensus in relation to how exemplars are efficiently and effectively shared with students. Different modes of implementation discussed above include: additional optional workshops; part of regular class; and annotated online or offline resources. My position is that dialogic use of exemplars in which discussion of samples is embedded within regular classroom teaching is a sensible starting-point for student appreciation of quality.

The field of exemplars research seems to be gaining some impetus, and I anticipate its steady expansion in view of its importance to learning-oriented assessment. Remarkably little is known about teachers' orientations towards exemplars, and this could be a particular focus of future research. A useful starting-point might be the development of a questionnaire which identifies teachers' perceptions of exemplars and their rationale for using them or not.

Summary of chapter

This chapter has focused on the nature of teachers' judgements and how criteria are used to clarify the nature of quality in the discipline. Exposure to criteria has been shown to be insufficient to support students in developing firm understandings of what is required in assignments. A case has been made for dialogue around exemplars of student work to facilitate student understanding of the nature and characteristics of quality work.

Main implications for practice

- The complex nature of academic judgements needs to be acknowledged
- Complex judgements are best represented through holistic marking schemes.
- Effective moderation processes can be useful for teachers in rehearsing the nature of judgements.

- Criteria need to express specific levels of student achievement and avoid overuse of generic language.
- Criteria need to be accompanied by activities which enable students to discern quality in the discipline.
- A powerful means of developing student evaluative expertise is through dialogue around exemplars of student work.
- The key to productive use of exemplars is to engage students in forms of dialogue which help to induct them into academic discourses.
- Students can also be profitably involved in drafting criteria.
- Peer dialogues can help students to engage with quality.

Chapter 8

Engaging with criteria in History and Geology

Lists of criteria are all the same. It's all very vague.

(Penny, Geology student)

Scope of chapter

In this chapter, I discuss evidence from two cases which usefully cast light on how criteria are interpreted. From the History case, explored in Chapter 4, I discuss the criteria and students' perspectives on them. From the Geology case, described in Chapter 6, I discuss how teachers and students interpreted criteria in relation to the group project.

Criteria in the History case

As discussed in Chapter 4, there were three components of assessment in the History case: fieldwork report; participation; and individual project. Due to space constraints, it is not feasible to reproduce full lists of criteria for each task, so instead I present extracts of the stated criteria for each of the assessment components to provide an indication of how quality performance was intended to be judged. I then present student data which provides indications of how they interpreted or perceived criteria for the different tasks.

Project

The criteria for excellence (i.e. a grade A) in the project are presented in Box 8.1. By way of contrast, the criteria for a grade C (satisfactory) response are provided in Box 8.2.

I evaluate this to be a fairly well-balanced list of criteria which contains generic elements as well as specific points, such as the reference to the intended learning outcome of engaging with representations of the past.

In order to clarify the criteria for successful completion of the project, David Pomfret organised an optional supplementary workshop. About forty students attended the workshop, which aimed to elaborate further the processes and

---

Box 8.1 Criteria for excellent History project

This project shows clear evidence of independent thinking, a refined and critical approach to its sources, and wide reading in the relevant scholarly fields. It engages critically with representations of the past using a consistently high level of analysis, and may also show evidence of originality. It demonstrates accurate, judicious and convincing use of evidence to construct and back up its arguments. Its structure is clear and this helps to convey the argument in a balanced and effective way. Concise citations of source material support the project but do not dominate it. The project is attentive to other interpretations while questioning and challenging them.

Box 8.2 Criteria for satisfactory History project

The project is sound and competent, showing some knowledge of the literature from relevant fields. It is appropriately organised and presented. It attempts to answer the question, but tends towards a narrative, factual and descriptive approach to representations of the past and provides a general engagement with the issues raised, rather than a focused and analytical approach. The project lacks a certain focus in its discussion, and the argument is not always convincing. Some of the material selected as evidence is irrelevant or has been poorly used in support of the main arguments owing to inadequate understanding or interpretation. The presentation may lose some of its clarity in places owing to problems related to grammar, spelling and style, and problems with structure and presentation.

---

requirements for the project. David began the workshop by revisiting the assessment guidelines and lists of topics (see Box 4.4). He then elicited from the students some of the steps in developing their project: choosing a topic; searching for source materials and readings; organising ideas; developing an argument. He emphasised that he wanted to see evidence of student voice in the work, not just a summary of what other people think. These elements are either explicitly or implicitly covered in the stated criteria in Boxes 8.1 and 8.2.

He displayed on the screen an exemplar student assignment which had received a B grade. He told me that he preferred to use a good assignment rather than an excellent one as he believed this facilitated more critique. In the workshop, he explained some of his annotations on the script and described the strengths and weaknesses of the exemplar. He also made some comparisons between plagiarism and citations. On the screen, the words appeared quite small, and it seemed difficult for students to get a clear sense of the quality of the work.

Wang offered the following analysis in her field notes:

> Only one exemplar might not be enough to demonstrate the wide range of the characteristics and levels of essays. Especially for first-year students who have little knowledge and experience of academic essays, they might need more exemplars of various features to enrich and contextualise their understanding of the quality of essays. It might also be worth the time to have the students read and evaluate the exemplar before revealing the teacher's assessment of it.

I also asked David about the use of exemplars and he stated that they are useful because they help to make the qualities of assignments visible and comprehensible to students. He reported working with exemplars in different ways, such as arranging students in groups and then comparing grades. I asked him whether he was concerned that students might see an exemplar as a model answer. He acknowledged that this was a potential problem which he tackled through using examples drawn from questions which are no longer part of the current options. In this way, he can illustrate pertinent issues whilst minimising the prospects of direct plagiarism.

During the workshop, a student asked the teacher how they would be graded. The teacher showed the class the grade descriptors on the LMS and explained them sentence by sentence. Bonnie was one of the attendees at the workshop because she wanted to know how to do the project and obtain a high grade. She commented on assessment criteria for the project as follows:

> The prescriptions are a bit inert and just state the basic requirements which one must exceed if one wants to get a good result. I wanted to know the teacher's interpretation of these criteria and his personal preference, but the teacher basically just repeated the descriptions on the website. I had also expected to see more examples.

She referred to the 'personal preference' of the teacher as being a supplement to the criteria. She seems to have tuned it to the way teachers personalise criteria, as discussed in Chapter 7. We followed up by asking her what she meant by 'inert':

> The descriptions of assessment criteria and standards are almost the same for every subject. They have the same key words, like 'critical' and 'analytic'. The criteria are not that important on their own; it's how to apply them that is important.

Another student commented:

I have had a quick look at the requirements of the project assessment and have got a general idea about what the assessment criteria are but now I've almost forgotten them. The sentences are quite long and I find them difficult to understand as they are vague rather than concrete. I attended the workshop to see if the teacher would add any more points to them. Teachers also tend to have different preferences.

This student seemed to be looking for clues as to what David is looking for and also reiterated the point about personal preferences.

We also talked to other students, including several who did not attend the workshop. Juliet commented:

It's been quite a long time since I've read those criteria and I cannot keep track of them that clearly. I would say the criteria for the project tended to be brief and general ones. It's like you have read nothing after you've read it, so I expect more explanation for that.

I infer a number of points from this. First, it seems that Juliet reads the criteria at the outset but then does not refer to them again. She also seems to find them general and somewhat empty. I feel her description of them as 'brief' is inaccurate, however.

Similarly, Deirdre seemed rather dismissive of the criteria and grade descriptors, referring to them as 'that thing'. We interviewed her after she had received her grade and feedback, and she commented as follows:

It is an essay and its assessment has to depend on the professor's mood as well, doesn't it? He has so many requirements and these are *his* requirements, so he has the final say on whether I have met them. I think that I have done what he asked, but he doesn't think so.

From this comment, we inferred that she felt the assessment was based on some combination of personal elements, such as mood and teacher preference, as well as criteria. Another undercurrent is her sense that she merited a higher grade and/or was unclear about why she had been awarded the grade she did receive. An inference is that the criteria have not been particularly well communicated to the students. As I discussed in the previous chapter, sharing grade descriptors needs to be supported by some dialogue with students and activities which engage them with the nature of quality.

Liu talked about the notion of critical thinking or criticality which often recurs in some form in lists of criteria:

I didn't look carefully at the criteria, but if I take the example of 'critical thinking', I don't understand how to distinguish degrees of criticality. I feel that such descriptions are hard for me to understand. I don't know what he considers as critical thinking.

This resonates with the discussion in Chapter 3 of the work of Campbell et al. (1998) in terms of the difficulty students experience in coming to terms with the notion of criticality. When asked how she could be helped to develop this understanding, Liu referred to another course:

> In an earlier semester, a tutor gave us some previous students' projects for reference, so that we could look at what standard will get a grade A. I think this is better. He can let you look at some samples during the lecture. This can make it more concrete.

This provides some tentative support for the recommendations concerning the use of exemplars in Chapter 7. My related inference is that David felt that he had done what the student suggests during the optional workshop (which Liu was unable to attend).

Fieldwork report

For the fieldwork report, students had a choice between reporting on the museum trip or the scavenger hunt, as discussed in Chapter 4. Box 8.3 indicates how quality performance in this task is assessed by the tutor.

Box 8.3 Performance indicators for fieldwork assignment

To get a good grade, you need to use the work you have done in the field to provide *not just a descriptive account* of what happened, but you need to cover:

- the interconnections between past and present that you found evident in the context of the museum/scavenger hunt;
- a critical approach to the historical 'artefacts' examined;
- a critical engagement with how the past has been represented and an analysis of the value and uses of history today.

We asked a student if he understood the assessment criteria for the fieldwork report and he replied:

> Yes, I understood the criteria, but when I was doing the report I did not always check if I had achieved them. I just took notes from readings and organised them into the report, which I see as a real learning process. I think that if you see it as a mission to meet the criteria, it will limit your learning.

I found this last point quite striking, in that it seemed to resonate with the view of Torrance (2007) that learning should go beyond criteria compliance.

This student went on to state his expected grade and also compared History with other subjects:

> I think that my report will get a B minus, at best. Although I know the assessment criteria and I know what the teacher wants, I don't know how to achieve the standard of A. It's hard to get a very high grade for subjective subjects like History and Literature. For objective subjects, like Physics and Science, the criteria are clear and concrete and I know how to get full marks.

This comment speaks to issues of teaching, learning and assessment in different disciplines. The student seems to be saying that the hard disciplines have more concrete assessable knowledge, whereas the soft disciplines rely more on what he terms 'subjectivity' and others might call 'professional judgement'.

Geoff commented on the standards required for the course as follows:

> I think that one has to work very hard to achieve a high standard for this course. You have to make a lot of extra effort to improve your work from B to A. For me, the effort you have made is disproportionally higher than what you might gain, so I don't think it is necessary.

This is indicative of a low intensity of grade-related desire. Later, when he received the grade for his fieldwork report, Geoff expressed disappointment (he scored 60: a B minus or lower second-class honours). He told us he had not referred to the grade descriptors or criteria. When we asked him why not, he replied: 'It's difficult to say. I did it quite casually. I just write whatever I want.' My inference is that Geoff is a cue-deaf student. I discuss his related difficulty in interpreting feedback messages in Chapter 11.

Tutorial participation

How tutorial participation is graded is an important consideration, particularly in view of the challenges in assessing participation discussed in Chapter 3. Lengthy grade descriptors were posted on the LMS. I present the criteria for a B grade as an example in Box 8.4.

This is a comprehensive and detailed description of expected performance. It denotes qualitative indicators of the kind of performance which is desired: coherent, relevant, insightful, analytic, and so on. 'Makes an effort', in the final sentence, is not an obvious quality indicator, although obviously this is something teachers encourage in practice. Whilst the list of criteria is admirably comprehensive, it is quite a lengthy descriptor for a single grade. This might make it hard for students to discern the essence of such criteria, and could lead to them misinterpreting what is expected of them or failing to engage. Lengthy criteria may also serve to make judgements more difficult, rather than easier, which might become a problem if there are multiple tutors for a course.

Box 8.4 Criteria for grade B for tutorial participation

The student makes coherent and relevant contributions in debates, and offers insightful, well-supported interpretations to the group. Most points are clear, well explained and convincingly argued. Contributions provide evidence of reading in the relevant fields and independent thinking. The student displays good communication skills and delivers contributions in an interesting, coherent way. Contributions demonstrate sound understanding and comprehension of the issues discussed. The student provides generally convincing analysis of key issues, such as the interconnectedness of past and present, the value and uses of history and historical awareness today, the validity of representations of the past, and the use of evidence to construct historical accounts. The student makes an effort to convey ideas and interpretations in an interesting, dynamic presentation style.

Liu commented on this kind of grading scheme as follows:

> He provided grading criteria. They usually say that if you participate very actively or you express your opinions very accurately, you will be given a good grade. However, such criteria are rather vague to me, because I don't know how active can be considered as 'very active', or how accurate is 'quite accurate'.

Here, Liu is overgeneralising, because the terms 'active' and 'accurate' do not actually appear in this particular rubric. However, she perceived vagueness in criteria and the difficulty of making judgements from them. As our conversation unfolded, she also showed some awareness of the challenges in setting criteria:

> It is not easy to set the grading criteria for discussion because it cannot simply prescribe the times that you must talk. What he did was all right. If he said, 'I will give you an A if you talk five times,' that would be too mechanical. A tutorial would lose its value if the tutorial participation was assessed by the number of times you did something.

Clearly, Liu appreciates some of the challenges inherent in marking schemes and criteria. There is a danger that if criteria specify performance requirements too rigidly or numerically, then meeting them becomes rather mechanical.

We also asked Liu about fairness of grades and students' acceptance of them. She mentioned that students' perceptions of grades relates to how ambitious they are and their expectations for their grades, and this could impact on how they perceived a grade. She exemplified this perspective as follows: 'When you have higher expectations of yourself, you may feel the grade that the teacher gives is relatively low.'

Nicole was unaware that tutorial participation was assessed, suggesting that she was another cue-deaf student. She said: 'No one explained it to me, but I guess that if you are active and volunteer to speak, and you do the tasks seriously, you will get a good grade.' Some tensions arise. If teachers have provided detailed grade descriptors in the written documentation or LMS, is it desirable to devote classroom time to explaining them further or exemplifying them? My answer would definitely be 'yes', but I sense that in practice teachers often do not support students in unpacking the meaning of criteria. What is the student responsibility in engaging with criteria? Our data showed that students often misunderstood the assessment aspects of their courses, even when the relevant information had been made available to them. This could be a drawback for multiple assignments in a course in that it places additional strain on students to engage with multiple sets of criteria. Effective constructive alignment may help to overcome this challenge in that learning activities will indicate to students what is important and emphasised.

One-sentence response

The full criteria for OSR are presented in Box 8.5.

I feel this is a clear and comprehensive statement highlighting the need for students to take a position and justify it in relation to the issue posed. One might feel that the descriptor is quite lengthy in relation to the short task, but it does make the requirements clear to the students.

I asked a number of students if they knew what made a good OSR. Below are three of the responses:

> Yes, the teacher already explained it clearly at the beginning of the module. He said that we need to give a reason for our answer so as to explain why we think so. There is no right or wrong answer because we are encouraged to express our own ideas.
>
> It should have a structure like introduction, topic sentence and conclusion. There should be a beginning, middle and ending. And there needs to be an argument.
>
> A drawback is that we don't really know about the criteria and how the mark is given.

The first quotation seems to be along roughly similar lines to the teacher's conception of a good OSR; the second begins with elements which do not seem to relate to the teacher's criteria for a good OSR, although the final sentence about the importance of argument is relevant; and the third ignores the fact that grade descriptors for OSR are clearly displayed on the LMS. The novelty of OSR may be an additional barrier for student understanding of its requirements

---

Box 8.5 Grade descriptors for OSR

- A: The one-sentence response shows clear evidence of independent thinking, a critical approach to the question posed, and perceptive reflection upon the issues it raises. It leaves the reader in no doubt as to the position of the author and why she or he has adopted it. It presents a clear, well-developed and effective justification for the author's position.
- B: The one-sentence response is interesting and purposeful, providing a generally critical engagement with the question posed. It is possible to discern an argument. The one-sentence response is presented in a generally clear style.
- C: The one-sentence response is competent, showing some evidence of engagement with the question posed. It reveals something of the opinion of the author but tends toward a narrative, factual and descriptive approach, rather than an analytical approach. The one-sentence response lacks a certain focus, or is too short to make the argument altogether clear or convincing.
- D: The one-sentence response is limited in many respects. It includes irrelevant material, and adopts a descriptive approach, or is too short to communicate the view of the author effectively. There are problems of comprehending what has been written owing to problems with presentation (e.g. poor style, grammar).
- Fail: The one-sentence response is poorly written, inappropriate or inadequate, and shows very little evidence of reflection on the question posed, or fails to address this altogether. The one-sentence response lacks a clear or coherent argument or pertinent reflections. The response may suffer from a serious lack of clarity owing to flaws of presentation, such as grammar, spelling and style.

(see Gibbs and Dunbar-Goddet, 2009). David stated that one of the reasons why he showed OSR samples in class was to give the students opportunities to see the qualitative variation in different responses and help them to appreciate why different grades are awarded.

I now present some evidence from the Geology case before highlighting the implications of both cases at the end of the chapter.

Criteria in the Geology case

In Chapter 6, I discussed a group work assignment in the Geology class. Now I analyse this further in relation to the assessment criteria in use and how they were interpreted by students and staff.

Teacher's introduction

In the first introductory lecture to the course, Lung-Sang Chan gave an introduction to the group project. The following represent the main points he made:

- Students should form groups of three or four and try not to work with friends, because diversity of views is an advantage.
- Each group should formulate a topic, something focused and novel – preferably something that the professors have not already considered.
- Groups should provide a short outline for teacher feedback, stating the project topic and why it is significant.
- The project will mainly be marked on its level of insight, the novel ideas that are proposed: 'I want to learn something new and I am interested in what you think and how you integrate knowledge.'

Finally, Chan clarified the timelines and issued warnings about plagiarism.

Two of the elements covered in this introduction appeared challenging for students: a topic which the teachers have not already considered or thought about; and, related to this, the notion that the students should integrate knowledge to provide new insights. I shall return to these issues later in the discussion.

The class was quite large and some students had to stand to hear this introduction, which lasted about ten minutes. Some whispered or gestured to their classmates, from which I inferred that they were making suggestions about forming teams. Many of the students did not seem particularly attentive, even though the introduction related to their assessment, which is usually thought to be a major priority for students. Overall, on the basis of the student reaction to this short introductory lecture, I judged the cue-seeking/cue-consciousness of the group to be quite low, although it may have been that the students had strategically realised that the composition of their group would be a significant factor in achieving a high mark on the group assessment.

Marking criteria

Chan's position on assessment criteria was: 'I like to keep the descriptors short and simple. Grading is a holistic judgement and it involves subjectivity and experience. It cannot be broken down into detailed descriptors. Descriptors can't convey our experience as teachers.' This comment seems roughly congruent with the position of Sadler (2009b): there is a tacit dimension which is difficult to express, and when teachers assess they are using their accumulated experiences to make a reasoned judgement of the holistic quality of a piece of work.

The main general quality indicators were 'contents' and 'quality of presentation'. These were defined as follows:

- *Contents* are based on informativeness of presentation, accuracy of information, whether information is interesting, insightfulness.
- *Quality of presentation* includes style of presentation, organisation, coordination of speakers, quality of graphics, ability to stimulate questions and interest.

Boxes 8.6 and 8.7 illustrate how these general statements were broken down into slightly more detailed descriptors which were suggestive of how numerical marks were awarded.

Box 8.6 Examples of grade descriptors for content of oral presentation

- 9–10: Rich contents. Thorough discussion. Insightful and interesting. Much individual ideas and clear evidence of critical thinking.
- 7–8: Useful contents and informative. Limited insights. Some evidence of careful but not critical analysis.

Box 8.7 Examples of grade descriptors for quality of oral presentation

- 7–8: A generally clear presentation with legible graphics. Coordination and teamwork are evident but not particularly smooth. Presentation is dominated by one or two individuals.
- 5–6: Presentation is a bit boring or has too many focuses. Main points not clearly articulated. Poor timing.

This is an analytic marking scheme in that separate scores are awarded for different elements. I note the use of numerical indicators and relative brevity of the descriptors in comparison with the rather more extended qualitative approach adopted in the History case. The hard disciplines tend to adopt a mainly quantitative orientation, as noted in Chapter 1. A further noticeable feature of these criteria is that students do not seem to be required to produce a particularly high level of performance to obtain a mark of 6 or even 7 out of 10. For instance, the criteria presented in Box 8.6 suggest that students are able to obtain 70–80 per cent for a presentation with 'useful contents and limited insight'. This may reflect that the group project task is quite challenging, especially for a cohort mainly comprising students in their first semester of tertiary study. There also seems to be quite a large gap between the requirements for marks of 9–10 and 7–8.

Student perceptions of criteria

We asked the six student informants whose views were reported in Chapter 6 about the criteria and their engagement with them. Penny commented:

> Lists of criteria are all the same. It's all very vague. For an A, it is excellent mastery and correct application, and then B plus would be above average mastery and good application. You don't know what it means, so you just do what you can. Once you know how to get good academic results, you don't need to rely on criteria any more because the criteria are always the same!

By 'the same' I infer that she means that they all look similar and carry similar gradations of meaning in relation to qualities of performance. The academic discourse may make it appear the same to students, even though, from a tutor perspective, there are nuances of meaning. These nuances do not seem to be readily apparent to students, even a motivated high achiever like Penny. Her final sentence seems to be quite an astute comment that obtaining a feel for quality and the application of criteria may outweigh the value of a specific rubric. What constitutes quality work is more important than understanding and interpreting criteria. When asked if she would request more elaboration from teachers to increase her understanding of the meaning of criteria, she indicated she would not, for the following reason: 'I don't think that they can explain what the criteria really mean unless they tell you exactly what to write; because it's not only about the content, it's also about the style of presentation.' This comment reinforces the opaqueness of criteria and the difficulty of explaining or demonstrating what they mean.

Penny and Wan both commented on the criteria in relation to their report:

> At the current stage, our writing is just description of the facts. But to get a good grade, we have to go beyond description. Because the professor said clearly that we should not only describe the information, but also need to be critical and analytic.
>
> (Penny)

> The professor said that the project should contain our own work. We cannot simply search for a variety of reports and then select some useful bits from them. Instead, we need insights and personal effort.
>
> (Wan)

Penny used the terms 'critical' and 'analytic', which I see as similar to the notion of insight mentioned in Chan's descriptors. Wan also referred to the importance of producing some kind of insight, and described some effort she had invested to meet this criterion. In a journal article she found a formula to calculate the rate of mass extinction and tried to apply it to calculate the mass extinction for the year 2012, but found that she was unable to do so. In the end, she just summarised the researchers' report. She expressed her disappointment that she 'did not add anything new but just copied others' work'. I infer that she was able to understand the teacher's expectations and made efforts to meet them, but eventually came up short. It is unlikely that this process was reflected in her grade, as grades tend to focus on final product.

It should also be noted that Wan referred to personal effort as a criterion, and that Chan highlighted effort in his overall evaluation of student performance. In principle, effort should not be a criterion in an outcomes-based context, but in practice teachers are likely to be influenced by the amount of student effort invested. This represents a further example of criteria not representing all the dimensions which teachers might reward. I return to this issue of hidden criteria in the 'Implications' section, below.

When asked about the extent to which she understood and used the criteria, Ming commented:

> The teacher explained it clearly and gave us a handout which provides detailed explanations about the assessment criteria. The writing for the project should be original, insightful and critical. They were similar to previous criteria descriptions, so I didn't study them carefully or consult them when preparing the assignment. I think that our content is quite original but the organisation may be problematic.

Ming was quite clear about the required qualities for the project. She reinforced Penny's comments in relation to the 'similar' nature of lists of criteria. Although she stated that had not studied them carefully, she seemed to have quite a good grasp of their main points, and in her final sentence she showed some application of them to the work of her group.

Tsang saw the essence of the criteria for the group project as follows: 'The information or content is not that important for the report; instead, it is our own opinions and thinking that matter.' Here Tsang seems to reinforce the issue of content versus insight, with the emphasis on insight being most central to the project. In a later interview, conducted after the presentation, Tsang elaborated his understanding of the criteria: 'To get a high grade for the presentation assessment, I think that the topic should be novel and original, the slides should be smoothly connected, clear in logic, and attractive.' Here, he re-emphasises the notion of originality, which the teachers had mentioned at the outset, and adds some comments in relation to presentation skills: for example, the adjective 'smooth' is also used by the teaching team (Box 8.7).

Fung understood the criteria as follows:

> I read the criteria descriptions some time ago and I've already forgotten them. I am not clear about the criteria but I think that being relevant to the topic is most important. I will try to produce rich content, coherent writing

and some practical significance. In reality, the criteria are not that important; a student has to be clear whether he or she has learnt something or not.

Fung mainly seems to have derived an interpretation of the criteria from his own general views of what he thinks a good project should contain. I found his final sentence particularly interesting because it downplays the importance of criteria whilst seeming to prioritise student self-evaluation of their learning. Fung seems to be implying that what is written down as the documented criteria is much less important than the extent to which students understand what they have learnt. The criteria may represent the teacher's general expectations for the students, but Fung seems to attach more importance to his own progress. This resonates with the notion of ipsative assessment, which focuses on comparing current performance with previous performance.

In her interview, Jackie commented on the teachers' application of the criteria:

> It seems that most of the groups cannot meet the criteria. Most of the things they present are quite factual; there are not enough insights. The professors seem to be looking for different things: some are looking for some new ideas or new knowledge, whilst others seem less critical of the content of the presentation and more concerned with fluency and communication skills.

I found these comments quite insightful. Jackie has recalled one of the key issues which Chan stated at the outset: tutors wish to learn new knowledge from the students' projects. Her interpretation seems to have some consistency with the teacher-identified aims of the project as exemplifying qualities, such as insight and originality.

Application of the criteria

We attended the student oral presentations for the project in order to try to understand the products of the group assessment, and to observe how assessment criteria were applied. Due to the large number of students, the assessment of oral presentations was conducted on two separate days in three parallel sessions (i.e. six groups with between twenty and twenty-five students in each group). I attended one session and Wang attended two, each of which lasted for two hours. Before the oral presentations start, one of the teaching team issues a reminder that each group must complete their presentation within twelve to thirteen minutes and that this will be followed by a short question and answer session. To encourage student participation, they are told that extra marks may be awarded if students ask insightful questions. One of the teaching assistants explained that the teaching team thought it was beneficial to motivate the students to ask questions, rather than just listen passively to the presentations. This seemed like a good idea, but in practice it would represent considerably less than 1 per cent of any student's overall mark. In addition, due to lack of time, the question and answer session was sometimes abbreviated.

A teaching assistant notified every group when they had two minutes left, but a number of groups still had to be stopped before they could finish their presentations. Marks for the oral presentations mainly ranged from 6 to 9. For the whole project, marks ranged from 19 to 27 (out of 30). In other words, all of the students scored relatively highly. Chan commented:

> I was satisfied with what they did. Some of them showed some originality. For example, a group went into the field and did some field measurement, which was good. The groups made an effort. The performance was generally quite good.

Here, Chan first focuses on the notion of originality, which he had stated as a requirement at the outset, and provides an example of something original and evidence-based ('a group went into the field'). He also introduces a further criterion of 'effort'. Although effort is rarely part of formal grade descriptors, it seems likely that it is very much in the minds of both teachers and students. If students feel that they have invested considerable time and effort, they probably expect to receive satisfactory – or better – grades.

With respect to student performance in relation to the criteria, one of the teaching assistants commented:

> I think the students understand the criteria but they lack the confidence to carry out all the requirements. They understand that they need to present their own insights, but they dare not. When they read different opinions about a topic, they lack the confidence to judge which point of view is most reasonable. They want to find a model answer, but, of course, there is no model answer.

Here, the teaching assistant emphasises student confidence to develop insight. To my mind, other factors include experience and ability in synthesising critically, especially if the student's experience of secondary school has not developed such dispositions.

Chan expressed a similar perspective to that of the teaching assistant in relation to student understanding of what the teaching team expected:

> I think students mainly grasped the idea that we are looking for insight, but they are not always confident or comfortable in expressing their insights and supporting them with evidence. Sometimes they stop at offering an opinion without showing evidence to support their argument.

I infer two main issues from these two comments from the teaching team. The main issue they raise relates to insight. This is consistently identified as a key element in the project. The teaching assistant highlights students' lack of confidence in presenting their own insights. Chan concurs and adds that students need to develop the skill of showing evidence to support their insights or opinions. These are both quite challenging for first-year students, which perhaps explains why grades were relatively high even though there were considerable limitations in the extent to which students met the key criterion of 'insight'.

My perspective is that the teachers set appropriately rich and challenging objectives for the group project, especially by emphasising 'insight'. These provided a sense of high expectations and challenged the students to produce high standards. However, there seemed a slight mismatch between the verbal encouragement for 'insight' and 'novelty' and the written descriptors, which were pitched at a lower level. In other words, there was some variation between what the teachers said they wanted to see and what the criteria demanded. This may have been a realistic compromise, as novelty and insight are sure to be challenging for first-year students to achieve. Jackie's comments above resonate with the reflections of Wang and myself that the presentations did not seem to exhibit the insight and novelty which were stated as primary targets at the outset. The teaching team was aware (and understanding) of student difficulties in meeting this challenge.

I felt the marks were relatively high, although they were roughly in accordance with the criteria presented in Boxes 8.6 and 8.7. When I asked Chan about overall student performance for the whole module, he stated that 20 per cent received an A, just over 40 per cent received a B, and the majority of the remainder achieved a C. He seems to have adopted some form of compromise between criterion-referenced and norm-referenced assessment, as noted in Chapter 6.

Implications

The evidence from these two cases illustrates that grade descriptors are limited in conveying the concept of quality. Students studying both History and Geology generally felt that criteria were vague and unclear; and that different sets of grade descriptors had similarities which reduced their meaningfulness. From the student perspective, we infer that few students studied the criteria in great detail because they always appear similar as they are generally set out in a standard style and use similar terminology (critical, insightful, coherent, etc.). For example, some of the History students made inaccurate comments about the criteria for their assessment based on generalisations about what criteria *usually* entail. It is also possible that the presentation of criteria in blocks of relatively dense text is unattractive to students, which may be a further barrier to their engagement. The evidence seems to indicate that students often do not engage seriously with criteria. This reinforces the arguments in the previous chapter that exposure to grade descriptors in itself is relatively limited in providing students with a sense of what quality entails; and that the development of evaluative expertise is more important than interpreting criteria.

The evidence also seems to indicate that students missed many cues and hints about criteria and required performance. The students sometimes seemed to have no more than a moderate understanding of assessment requirements, even when these had been explicitly explained to them by the teacher and the relevant information was available on the course LMS. It should be remembered that these were first-year students, so their cue-consciousness was probably not highly developed. For students who are less cue-conscious or cue-deaf – especially those who also have a modest intensity of grade-related desire – what a teacher is looking for can remain something of a mystery. If descriptors are to communicate well with students, strategies must be developed to engage with the nature of quality work which is embodied in the assessment criteria.

Analogous to the notion of the hidden curriculum, my interpretation of the data in the Geology case suggests the presence of 'hidden' criteria. These are those aspects which are not part of the official assessment apparatus and may not appear in the assessment criteria, but may be taken into account when awarding a grade. Effort was one of these (see Sadler, 2010b). There were also complexities in relation to requirements for novelty and insight in Geology. These were encouraged verbally, and were partially present in the criteria, which showed admirable ambition on the part of the teaching staff. However, even though the students were rarely able to achieve either, they still obtained relatively high marks. The hidden criteria seemed to be that the official requirements were a tall order, and if they were rigidly enforced they could disrupt harmonious social relationships between staff and students. This resonates with Shay's work on reinforcing the socially situated nature of academic judgements.

Hidden criteria might operate in different ways under different circumstances. A negative aspect of them would be if a teacher used them to downgrade a student they disliked or upgrade one they found attractive. Alternatively, hidden criteria may bring some flexibility to what would otherwise be a rigid process: for example, understanding a particular student's personal circumstances may be used to compensate for their underperformance in a formal assessment. Some may view this as undermining standards, whereas others may perceive it as a flexible, pragmatic acknowledgement of real-life issues in education.

Another aspect is variation in teacher application of criteria. Teachers have a feel for quality which can be demonstrated in a variety of ways, so they are likely to interpret criteria in different ways, too. In the same way as teachers practise academic freedom of expression, they have freedom to interpret criteria according to their own values and emphases. The criteria represent a basis for evaluation, but teachers are mainly making grading decisions based on their experience and professional judgement (see Bloxham et al., 2011).

To sum up, the discussion has reinforced some of the complexities of academic judgements. Criteria are not merely technical artefacts; they are socially constructed guidelines which are implemented in different ways according to teachers' values, prior experiences and subjectively informed professional judgements.

Summary of chapter

This chapter has provided examples of criteria and their use in the History and Geology cases. It has highlighted some of the difficulties students experience in engaging with criteria and has discussed hidden criteria which occur when there are mismatches between stated criteria and how these are applied in practice.

Main implications for practice

- Criteria should be task specific rather than overly generic.
- Classroom activities could be designed to counter student perceptions of similarity in criteria.
- Students need to be involved in activities which encourage them to engage with criteria and the nature of quality work.
- Teachers should try to minimise the impact on grades of hidden criteria and reduce the impact of covert norm-referencing.

Chapter 9

Critical reviews in Architecture

All teaching is based on some kind of dialogue.
(John Lin, award-winning Architecture teacher)

Scope of chapter

From the Architecture case, I analyse critical reviews, commonly referred to as 'crits', which are a major means of prompting Architecture students to engage with the nature of quality in their discipline. The chapter fits into the overall structure of the book by illustrating the interplay between learning-oriented assessment tasks, the development of evaluative expertise, and student engagement with feedback.

The crit in design-based subjects

The Architecture case represented a rather different (studio-based) system to those of the other cases, and I first discuss selected relevant issues in relation to teaching, learning and assessment in design-based subjects. A major feature is the crit – or critical review – during which, in front of their peers, students present a design project to a jury of teachers, respond to questions and receive commentary on their work. The crit is part of the signature pedagogy of design-based subjects (Schrand and Eliason, 2012) and relates to the notions of WTP and authenticity in that pitching designs is a core task in the profession. In the crit, students explain their work to the teachers, in contrast to a more conventional classroom setting, where the discourse tends to be the other way round (Orr, Yorke and Blair, 2014).

Carrying implications for how students approach their studies, discussed in Chapter 2, the public nature of signature pedagogies in design generally prompts high levels of student engagement (Shulman, 2005). The creative freedom afforded by design projects can be a source of powerful intrinsic motivation and emotional investment in the work (Schrand and Eliason, 2012). However, open-ended creative pedagogy may also result in a certain amount of puzzlement, which seems to affect each generation of students entering the studio (Akalin and Sezal, 2009).

The studio crit is a major formal opportunity for feedback, with teachers, and sometimes students, providing individual comments in a group environment about the strengths, weaknesses or areas of concern during the development of a studio project (Blair, 2006). The feedback is often focused not just on how the work might be improved but on extending its potential (Orr et al., 2014). The public crit as a site for feedback is also complemented by preliminary critiques, often called desk critiques, where the teacher visits students at their desks during studio sessions for informal discussions about work and progress (Schrand and Eliason, 2012). Therefore, desk crits entail private feedback as opposed to the public nature of the formal crit.

The crit also represents a ritual or rite of passage in the study of Architecture that socialises students into a culture of long hours and vocational commitment via its intensive preparation (Webster, 2006). In the social environment of the design studio, while experiencing design as a process of creativity within a contextual framework, students learn to communicate, critique, respond to criticism and collaborate (Akalin and Sezal, 2009). Learning in Architecture has particularly visual and social dimensions (Shreeve, Sims and Trowler, 2010). Processes of socialisation can play a role in developing close relationships between participants which may carry positive implications for formal or informal peer-feedback elements. For example, peer feedback was evaluated more positively in design subjects than academic writing classes due to higher levels of student engagement in peer reviews, perceptions of greater student expertise, and more trust amongst students (Schrand and Eliason, 2012).

The socialisation processes also represent a form of hidden curriculum which may involve the teacher modelling various habits or behaviours related to the study of Architecture. The teacher exhibits much of the expertise that students are trying to develop, so often becomes a role model. Negative aspects of a hidden curriculum might arise if anxiety and emotional responses before and during the crit inhibit student learning (Blair, 2006). In design education, the capacity to overcome the emotional stress of being critiqued is an important aspect of the learning experience: without a certain amount of anxiety and risk, there are often limits to how much learning occurs (Shulman, 2005).

Elements of power and authority which reside in teachers sometimes carry a repercussion that the critique operates in a largely hierarchical manner and that a resulting function of it can be for students to witness a virtuoso performance by their tutor (Percy, 2004). Based on ethnographic data, Webster (2006) found that students sometimes agreed with critics, yet later admitted that they did not understand the comments because of the complexity of the critics' discourse. This was particularly prevalent amongst the less confident and less competent students, whereas high-level learners were more likely to view the crit as a constructive and dialogic experience in which they could engage with the ideas of the jury (Webster, 2006). When the pedagogy of the crit involves co-production and co-construction, the student understanding of their own design can overturn traditional power relations by highlighting the role of student agency in relation to their work (Orr et al., 2014). A related development lies in alternative formats for crits, such as student-led crits, where students rather than tutors take responsibility for commenting on their peers' work (Parnell and Sara, 2007). This has the potential to enhance student participation, encourage constructive criticism, decrease defensiveness, and develop an appreciation of what it is like to be in the teacher's shoes (White, 2000).

A number of useful additional potentials and challenges for the conduct of a crit are summarised by Orr, Blythman and Blair (2007) in their staff guide for the Higher Education Academy entitled 'Critiquing the crit'. Positive elements of a crit include: opportunities for students to see each other's work; students can identify that staff have a variety of perspectives; crits teach students to prepare for talking about their work and responding to others; and the process acculturates students to receiving critical judgements about their work. Challenges include: the term 'crit' can be interpreted negatively (as criticism); introverted students may find it difficult to benefit; crits are mainly focused on one student at a time, so even if the intention is to highlight overarching issues, it can become like a public mini-tutorial; related to this, it can be difficult to maintain student interest in the crit over a period of time; and crits take up a lot of staff time and are often teacher-dominated, which accentuates the problem of limited student participation.

The crit also brings to the fore differentiation between public and private modes of assessment. Public modes of assessment recall Hounsell's notion of 'on-display assignments', discussed in Chapter 3. The public nature of an assessment event, such as a crit, can bring transparency to assessment by exemplifying the kind of criteria and standards which are being applied, and provide potential for students to learn from peers' presentation of their work.

Crit processes also bring to mind the notion of educational connoisseurship which I introduced in Chapter 7. Eisner (1985, p. 93) sees educational criticism as representing the art of disclosure and talks about the role of the critic as follows: 'The task of the critic is to adumbrate, suggest, imply, connote, render . . . [T]he language of criticism is measured by the brightness of its illumination. The task of the critic is to help us to see.' So critique, as embodied in an architectural crit, is a means by which the connoisseur makes public their perceptions so that others can appreciate their work and its qualities or deficiencies. This often involves some combination of intuitiveness and more technical know-how.

To conclude this section and as an introduction to what follows, I raise a key issue of particular relevance to learning-oriented assessment: how can crit processes facilitate the development of student evaluative expertise in Architecture?

Setting the scene

John Lin is both a practising architect and a teacher of Architectural Design. He was a recipient of a University Outstanding Teaching Award in 2010, and four years later won a prestigious teaching award which spans all the universities in

Hong Kong. John's high reputation as a teacher is based partly on his emphasis on experiential learning: he involves students in real-life experiences of architectural planning and design. For instance, he won a major international award for a prototype of a self-sufficient home in China which he developed with his students.

The Architecture course and its portfolio assessment

John teaches a first-year Introduction to Architectural Design course. Timetabling is flexible and open, with students seeming to work with diligence and intrinsic motivation in a spacious design studio. One of the students told us, with some pride, that the lights and air-conditioning of the design studio are never switched off because students work around the clock. This probably contrasts with other international contexts, where students are more likely to work at home or outside the studio. Sixty-five students took the course and they were divided into six tutor groups of eleven or ten students per group. The course was organised around architectural planning for a Chinese village within a few hours' travelling distance from HKU. The project had a number of interrelated stages: a design for the village as an overall structure; the design of a house as a contemporary alternative to generic house types; and a one-week project workshop, which involved discussions about the consequences of the students' interventions into the village and the house designs. Site visits were also carried out to the actual village. The course was assessed by portfolio assessment, as set out in Box 9.1. Crits were stepping-stones in the public development of the portfolios.

Box 9.1 Assessment design in the Architecture case

Assessment is by continuous coursework assessment of drawings, diagrams, photos, renderings, animations, physical models, prototypes and project presentation. The work is presented in a portfolio, including series of designs: a design for the village as an overall structure; and the design of a house as a contemporary alternative to generic house types (100 per cent).

John explained:

> The portfolio provides students with a final opportunity to present their work. It can only help them. However, the final crit and the other presentations are also considered. The portfolio is the chance to visually integrate all the work together in a final output.

My overall judgement was that the assessment for the course involves not just the portfolio but the students' overall performance over the semester. I infer that John's comment 'It can only help them' refers to the grading: in other words, the portfolio provides an opportunity to present a stronger case for a high mark than has been evidenced by the teacher's continuous observation during the semester.

John explained the grading of portfolios as follows:

> The portfolio is useful for standardising the grades across six groups. We discuss with colleagues in the teaching team because the grading is done collectively. Students are evaluated against the whole class. We take all sixty-five portfolios and we first rank them ourselves and then we benchmark the grades; it's a long process.

I inferred from our wider discussions that there was interplay between criterion-referenced and norm-referenced approaches. I asked John about the anticipated spread of grades and he expected two or three A grades, approximately six B grades, and two or three C grades for his tutor group of eleven.

Assessment by portfolio was seen as a default means of assessment in Architecture so was accepted readily by students as they perceived it as an effective way to collate their work and demonstrate improvement in their designs over time. It is also how they are judged in the workplace or when looking for a job. One of the students, Laurence, spoke about portfolio assessment in Architecture as follows:

> It is the best way they have to understand you and your ideas. There are infinite possibilities and your own process is the only thing that shows how you tackle the task. Everyone's path is different; that's what makes a designer unique and interesting. So the portfolio is an argument for you as a designer to show that you are developing your process, you can understand problems and tackle them in a meaningful way.

In the first sentence of this comment, Laurence is suggesting that both the individual and their work are being considered and evaluated. This perception is reiterated by Orr and Bloxham (2012), who suggest that assessment of a design portfolio involves assessing both the portfolio itself and the person who compiled it. This is different to trends in most other disciplines, where, in theory, only the work is assessed.

The students generally felt that assessment considered both the final portfolio and their performance during the semester. For instance, Ying commented:

> I don't think the portfolio really had 100 per cent weighting. Every desk critique with the tutor is important as they represent the process of evolution of our thinking, which is important for Architecture students. The final

review is also very important as it displays your product for other people to comment on.

She also elaborated on what she thought the grading comprised:

> Our grades do not depend solely on how good the project is, but also on how diligent we are, what alternative designs we have attempted, procedures as well as product, how well we expressed our ideas, and what progress we have made. It is quite comprehensive.

Derek commented on how students' performance is evaluated:

> I do not think that the assessment for this course is decided by the portfolio that we submit at the end of the semester. Instead, I think that our tutors have already formed their opinions and judgement about the quality of our design through all the reviews they have done with us throughout the semester.

Derek perceives that teachers have formed an impression of the quality of student work *before* the submission of the formal portfolio, because they have seen it throughout its development.

Gloria did not share this perception, and felt that she would be assessed on her portfolio, rather than any other factors. She expressed the view that packaging a portfolio was a skill in itself and expressed her intention to highlight the design aspects in which she was strong and try to camouflage those in which she was less adept. She was confident that her tutor would not see through this strategy, as they would not understand every detail of her work or her thinking processes.

John's view was congruent with that expressed by Derek and Ying: students were assessed on the overall process, including their presentations and iterations of designs. He saw the role of the portfolio as clarifying and providing substantiating evidence.

Some issues arise here. Should there be greater explicitness as to the balance between the assessment of the portfolio and continual assessment during the semester? Is it fairer and more valid for assessment to arise from an extended period of relatively informal evaluation rather than a single portfolio? What is the relationship between architectural skill and adroitness at presenting a portfolio? Are some students better at making a case in a portfolio than they are at design and vice versa? In passing, I also wonder whether award-winning teachers are unusually skilful at presenting a persuasive teaching portfolio.

Quality in architecture

John highlighted three aspects of quality in architectural design: craft – the quality of the craftsmanship in the designs; contribution, including originality and creativity; and concept, as embodied in the overall design process. From the Architectural Design Curriculum Guide he shared with us, the most relevant set of related descriptors was a marking rubric for design reviews which listed five overarching elements: quality of analysis; quality of design; comprehensiveness of design process; clarity of ideas; and effectiveness of communication. The specific criteria for grade A (excellence) in the course we observed sometimes overlapped with and sometimes slightly differed from these criteria. For illustrative purposes, these are set out in Box 9.2.

Box 9.2 Criteria for grade A in Architecture

The student demonstrates excellence in research, analysis and design. The drawings, models and other visual material must be completed to the highest level of craft. The work must demonstrate originality, creativity and critical thinking. The student must show evidence of a design process that clearly influences the final design.

These are abstract general statements of excellence in architectural design. Following from the discussion in the previous two chapters, they are unlikely to be sufficiently specific in themselves to act as a guide for student work.

I asked John how students come to develop a sense of quality in architecture in the context of crits:

> I think it's a balance between rationale and intuition. In some sense it has to be rule-driven but then you also have to know the limit of those rules [Carless, 2014, p. 9]. For a creative phenomenon, it can still be structured and there is technique. And there is also craft and creative expression.

I infer from this that architecture involves a balance between more technical rule-governed aspects and more creative intuitive elements. The latter might be rather subjective, so I raised this issue with John:

> I think the idea is to work against subjectivity through personal rationale. That's the difference between a good critic and a weak critic. If a critic says, 'You should do this' or 'This is better than that', then this is weak because you are only learning their personal, subjective views. The good critique is really about explaining the why.

This resonates with the discussion of subjectivity in Chapter 7 in that professional judgement inevitably involves some embodiment of the assessor but its potential drawbacks are minimised when reasons, criteria and evidence are brought to bear.

John also talked of the interplay between argument and evidence:

> In the reviews, we are using the evidence displayed on the wall. It's like being a detective: you are arguing the case. It is subjective in that you don't know the right answer, but it isn't totally subjective because you have evidence. So what you try to do is to argue using the evidence, present it and piece together that evidence. There are degrees of interpretation, but that's different from being subjective.

I infer that, for John, subjectivity is a personal view; but the subjectivity is reduced when that view is supported by argument and evidence.

We also asked students about related issues. When I asked Laurence what he thought the tutors wanted to see in terms of quality work, he replied:

> I think they are looking for consistency throughout the body of work, not just one good design; depth of thought; and craftsmanship, the quality of the drawings. It's also about communication: how good your drawings are and the clarity of the intentions.
>
> (Carless, 2014, p. 9)

Here, Laurence echoes some of the qualities mentioned by John and found in the documentation: craftsmanship, effective communication and clarity. He also acknowledged difficulties: 'What the tutors are looking for is somewhat unclear to me and sometimes I get frustrated . . . [T]here are an infinite number of permutations.' Other students expressed similar doubts or insecurities: 'I am really not sure what I have learnt about architecture' (Yeung); 'I am puzzling over what I am doing' (Ying). This could mean that goals are sometimes unclear to students, or that in a creative discipline like Architecture it is difficult to feel secure. These comments resonate with the views of Akalin and Sezal (2009) about the puzzlement commonly experienced by design students. In addition, a certain amount of insecurity and challenge can be a stimulus to engagement, analogous to Shulman's (2005) perspectives in relation to anxiety and risk alluded to earlier.

In subsequent sessions, we elicited conceptions of quality in architecture from other students. For instance, Yeung argued:

> Architecture does not have a concrete answer. Even the judgement of whether it is good or bad varies with people, and there is no such thing as universal criteria for good architecture design because everyone has philosophies of their own.

It is probably fair to say that there are some design issues on which architects can reach agreement, but to some extent Yeung's point echoes the infinite permutations mentioned by Laurence. After further discussion, Yeung outlined what he saw as quality criteria:

It is important to present the design clearly and persuasively, and whether one can create 'architectural possibility'. This is a term the tutors use a lot and I think it relates to the creativity of one's design. A design which just repeats some commonplace things and has nothing new is obviously limited. Overall, I think an architect can be judged by the proficiency of techniques, the depth of thought and the degree of creativity.

Here, Yeung notes some of the criteria in the rubrics for the Faculty of Architecture: for example, creativity and clarity. He uses analogous terminology, so 'persuasively' may relate to the communication aspect; 'proficiency of techniques' probably relates to 'craftsmanship'; and 'depth of thought' could be linked with 'quality of analysis' and 'critical thinking'.

Another student, Serena, felt there were no standard rules for a good design because 'everyone's design is different . . . [T]he subjective nature of design makes it difficult to understand what is quality . . . [T]he tutors have different opinions and I can't see a consistent pattern in what they are looking for.' She noted that one of the reasons why a jury has more than one member is because of the inherent subjectivity of the judgements.

An inference I drew from these discussions with students was that those who were most adept at defining and understanding quality in architecture seemed to be the most capable members of the cohort.

Critical reviews

Now I focus on the processes of the crits and related teacher and student perceptions.

John's views of crits

I asked John about some of the main features of crits. He explained that design is an individual process, so it is important to treat students as individuals. He also emphasised the dialogic nature of the crit and how it enables this dialogue to be a personal one that reflects the students' intentions and is responsive to the problems generated by their work. The overall goal was for students to learn how to structure a design process.

I asked John what the student audience might gain from observing a crit session:

> We are trying to teach the students how to critique. It's sometimes easier to look at somebody else's work than your own, so we discuss with students – 'How do you evaluate the project critically? What would cast it in a new light?' – and then listen to what the critics say. See how that matches with your instinct, because the more you can critique, the clearer you can judge your own work, which is fundamentally harder than judging others' work.

The main point I infer is that the aim of the process is to teach the students how to critique, and that reviewing the work of other students in partnership with the teachers is a means to this end.

John also elaborated on the public dimension of the crit: 'You are opening up the student work to the outside view of the audience.' So the crit is both specific to an individual student and reflective in relation to bringing together wider public ideas about architecture. When I asked about the nature of a perceptive crit he explained:

> An insightful crit is to let the students see the project a little differently, a bit clearer. You would evaluate the crit based on the discussion that it provokes around some core issues: that is, by being provocative, by bringing up certain issues and questions. Projects need to have a sense of questioning and an opening up of discussion.

I infer that a crit seeks to open up and provoke discussion in order to enable the students to see things in a different light. The emphasis on questioning and dialogue also bears some similarities with the approach in Ali's teaching of Business, discussed in Chapter 6.

The interplay between individual and collective insights is also apparent in John's analysis:

> The crit is not just about showing up and having your work reviewed; it's an ongoing discussion from morning to evening which is stimulated by specific approaches to a problem. There is an overall problem of rural house recon-struction that is being solved both on individual scales and on a collective scale.

Some interesting points emerge here. First, there is the practical issue of the time spent on the crits, which last for many hours. Second, there is interplay between individual and collective in terms of students presenting their own individual designs within a collective project. By working on collective issues, there is the potential for relevant insights to emerge, which might stimulate student reflections or critical thinking. How these collective insights might emerge and the difficulties of unravelling them are discussed later in the chapter.

I also asked John about the challenges involved in developing effective crits:

> The main challenge in a crit is to treat each situation as a specific one and this requires a lot of concentration and effort as there are many crits in a single day and you need to avoid falling into a generic critique, with preconceived ideas.

Our observations confirmed that the crits were a lengthy process, and we felt that this might have implications for attentiveness and concentration. I went on to ask John how the process might be improved:

The main way is to make the crits more interesting by discussing contemporary issues. If you listen to a lot of critique on the placement of windows, then that is boring. It is better to create an open spirit of enquiry where the students are there to look at other solutions to a problem they have worked on, to develop a wider discussion and to get more students to participate actively.

This comment seems to reinforce John's earlier point that good crits bring up wider issues for discussion, rather than focus narrowly on the specifics of a particular design. Involving students more actively in crits is explored further in the 'Implications of crits' section below.

The processes of individual crits

The processes of critical review of student work took place through different kinds of review. The first of these comprised desk critiques of work in progress with an individual tutor, roughly analogous to a personal tutorial in humanities subjects. There were also a number of crit sessions: two crits at an interval of about one month when the student presents their work in front of an audience of peers, with two groups of students joining together and two tutors providing commentary; and a final crit presentation in front of peers and a jury of four tutors, including at least one from outside the university. In our fieldwork, we observed all of these critical reviews of student work in the Architecture design studio.

The basic structure of a crit in John's practice was for the tutor group to gather around the display boards. The arrangements were flexible and students often came and went during the session. Before one of the crit reviews we observed, John began with some reminders: 'We are here to help you. It's work in progress. It's about developing a house. The real meaning of review is to move forward.' The student presenter then shared their design for about five minutes before John and his partnering tutor offered comments on the design to the presenter. John always went first and commented in a friendly tone, raising some issues and providing some critique.

The following is an extract from Wang's field notes on this process:

Sometimes the tutors spoke loudly or even turned to the audience to speak so that everyone could hear them clearly. At other times the tutors seemed to be deeply absorbed in the presenter's design and the other students seemed neglected, as tutors engaged mainly in a private conversation with the presenter. The student audience sat, or sometimes stood, quietly. There is sometimes some background noise and it is not always easy to hear what is being said. Some students seemed to be listening to and engaging with the presentations and the tutors' comments; some were busy preparing for their own presentations; a few students were accessing information on their iPhones; some chatted with their friends, especially when the tutors were engaged in forms of private conversation with the presenter. The sessions continue until night-time.

So, our impression was that the setting for the crit was not ideal for wider learning beyond the presenter. Seating was somewhat cramped and for students who do not get a seat near the front audibility was occasionally an issue.

The first two students we observed taking part in a crit both seemed rather anxious. John made a number of comments in his usual friendly and constructive tone. The students made minimal responses but occasionally jotted down some notes. There was no interaction between the student presenters and other students. The students told us that the main reason for this was that it was difficult for peers to provide insightful comments when they were not deeply familiar with a particular design. Another reason was the time factor. The crits we observed took about twenty minutes on average, and there were clearly limit-ations of time available. If the students had participated in all of the discussions, it would have been impossible for every scheduled presentation to be made in the available time. John acknowledged that time was a factor, and he reported that some students were reticent in critical open discussion.

The third student we observed undertaking her crit was Gloria, who seemed more confident. Her design attracted some quite positive comments from John, such as 'interesting', 'intriguing', 'very rich' and 'good intuition'. However, he also suggested that the goal of the design could be sharper and that Gloria could develop a more ambitious conceptual storyline. Gloria interacted a little with John and tried to explain more about the rationale for her design. Together, they discussed some ideas for moving the design forward.

Student perspectives on crits

After her crit, we discussed the process with Gloria. She expressed the view that it is important to interact with the tutor and try to justify the design because that is an important aspect of being an architect. Persuasive presentation and the ability to 'sell' your design to a group of observers are skills which students need to develop. She also spoke about the idea of becoming your own critic and self-evaluating your work, which she saw as crucial when studying Architecture:

> I need to ask myself how I can make my design better. It is part of learning to be self-critical. We learn to be critical from listening to their analysis and so we can start to see things from another viewpoint.
>
> (Carless, 2014, p. 9)

When asked about affective issues in presenting in front of peers and being critiqued, she stated, 'It is a bit nerve-racking but it helps you to face clients later, which would be even more daunting.' This link to the workplace made me think of the notion of WTP, highlighted in Chapter 3.

Zhou highlighted the comments she received from multiple experts in her final review:

> All the tutors are interested in different aspects and want you to develop along a different direction . . . After listening to their comments, I feel my thinking is conventional . . . Their suggestions are not standard answers, but just some ways to solve the problems.

By listening to the experts' contrasting opinions, she realised that there were many different ways in which she could develop her design, and she was also aware of the limitations of her own thinking and the distance between herself and the experts.

In his crit, Yeung kept smiling and persistently tried to explain and justify his design. He commented:

> The crit is an occasion to explain one's work systematically in public. It is hard to convince the tutor that your idea is better but we should learn to make decisions for ourselves. I shouldn't give in too easily at the outset of the discussion even though I know that I may yield to his ideas eventually.

Yeung also saw value in the process of debating with tutors:

> The purpose of debate is to get more opinions from the tutor. Sometimes the debate goes beyond the specific issue we are discussing. Debate skills are important for architects as we need to convince different kinds of people about our design.

Again, I infer the relationship between the activity and the eventual disciplinary needs. Yeung felt that his crit provided 'some concrete suggestions and inspirations, which I think are useful. However, I don't know what to do next to make it better, even though my tutor gave me a lot of sensible and specific suggestions.' We asked him to elaborate on this issue:

> You can adopt the tutor's specific suggestions and develop from them, but that is too simple and is different from learning through exploration. Some of us prefer to work out a programme by ourselves, which gives us a stronger sense of accomplishment. Exploring a variety of possibilities under a major premise is the manifestation of a good architect.

We were quite impressed by the thoughtful way in which Yeung reflected on his ongoing exploration of possibilities in his design work.

I also asked Yeung what makes for a perceptive crit. He felt that an insightful crit could suddenly make a student realise something new, comparing it with Columbus discovering America. He said that the main purpose of a crit is to help the student 'jump out of the box', and exemplified this by saying that one might start with a definition and then redefine it by thinking in a different way. There are some parallels between this position and that of John, who felt a perceptive crit should enable students to see a project differently and provoke some discussion.

Learning from other crits

The public nature of the crit provides an opportunity for students to listen in to the conversation around design issues. This might provide some general insight into architectural thought processes and might stimulate ideas for one's own work. We also sensed, however, that it might be difficult to derive any relevant insights and that some students might find it hard to benefit from what looks like a public individual tutorial. We were curious about this aspect of the crit, so asked a number of students how they felt about attending their classmates' crits and what they might learn from them.

Ying felt she could learn from other students' presentations and the teachers' comments on them, but found it difficult to remain attentive throughout a long review period. She stated that if she found it hard to understand a design, she would generally be motivated to listen and engage with it. She also perceived that it was common for teachers' comments to relate to specific problems and that 'There are rarely general rules that can be applied to other projects.'

Celine felt that students tried hard to listen to the tutors' comments, but sometimes they were too tired to concentrate fully; some students' designs were not particularly interesting; and students were often busy preparing for, or thinking about, their own presentations. Serena thought that the tutors' comments on other students' work were useful because they helped her to determine why something was good or poor, and what was working well in her peers' designs. It was difficult, however, to learn much because 'everyone's design is different'. Laurence elaborated that he could form his own perspective on a piece of displayed work and learn something meaningful for his own work or his development as an architect. Yeung observed that he could see different kinds of design, form an impression of the variations, and learn how his classmates organised their work.

Gloria said that it was not particularly easy to gain much insight from comments on other students' work, but the whole class was trying to develop an overall impression of major issues in architectural design. She did not usually spend much time listening to other crits as she preferred to focus on her own work. This comment revealed some of the flexibility of the design studio.

Derek said that Architecture students learn more from seeing than from listening. He told us that a main reason why he continued to attend the crits for extended periods of time was that he thought tutors might form a positive impression of those students who were regularly present. This relates to the notion of hidden criteria, cue-consciousness and the making of positive general impressions on tutors (see Miller and Parlett, 1974).

To sum up, I had little difficulty in seeing the benefits of crit feedback for individual presenters, but I found it hard to identify how students were engaging with the public feedback. There seem to be three main challenges for gaining collective insight from the crit. First, students may perceive that a crit is contextualised and focused on someone else's work and may not carry relevance for their own project. Second, students reported some difficulty understanding what was being said both at an architectural discourse level and physically because of the presence of background noise and space limitations in the studio. Third, exacerbating these challenges was a fatigue factor: sometimes students had worked long hours on their own designs and in preparation for their own crits. In the 'Implications of crits' section below, I discuss how crits might be organised differently to support wider student learning.

Peer review and peer learning

As discussed in Chapter 7, peer review is a useful way of understanding quality criteria and learning from the work of classmates. Given the open-plan nature of the studio, Architecture seemed to be a good site for peer collaboration. However, our discussions with the students provided mixed evidence. Some students commented that they could see what their classmates were doing and learn from looking at other designs. They could learn a different way of approaching a design and could observe different techniques or a different style of drawing. So it seemed that there was a certain amount of informal learning from the work of peers. However, students could be less positive about the value of receiving peer feedback on their own work in progress. For instance, Celine said she rarely solicited any peer feedback on her work because she did not like to show her projects to other students until they were finished. Similarly, Yeung said he did not particularly welcome peer feedback as 'it is very difficult for someone who is unfamiliar with your overall design to give you feedback halfway through'. Ying was sceptical about the reliability of peer feedback but said she liked to chat with classmates to garner inspiration when she was having difficulty moving forward with her work. She also told us of one classmate who 'likes hanging around to look at others' designs and then shares her intuitive feelings. Sometimes some valuable issues come up.'

Natalie commented on peer learning as follows:

> Learning Architecture is about knowing what other people are doing. It is common for us to discuss each other's designs in an informal way. I like to walk around the studio and ask for other people's opinions on my design.

This gives some indication of the social nature of learning in Architecture. Ying expanded on this when she revealed that there is a tradition of senior Architecture students 'adopting' junior ones for mentoring purposes. The two parties in this informal arrangement provide mutual help and support, particularly during busy periods or when facing difficulties. For example, Ying's senior taught her how to use some computer software for graphic design and, in return, Ying contributed to the design work for the senior's final-year project. Similarly, Laurence helped his mentor make some models and tried to learn some techniques and strategies from him. He particularly sought advice on those aspects which he found challenging: clarifying the nature of design processes; how to approach new projects; and time management.

At the end of the course, students with similar designs were paired up by the tutors to do a final review which lasted from morning until evening. This time the jury comprised four people, including external members from the profession and another university. John talked about jury members' willingness to devote their time to this process because there was a good chance that they would encounter some thought-provoking ideas:

> Even though the students are only first-years, there is often some creativity or imagination which means that jury members can garner some inspiration for their own work. They can also gain insights from what other jury members see in a certain design.

I found it hard to imagine many disciplines in which university teachers would give up almost an entire day to advise students from another university. Perhaps this is a consequence of vocational commitment, the norms of the discipline, and the co-constructed nature of learning in Architecture. The boundaries between teaching and learning are possibly less defined in art and design than they are in other disciplines (Shreeve et al., 2010).

The final review seemed to create a lot of interest and excitement in the studio. Seeing all of the students' work at one time and listening to some of the final crits appeared to provide a valuable opportunity for peer learning. Many of the students walked around and examined their peers' designs, which were displayed on the walls and as models on the floor. Some took photos of the designs and understood the benefit of seeing all the designs at the same time. We inferred that the visual sense is quite powerful for Architecture students: looking and taking photos are aspects of how they determine or appreciate quality. For example, pairs or groups of students discussed designs or shared photos of designs that they had taken. In this way, they seemed to participate in a version of the spontaneous collaborative learning noted in Chapter 3 (see Tang, 1993).

Ying explained that she learnt how to tackle some technical problems by looking at others' drawings and models. She reported that looking at the models was much more efficient than discussing designs with classmates one by one. She did not take any photos but sometimes stopped in front of a design that she found especially interesting and studied it carefully for some time. Natalie's design seemed to catch the eye of many of her fellow students, who stood in front of it and discussed it at length. Ying was particularly impressed, explaining that she thought it was 'a combination of creative design and high practicality'.

Zhou held that:

> We should take a good look at other students' projects. I feel that my design is squeezed out bit by bit, like toothpaste, by my tutor and me. What I can think of is limited and I have a habitual way of thinking. Other people's designs can inspire me to think differently.

So, it seems that Zhou was looking for inspiration from some her peers' designs.

Both Zhou and Ying expressed a desire to attend the final crit review for a particularly innovative design, as they were eager to hear the jury's comments. They were not alone, as this review session attracted more students than most of the others. The general consensus was that the design was creative but not particularly practical. We inferred that the students paid selective attention to their classmates' crits: for example, they engaged with work that interested them or which they found attractive. This seems to be an advantage of the flexible approach to crits, as students can attend those they find interesting and continue with their own work at other times.

I asked John about the potential for students to learn directly from the work of their peers:

> I try to create an open spirit of enquiry. When you have that, then you are interested in other people's work. It is a bit limited if you are looking at other people's work in a direct manner of how it can improve your own; that's just too self-centred in a sense. One has to be aware of a broader set of issues.

John also mentioned that he provided structured opportunities for students to comment on each other's work: 'I actively try to encourage students to carry out peer review, but sometimes there are barriers of time and culture. It's easier in a small group and I often have them critique each other.' Overall, we felt that the final review provided a particularly rich environment for spontaneous peer learning.

Implications of crits

The Architecture case exemplifies the unified nature of the learning-oriented assessment framework. There is a coherence between the portfolio assessment task, the development of evaluative expertise through learning to critique design work, and the processes of dialogic feedback. The iterative development of the portfolio design for village houses also involves students in WTP in the discipline.

The processes promote deep approaches to learning: students seemed to be intrinsically motivated to develop their designs; they generally seemed to have high aspirations; and they appeared to be charting their own individual paths in maximising the architectural possibilities of their designs.

Crit processes seek to develop an evolving understanding of the nature of quality in architectural design through students learning how to critique and evaluate their own work and that of others. At its best, the dialogic communication in the crits acted as an exchange of ideas which could stimulate student self-evaluative capacities. There are also some similarities as well as some differences between the crit sessions and the analysis of exemplars of student work. They are similar in that both involve displaying and publicly discussing a piece of work. The main difference is that the crit focuses on work in progress, whereas analysis of exemplars generally entails the study of completed pieces of work, usually by students from a previous cohort.

The focus on student work in progress in Architecture carries positive implications for student action on feedback. The crit facilitates student engagement with dialogic feedback as they defend and justify their work before considering whether, and how, to revise it. This sense of ownership of work in progress seems to act as a facilitating factor for engagement in the crit discussion and its aftermath. I return to the issue of feedback in Architecture in Chapter 11.

The crits seemed more useful for individual student presenters than for the wider group of observers. Although students seemed able to self-evaluate their own designs, we did not see much evidence of them critiquing the work of others insightfully. This begs the question of how crits might be organised more effectively. Possible alternative arrangements include crits led by peers: for example, student-led crits without the presence of the tutor might bring additional student voices and ownership into the process (Parnell and Sara, 2007). Peers might also provide written comments to classmates rather than verbal ones (Blair, 2006). A related variation would be for students to prepare a written summary of the crit dialogue for the benefit of the student presenter (Orr et al., 2007). There are also different ways of carrying out teacher-led crits. Comparisons and contrasts between different student designs could promote sustained engagement (Orr et al., 2007). Teachers could strive to communicate the generic issues which emerge from particular crits to students so that wider messages are signposted clearly.

In Chapter 2, I emphasised the potential of learning-oriented assessment to mitigate unhelpful dichotomisations between formative and summative assessment. Orr and Bloxham (2012) reinforce this position in relation to art and design when concluding that students' developmental and final work are assessed as a whole, suggestive of productive integration of formative and summative assessment. The evidence in this chapter provides further support for this position in that the portfolio represented a final product which is also evaluated through the iterative processes underlying its development. The interweaving of teaching, learning and assessment in Architecture is something teachers in other disciplines might like to replicate.

Summary of chapter

This chapter has mainly explored the crit, which is part of the signature pedagogy in Architecture. It has also analysed some of the processes by which students try to develop evaluative expertise. I have more to say about this case in Chapter 11 in relation to the related issue of student engagement with feedback.

Main implications for practice

- Portfolio as an assessment task provides potential for the productive merging of formative and summative assessment.
- Involving students in dialogue around their work in progress promotes student engagement.
- Activities which involve students in developing their ability in complex appraisal support continuous improvement.
- Productive critique focuses on opening up possibilities for students to move forward in their work.
- On-display assignments provide a fruitful means for spontaneous peer learning.

Part IV

Reconceptualising feedback and ways forward

Chapter 10

Promoting student engagement with feedback

Changing feedback is at the heart of pedagogy – it is never marginal.

(Boud, 2000, p. 158)

Scope of chapter

In this chapter, I explore how students might be prompted to engage more effectively with feedback. I begin by charting some directions in feedback research, considering what feedback means, and reviewing some of the key challenges for productive feedback processes. Then I make the case for re-engineering feedback to promote dialogue. I examine some strategies to promote dialogic feedback and analyse the main barriers that may arise. I also re-analyse unpublished data from my previous interview study of award-winning teachers to propose a continuum of conventional and sustainable feedback practices.

Making sense of feedback processes

First, I review some key issues in relation to the theory and practice of feedback. I distinguish between feedback as comments and feedback as dialogic processes. I then explore some major difficulties in implementing effective feedback processes.

The feedback issue: interest and invisibility

Feedback is simultaneously a core aspect of improvement and something which is extremely difficult to manage effectively. It represents a learning-oriented assessment topic that was relatively neglected for a long time but has attained a higher profile in recent years. A major stimulus for increased interest in feedback emanates from the influence of accountability forces: the consistent results of institutional surveys in Australia and the UK (e.g. ACER, 2010; HEFCE, 2010, 2014), which indicate that students find the effectiveness of feedback one of the least satisfactory aspects of their university experience. It is not clear from these surveys exactly how student respondents define feedback; and it is also likely that one can never receive enough good-quality feedback. What is clear is that these surveys are politically and economically important to institutions as they position themselves in the market for student intake; and feedback on student work is a component of perceptions of value for money in higher education (Yorke, 2013). Satisfaction with feedback seems to be improving in those institutions which have responded proactively to the student voice (Barker and Pinard, 2014).

A couple of decades ago, feedback was an under-explored and under-theorised issue, but the literature on the subject has mushroomed over the last ten years or so. The studies are often small-scale in nature, but they have explored a variety of institutional settings. There have also been a number of significant review articles (in chronological order): Hattie and Timperley (2007); Shute (2008); Li and de Luca (2012); Boud and Molloy (2013a); Yang and Carless (2013); and Evans (2013). Navigating one's way through this expanding literature is not a straightforward task. Among the sources which I have found particularly informative and which have influenced my current thinking are: Nicol (2010); Sadler (2010a); Price, Handley and Millar (2011); and Boud and Molloy (2013a). In what follows, I provide an entry-point to the relevant literature and prepare the ground for the discussion of award-winning teachers' feedback practices.

Whether the interest in and research into feedback have fully transformed its modest status and relative invisibility is another matter. In a study of fourteen teachers from various disciplines, Tuck (2012) claims that written feedback is a marginalised aspect of academics' work which is largely invisible in terms of recognition, and reports that teachers feel that marking numerous students' scripts is largely unproductive work. A further level of invisibility represents what students do with feedback from their teachers, particularly end-of-semester written feedback (Price, Handley and Millar, 2011). It can be difficult to establish the effectiveness of feedback processes because subsequent student actions are often private and unknown (Parkin et al., 2012).

Conceptualising feedback processes

Before going any further, I wish to work towards a definition of feedback by discussing some different ways in which it has been conceptualised. As a preview of what follows, I shall suggest that there are two overlapping ways of referring to feedback: a focus on feedback as comments; and a view of it as some form of dialogue.

In their important review of research evidence related to feedback from both schooling and higher education, Hattie and Timperley (2007) conceptualise feedback as being information about one's performance or understanding. They suggest four levels of feedback which, with minor adaptations, I summarise in Table 10.1.

Hattie and Timperley's evidence suggests that feedback at the self-regulation and process levels tends to be the most effective; feedback at the self level is the least effective; and a key limitation of feedback at the task level is students'

Table 10.1 Levels of feedback

Level	Actions
Task level	How well tasks are understood or performed
Process level	The main processes needed to understand or perform tasks
Self-regulation level	Self-monitoring and regulation of actions
Self level	Personal evaluations of the learner, frequently praise

Source: Adapted from Hattie and Timperley, 2007

difficulty in generalising messages to other tasks. The importance of feedback at the self-regulation level is a major theme of this chapter. This is consistent with a major purpose of feedback being to support students in developing their ability to monitor, evaluate and regulate their own learning (Nicol and Macfarlane-Dick, 2006). In current mass higher education systems, many incoming students arrive unprepared for independent self-reflective learning and so the aim of first-year feedback practices should be to develop their capacities for self-regulated learning (Beaumont, O'Doherty and Shannon, 2011).

A further useful way of organising thinking about feedback is a four-category taxonomy of feedback components proposed by Chetwynd and Dobbyn (2011), building on previous work by Brown and Glover (2006) and Walker (2009). The four categories of comments on student work are: retrospective on content; future-altering on content; retrospective on skills; and future-altering on skills. Future-altering comments, especially on skills, are more likely to be useful in moving students' work forward, whereas retrospective comments are more likely to help students understand the strengths and weaknesses of their work and why they received a particular grade. This represents part of the challenge for feedback in that it is trying to achieve several goals simultaneously. Analogous to Boud's concept of double duty, discussed in Chapter 1, is what I call 'double feedback duty' – to indicate that feedback serves a number of different, and possibly competing, functions. These functions might include: feedback as advice for student improvement of the current or future work; comments as justification of the mark and/or to provide protection against student complaint; feedback for quality assurance purposes envisaging an auditor or external examiner as part of the audience; comments to demonstrate diligence and/or respect for the student work; and, most importantly, feedback for enhanced development of self-regulative strategies.

What I have discussed so far mainly relates to views of feedback as information that is provided: comments for students, as it were. This is a natural and conventional way of thinking about feedback and is useful in framing the ways in which comments may play different roles and have different functions. I shall call this the 'old paradigm' of thinking about feedback because it has dominated conventional thinking over the last few decades. In recent years, however, assessment researchers (e.g. Nicol, 2010; Sadler, 2010a) have produced a body of work that indicates limitations of views of feedback mainly predicated on providing information to learners in the form of comments. Instead, they have proposed that ways forward involve seeing feedback as a process in which students engage with feedback from various sources and make use of it to improve their work and/or develop their learning. These views of feedback emphasise the dialogic nature of processes in which messages are negotiated and moulded with an aim of closing feedback loops. A key point is that information becomes feedback only when it is used productively. I refer to this way of thinking about feedback as a 'new paradigm' because it represents a different conceptualisation focused on interaction and student uptake. Of course, there is a certain amount of interplay and overlap between the two paradigms, but they have distinctively different emphases and implications which I explore further as the chapter unfolds.

Implicit in the above discussion is that feedback is a concept that has different meanings and interpretations; hence, it is hard to define. In previous work, I have emphasised the dialogic nature of feedback processes, adopting a broad definition of feedback as 'all dialogue to support learning in both formal and informal situations' (Askew and Lodge, 2000, p. 1). A recent state-of-the-art definition of feedback processes (Boud and Molloy, 2013a) shifts the emphasis to the student role in making sense of and using feedback and away from the inputs provided through comments. Following these dual strands of dialogue and sense-making, I propose the following definition:

> Feedback is a dialogic process in which learners make sense of information from varied sources and use it to enhance the quality of their work or learning strategies.

This definition has the following features: it establishes feedback as a process rather than a product; it emphasises dialogue which could be with a teacher, peer, other contact, or the self through some form of inner dialogue; and emphasis is placed on what students do with feedback in relation to their current or future work and/or in terms of modifying the kinds of learning strategies they are adopting.

An issue in what follows is that some of the research I discuss takes an old-paradigm view of feedback as comments provided to students, whereas other studies adopt a more process-oriented, dialogic, new-paradigm perspective. This is a reminder that when we refer to feedback, we need to be aware that it means different things to different people, which may lead to miscommunication.

Challenges for effective feedback processes

Reinforcing what I have discussed above, a major challenge for the development of effective feedback processes is the predominance of a view of feedback as the transmission of information, often in the form of a monologue. In other words, feedback which merely provides information about performance is likely to be insufficient to engage students and prompt them to take action. Just as learning does not occur through the mere transmission of information, feedback delivery on its own does not lead to learning improvement (Nicol, 2010). A related point is that transmission modes of communication may fail to engage with students' interests and needs. Feedback is too often based on what the teacher wants to say rather than on what the student is interested in hearing (Carless, 2013a).

Misgivings about the current handling of feedback processes are widely expressed. When feedback on coursework is provided after a course has finished, much expensively produced feedback goes to waste (Gibbs and Simpson, 2004; Price, Handley and Millar, 2011). A study of how many students accessed feedback after their grade was known found that it was a low percentage. Given the time implications of providing high-quality feedback, perhaps it might be reduced on certain summative assignments: for example, provided only to those who request it (Jones and Gorra, 2013). It is impossible to justify the time spent crafting feedback messages if it does not have a positive impact on what learners can do, so making feedback satisfying for teachers is as important as making it worthwhile for students (Boud and Molloy, 2013a). Implicit in this is a sense of some teacher unwillingness to devote time to unproductive feedback practices. This could be a facilitating factor in promoting change.

The efficacy of feedback in higher education often depends on the extent to which teachers and students are committed to the process (Barker and Pinard, 2014). Award-winning teachers might be expected or required to have that kind of professional commitment. A related point is the proposition that effective lecturers provide good-quality feedback (Poulos and Mahony, 2008). If this is correct, one might anticipate that award-winning teachers might possess a repertoire of useful feedback practices. This is explored in Chapter 11.

The issue of double feedback duty, introduced above, represents a further challenge. Teachers reported that assessment feedback should inform learning as well as justify grading, but they found it hard to balance these roles in practice (Li and De Luca, 2012). Tensions between providing useful formative comments to students and institutional quality assurance processes are also reported (Bailey and Garner, 2010). The multiple functions and expectations of what feedback can and will cater for tend to exacerbate staff and student dissatisfactions (Price, Handley and Millar, 2011).

A further challenge relates to criteria and academic expectations – the kind of issues I discussed in Chapter 7. These are relevant to feedback because when students are unsure of the nature of quality work or what teachers are looking for, they find it hard to understand and use teachers' comments. The notion of cue-consciousness is particularly relevant to feedback, as students often do not understand the purposes of feedback, sometimes privilege written over verbal feedback, and may have received little modelling or guidance on how to use feedback (Price, Handley and Millar, 2011). Cue-conscious students have the ability to identify signals in tutors' discourse about assessment requirements and are potentially able to act on them when working on their own assignments. The cue-deaf often find written feedback to be too deeply encrypted; may find comments hard to understand; and be unable to recognise implicit messages as comprising feedback. This paves the way for what comes next: a set of challenges for feedback processes which relate to students' perceptions and interpretations.

Student perspectives on feedback

The evidence from a number of studies is that students tend to express varying degrees of dissatisfaction with how feedback has been handled. Much of this dissatisfaction relates to the old paradigm of feedback and has contributed to the development of the new paradigm. Students' views of feedback seem to be rather different from those of their teachers (Adcroft, 2011; Carless, 2006). For example, academics seem to believe much more strongly than their students that feedback is a crucial element of the student learning experience (Adcroft, 2011); and staff perceive that their feedback is useful to a greater extent than their students do (Carless, 2006). Again, this can relate to how feedback is defined. For some students, feedback may be equated with grades, so dissatisfaction with it may indicate that they would like to have received, or felt they merited, a higher mark! Other students may conceive of feedback as something formal and summative, so they may not regard teacher in-class guidance or other verbal commentary as feedback.

So, how do students define feedback? Based on four focus groups involving thirty-three undergraduates in soft-pure or soft-applied disciplines, Scott (2014) infers a student definition of feedback as the means by which students are able to gauge how they are progressing in terms of the knowledge, understanding and skills that will determine their results in the course. In a phenomenographic investigation of Physiotherapy students' conceptions of feedback, McLean, Bond and Nicholson (2014) identified four qualitatively different student experiences of feedback: telling; guiding; developing understanding; and opening up a different perspective. Most of their interviewees identified conceptions of feedback in line with telling and guiding, with just one informant contributing most of the ideas relating to the other two categories. The telling and guiding perspectives resonate with the old conception of feedback as providing information, whereas the developing understanding and opening up different perspectives orientations are more in line with the newer, dialogic perspective.

Students often view tutors' comments on their work as difficult to understand. For example, a substantial number of the Business students surveyed by Weaver (2006) expressed the view that they were unsure of what teachers meant by such comments as 'more critical reflection needed' or 'superficial analysis'. Feedback comments are often shrouded in academic discourse which can remain opaque to many students. Due to its time-consuming nature, written feedback also tends to be relatively cryptic, which can exacerbate difficulties in student understanding. When students' interpretations of a task do not match those of their tutors, these challenges are also accentuated. A challenge for teachers is to make feedback accessible to students without denuding it of its capacity to signify, analyse and critique (Sutton, 2012).

Students often find feedback difficult to act upon (Gibbs, 2006; Poulos and Mahony, 2008). In many instances, feedback can only diagnose a problem rather than provide a recipe for development (Price, Handley and Millar, 2011), which can make further student action or follow-up difficult, except for the most motivated and well-organised students. Comments which carry impact beyond the task to which they relate may represent 'high-value' sustainable feedback (Hounsell, 2007).

Students often view feedback from one tutor as having limited transferable use because they perceive teachers as having varying individual preferences (Norton, 2004; Price, Handley and Millar, 2011). There is probably some validity in this perception, but it may also be that students sometimes overestimate the variation in teachers' perspectives. An unwillingness or inability to transfer possible insights from one module to another may also relate to what I called low intensity of grade-related desire in Chapter 6: avoidance of doing the hard graft which is required to improve work and learning strategies. If a student is content to attain marks close to the class average, feedback may not spur them on to raise the quality of their work further (Hounsell, 2003). They may also lack the know-how to transfer insights from one task to another, so this may need to be modelled for them.

The issue of timing of feedback is a particular challenge in modularised higher education, particularly in relation to end-of-module assignments. The timing of feedback is sometimes interpreted by students as a perversely belated revelation by teachers of things that they feel should have been revealed earlier in the assignment process (Crook, Gross and Dymott, 2006). The key issue in timing concerns the progress of work during the semester and how it relates to ongoing assignment tasks. Less significant is the turnaround of summative comments after a course has finished because their potential for student action is, by definition, limited or even non-existent.

Social and affective issues also impact on how students respond to feedback, an issue I highlighted in Chapter 2. Feedback is an essentially problematic form of communication involving social relationships, mediated by patterns of power, authority, emotion and identity (Higgins, Hartley and Skelton, 2001). Students feel comfortable with tutors who appear approachable, but wary of those whom they perceive as threatening and not open to alternative interpretations of assignment questions, as well as those who seem to award grades without adequate justification (Orsmond, Merry and Reiling, 2005). Feedback is facilitated by relationships of trust in which classroom participants value the views of others, respond empathetically and co-construct classroom atmospheres in which students can feel free to take risks (Carless, 2013b). When teachers indicate that they care about their learners, the possibility of student engagement with feedback is enhanced (Sutton, 2012).

For feedback to have an impact on the student there needs to be some action to close the gap between actual performance and required performance. At the level of feedback as information, if students have difficulties in understanding comments, are unsure about their usefulness and transferability, or react negatively to them in some way, then future action is unlikely or at least impaired. This is at the heart of the feedback conundrum. More communication is needed with students about the nature of productive feedback processes and their role as active users of feedback. I turn next to this notion of student engagement with feedback as dialogue.

Developing effective dialogic feedback processes

Thus far, the discussion has mainly focused on the old paradigm of feedback as telling or monologue. Now I shift to the new paradigm of feedback as dialogic interaction. New thinking about feedback holds that a major principle for developing effective feedback processes is to capture student attention and action because feedback is inevitably limited in its impact without this student engagement. By reconciling the definition of feedback earlier in the chapter and a previous definition of dialogic feedback (Carless, 2013a), I propose the following definition:

> Dialogic feedback involves iterative processes in which interpretations are shared, meanings negotiated and expectations clarified in order to promote student uptake of feedback.

An important step is to narrow differing staff and student expectations and perceptions of feedback through communication and dialogue. A convincing case for more dialogic approaches to feedback has been put forward in a number of papers emerging over the last five years or so (Beaumont et al., 2011; Carless et al., 2011; Price, Handley and Millar, 2011; Nicol, 2010). A key message is that dialogue can take various forms and involve different sources other than the teacher. I first discuss some ways of students interacting with the teacher and then other forms of self- and peer evaluation.

Teacher-led dialogic feedback

Dialogic interaction with a teacher could involve in-class interaction around issues, such as the nature of quality and standards, and the specific requirements for a module assignment task. These forms of dialogic feedback are embedded within the teaching of a course; they do not arise mainly at the end. This kind of preliminary guidance about expectations and requirements would be congruent with viewing guidance and feedback as an integrated whole and a series of feedback loops (Hounsell et al., 2008). The structural problem of timing of feedback is potentially well addressed by in-class guidance and feedback.

Another means of enhancing student uptake with feedback is through the way assessment tasks are designed and sequenced. As discussed in Chapter 2 and implicit in the learning-oriented assessment framework is the potential of assessment task design to facilitate student uptake of feedback. A recent example from a large first-year Business course involved two written essay tasks which were closely related in their content and conceptual demands facilitating the use of feedback by students in direct and meaningful ways (Vardi, 2013).

Designing assessment sequences which involve feedback on drafts is another common means of developing dialogue from written feedback processes. In this way, students' assignments are re-engineered to promote the iterative cycles of feedback and revision that normally characterise academic writing (Taras, 2006). If both a first and second submitted version of a paper count for marks, then this may be a way of increasing student engagement with feedback and encouraging greater dialogue, because action on feedback counts towards improved grades. An intervention in which 70 per cent of the assessment weighting was for the first draft and 30 per cent for the second draft is reported by Court (2014). The second draft was assessed on the criteria of the extent to which students engaged with and acted on the feedback they had received. The main drawbacks of feedback on drafts are its resource implications, so if feedback is provided on a draft, considerably less summative feedback should then be provided for a subsequent, final submission of a piece of work. Overall, comments on drafts are useful for students, but it is fair to say that the provision of such feedback is contentious in terms of drawbacks of teacher workload and student dependency (Beaumont et al., 2011). Perhaps feedback on drafts can be emphasised in the first year of a programme to support student induction and then gradually withdrawn or reduced.

In a thoughtful analysis of effective feedback on written assignments, Willingham (1990) makes a number of useful points congruent with a dialogic approach. Feedback comments should form a hierarchy of importance that the students can discern so that they are focusing on high-leverage comments rather than being overwhelmed with numerous comments. The most important principle in providing feedback is to encourage the student to be his or her own editor, congruent with the self-regulation role highlighted at the outset of this chapter. A further related strategy is for the marker to raise questions which initiate a dialogue between teacher and student, rather than set up teacher comments as the final words (Willingham, 1990). Raising questions is an interrogative way of learning implicit in academic life (Barnett, 2007b). In such ways, teacher commentaries aim to promote student thinking rather than merely provide judgements and instructions (Anderson, 2014).

Another means of developing dialogic written feedback is by providing students with the opportunity to take an active role by stating what kind of feedback they would like to receive. A small-scale study explored this strategy through the use of interactive coversheets in which first-year students initiated dialogue on issues they considered important (Bloxham and Campbell, 2010).

In this case, students' limited understandings of staff expectations and standards constrained their ability to engage in meaningful dialogue, and it was suggested that prior discussion with peers might have been a beneficial starting-point.

Peer feedback and internal feedback

Peers are potentially important sources of dialogic feedback. This is not just because teachers do not have the time to provide extensive feedback, but also because students need to involve themselves actively in generating feedback. Engaging with the work of peers is often helpful in supporting students to self-regulate their own work. Moreover, comments from peers can sometimes, although not always, be more palatable and congenial than those from authority figures, such as teachers. Involvement in peer-feedback processes transfers some of the responsibility for providing comments from staff to students, so potentially increases engagement. Producing peer feedback is more cognitively demanding than just receiving it, so constructing feedback is likely to heighten student engagement with feedback processes (Nicol et al., 2014). Justifying and negotiating feedback messages can also enable students to think more deeply about criteria, standards and the nature of quality work.

Social relations and trust are important factors in peer feedback. Some students see peer-feedback processes as constructive and motivational, whereas others are concerned about issues such as the competency of their classmates and possible plagiarising of their ideas (Beaumont et al., 2011). At the micro classroom level, a positive interactive class atmosphere facilitates the sharing of honest peer feedback, and this is largely dependent on the development of trusting relationships (Carless, 2013b). At the wider programme level, a target is to create course climates in which the giving and receiving of peer feedback is a regular aspect of teaching and learning processes (Boud, 2000; Liu and Carless, 2006).

There is interplay between peer feedback and the development of student evaluative expertise. At its best, peer feedback functions as external feedback to regulate students' monitoring and evaluation of their performance. This self-regulatory role in feedback relates to internal feedback (Butler and Winne, 1995) or inner dialogue (Nicol, 2010) which supports students in deriving meaning from feedback messages and using them consciously to influence future action. Feedback needs to support students in building their capacity to make their own judgements about their work; learners will change what they do only once they have made their own judgements that this is necessary (Boud and Molloy, 2013b).

Peer-collaborative learning can profitably be integrated with technology-assisted approaches to feedback. For example, Nicol (2007) reports on students responding to multiple-choice questions through an electronic voting system (EVS) system and then participating in peer teaching to justify their answers to classmates. Such processes involve dialogue and potential reappraisals as students revise their thinking when the correct answer is revealed. A recent example of online peer assessment using Moodle's Workshop module provided further evidence that providing feedback tends to generate more higher-order thinking than receiving feedback (Mostert and Snowball, 2013). Consistent with the general aim of feedback introduced at the outset of this chapter, technology-enhanced peer feedback is probably most effective when it encourages the development of learner self-regulation (Nicol, 2009).

Technology-enhanced dialogic feedback

The essence of feedback processes with technology should be congruent with the position taken above: dialogic, focused on student engagement with feedback, and with the aim of facilitating student self-monitoring of their own progress. Russell, Bygate and Barefoot (2013) provide a useful starting-point of strategies to support technology-enhanced forms of dialogic feedback: the use of blogs to enhance reflection and improve dialogue; the use of electronic voting systems (EVSs) to monitor student understanding and response; and the use of wikis and group areas within virtual learning environments to establish opportunities for collaboration and co-creation. Although there is quite a lot of small-scale research activity in relation to technology-enhanced feedback, a recent review (Hepplestone et al., 2011) concludes that the literature remains somewhat limited in terms of reporting effective uses of technology to enhance feedback processes.

LMSs, such as Moodle and Blackboard, are now in widespread use, although they are rarely deployed optimally to stimulate effective dialogue. They provide opportunities for teachers to return work more quickly and easily without the need to meet the students in person. They enable comments to be stored and accessed by teachers and students; and they may facilitate peer feedback or other forms of online dialogue. Atkinson and Lim (2013) explored the use of a semi-automated rubric stored on Blackboard to facilitate feedback processes and found positive perceptions from both teachers and students, as well as some teacher workload benefits. Carrying similar possibilities to an LMS is the use of Facebook, which students at HKU felt was more familiar and easier to navigate than Moodle (Deng and Tavares, 2013).

An adaptive release tool used at Sheffield Hallam University allows tutors to release feedback but withhold the grade until the student has produced a reflective account of the feedback (Parkin et al., 2012). Storing online feedback increases the likelihood of students revisiting the feedback and using it in future assignments; and the problem of students focusing more on grades and less on the comments is circumvented. However, some students perceived adaptive release as 'enforced reflection'.

The use of clickers or EVSs also provides opportunities to generate interaction within classes. The instant feedback aspect of clickers is generally perceived as attractive and motivational by students (Patry, 2009). In the context of a large undergraduate Mathematics class, King and Robinson (2009) report the use of an EVS to enliven the classroom atmosphere and increase student participation, although they found no correlation between EVS use and improvement in grades. To date, clickers seem to be used most commonly in the hard sciences, rather than other disciplines, often in relation to periodic multiple-choice questions during lectures (Patry, 2009). A related development involves students using their smartphones to submit instant responses (Voelkel and Bennett, 2013).

Audio feedback has generated a certain amount of interest in recent years. It carries some potential advantages: it seems to be viewed positively by students (Lunt and Curran, 2010); it allows more detailed and nuanced feedback and enhances students' perceptions of teacher concern for their progress (Savin-Baden, 2010); it permits greater personalisation and opportunity to provide detail (Gould and Day, 2013); and students may perceive it as resembling a form of dialogue (Nicol, 2010). Its limitations are: its potential to improve student learning was perceived only as 'moderate' (Gould and Day, 2013); it would be undesirable if it came to replace face-to-face tutor student interactions (Lunt and Curran, 2010); and there are concerns about implications in the event of a failure grade (Gould and Day, 2013). The results of these studies vary in the extent to which audio feedback might increase or decrease staff workload, an issue that is keenly debated in the literature (Hennessy and Forester, 2014). A possible way forward lies in generating dialogue from its processes: for example, students could receive audio feedback which serves as a stimulus and starting-point for face-to-face discussion (Hennessy and Forester, 2014).

In sum, there are various forms of technology-enhanced feedback. My interim conclusions are that strategies which promote interaction have the most potential to bring student engagement and dialogue into feedback processes; and those that are workload-friendly for teachers are likely to have the most potential for wide uptake.

Programme or institutional approaches to feedback

An important way forward for dialogic feedback processes would be a coherent, system-wide approach. In such a vision, feedback would permeate the curriculum and include scheduling of nested and incremental tasks which allow for learning to be demonstrated after the exchange of internally and externally produced critique (Molloy and Boud, 2013). This could be facilitated by a systematic and sustained implementation of all the principles discussed above: communication around purposes of feedback and students' active role in engagement with its processes; activating the roles of peers as a source of feedback; using technology-enhanced feedback to promote dialogue; and engaging consistently with quality in the discipline.

Worth noting as an institution-wide initiative to promote feedback in the context of the Re-engineering Assessment Practices (REAP) is the 'feedback is a dialogue campaign' (Draper and Nicol, 2013). Working in association with the university's student union, this involved a leaflet and posters explaining to students what feedback is; why it is important; and how it can be engineered to work for them. This was accompanied by a leaflet for staff summarising twelve principles of good assessment and feedback, with teachers encouraged to distribute leaflets to students themselves to indicate that they have bought in to the REAP principles. Web resources were provided which gave advice on how students could put REAP ideas on feedback into practice. This approach invites further implementation in other contexts.

Challenges for dialogic feedback

I have presented the case for dialogic feedback processes and illustrated different ways in which they might be implemented. There are, however, a number of challenges which need to be discussed. The first is that there is a risk of dialogic feedback *sounding* implausible. A first thought might be: how can teachers engage in dialogue with a large class of students with minimal contact and a lack of a personal interaction? This is a valid point, although it underestimates the potential of different forms of dialogue: whole-class as well as individual verbal dialogues; various forms of written dialogue, including interactive coversheets; and technology-enhanced dialogue. Nicol (2010) is exemplary in discussing a range of practical ways in which dialogic feedback could be implemented.

A lack of widespread assessment and feedback literacy is the principal barrier to the development of thoughtful dialogic feedback processes among teachers. Moreover, this is exacerbated by structural constraints, such as modularised programmes, large class sizes, the multiple demands of academic life and increasing workloads (Yang and Carless, 2013). These structural limitations in the organisation of feedback in universities represent a genuine challenge which necessitates the kind of re-engineering of feedback processes discussed above: careful task sequencing to provide feedback opportunities; in-class integration of guidance and feedback; and dialogues through various means, including peers and technology-enhanced. A further challenge relates to teaching approaches which emphasise the transmission of content – what was referred to in Chapter 2 as information transfer teaching focus. Such conceptions of teaching are barriers to a more dialogic learning experience.

The process of engaging with feedback is mediated by learners' relationships with their teachers (Sutton, 2012). A review of key elements of the architecture of dialogic feedback (Yang and Carless, 2013) suggests student-related barriers are salient: for example, convincing students that they want to engage in dialogue with their teachers. Sometimes unequal power relations discourage students from entering into feedback dialogues for fear of exposing their weaknesses or suffering threats to their self-esteem (Carless, 2006; Sambell, 2013). Critical comments can unintentionally discourage lower-achieving students who already lack confidence in their academic writing (Court, 2014; Wingate, 2010). Anodyne comments can fail to challenge students sufficiently. A useful strategy for modelling engagement with critical comment would be for teachers to share personal experiences of handling peer review feedback on their research and teaching (Värlander, 2008).

A further related challenge is how to enable lower-achieving students to access and engage with feedback. Lower-achieving students tend to be heavily reliant on external teacher feedback; unable to self-regulate their learning successfully; and have limited understandings of their own learning processes (Orsmond and Merry, 2013). Such learners are often locked into surface approaches to learning (Sutton, 2012). Supporting the lower-achieving learner defies easy answers, but starting-points may include the need to discuss the nature of learning, different learning strategies, and the relationships between learning, assessment and desired student outcomes. Orsmond and Merry (2013) make some useful suggestions: further development of social learning with peers; dialogue around exemplars to support understandings of quality work; and, most fundamentally, guidance and training in the development of self-evaluative capacities. The explicitly social nature of learning and dialogue could enable feedback to become part of a broader transformative student process, not merely an adjunct to assessment (McArthur and Huxham, 2013). How dialogic feedback can be developed supportively and effectively with students of all capacities represents an area for further research.

Conventional and sustainable feedback

An undercurrent running through this chapter is the distinction between an old paradigm of feedback as comments and a new paradigm of feedback as dialogic interaction. I now wish to take this further and suggest some of the interplay between these two paradigms by reanalysing data from a study of the feedback practices of award-winning teachers carried out in 2009–2010 (Carless et al., 2011). The main aim of this study was to identify teacher perspectives on key issues in feedback processes through in-depth interviews. The sample comprised ten award-winning teachers (seven male, three female), one from each of the ten faculties at HKU, including Rick (Law) and Ali (Business), both of whom feature in this book, too. For the purposes of this section, I draw selectively on previously unpublished data from the study to shed light on the issues under discussion and to add more award-winning teacher voices and disciplinary areas to those featured thus far in this book.

Our analysis suggested a continuum of feedback orientations amongst the ten teachers. At one end of the continuum were more conventional feedback practices: standard, well-established strategies which involve tutors commenting on aspects of student work through various modes (i.e. there is emphasis on what the teacher is doing). This approach is similar to what I have termed the old paradigm of feedback in that it focuses mainly on providing information to students.

At the other end of the continuum were more sustainable feedback practices, defined as: dialogic activities in which students generate and use feedback from peers, themselves or others as part of an ongoing process of developing capacities as autonomous, self-regulating learners (Carless, 2013a). This is compatible with what I have called the new paradigm of feedback, and through the notion of sustainability it emphasises the potential of students to monitor their work independently of teachers. In current forms of mass higher education, this might represent a way forward for feedback research and practice. So, if the ideal is dialogic feedback, might sustainable feedback support its implementation within current resourcing arrangements?

Informants reported a range of practices between the two poles, although generally there was greater emphasis on one or the other. For the purposes of exemplifying the range of practices, for illustrative purposes I have selected four of the ten informants to provide a flavour of the data.

Reported practices in Arts and Nursing

In Table 10.2 I present key practices and issues from the Arts and Nursing interviewees. 'Signature feedback strategies' represent the main practices they reported; while on the right-hand side of the table I note other salient issues

Table 10.2 Examples of feedback strategies (Arts and Nursing)

Discipline	Signature feedback strategies	Other issues or suggestions
Literature specialism, Faculty of Arts	Task design to promote student use of feedback: 30 per cent weighting for first assignment; 70 per cent weighting for second assignment. One-to-one or small-group tutorials. Peer review to reduce hierarchical power relations: 'students need careful instruction and modelling of peer review'.	Provide more feedback for first-year students. Students have misconceptions about feedback and their role in it. Inconsistency in teachers' handling of feedback. 'The practices are time-consuming but we have to devote time to the students: that is our job.'
Nursing	Task design: portfolio with two submissions to promote student uptake of feedback. After-class discussions with individuals or small groups. Responding to email queries about the portfolio assignments. Tried to promote self-evaluation 'but students are not good at doing it'.	Feedback should be timely to promote student action. Feedback is most usable if action can influence student grades. Claims to enjoy reading student portfolios. Believes feedback responses enhance student motivation. Describes giving feedback as 'hard work but it's worth it'.

which were raised. I mainly paraphrase the points they made, although there are a small number of direct quotations, as indicated by quote marks.

Both of these informants viewed providing feedback as a key part of their role as a teacher and they displayed considerable professional commitment, or even passion, in supporting their students. Reported practices included: written feedback on drafts or final versions of assignments; verbal comments in individual or small-group tutorials and discussions; and email responses to queries. These often carried elements of dialogue but were mainly premised on teachers providing comments or advice. This is an important part of student understanding of the expected requirements of university work in the discipline, but two challenges arise. First, such practices are relatively labour-intensive and strategies which require substantial additional work or commitment from staff may be suitable for enthusiasts but probably not for wider-scale implementation. Second, feedback in the form of teacher-led information provision tends to make students dependent and fails to encourage them to be active, self-regulating students. These two elements limit the sustainability of such practices.

Both of these informants also used or at least experimented with peer review or student self-evaluation practices, which are nearer the sustainable end of the continuum. Such practices place more emphasis on the active student role in generating or applying feedback and are congruent with a view of feedback as promoting student self-regulation. The two teachers also reported challenges for the implementation of these strategies, and I inferred that these caused some doubts in the teachers' minds about their feasibility.

Reported practices in Real Estate and Medicine

Selected aspects of the practices of the informants from Real Estate and Medicine are summarised in Table 10.3. These teachers shared some strategies with the two informants above, with the main differences being that they persistently encouraged students to become active agents in generating internal feedback and peer feedback, and attempted to stimulate learner independence and self-regulation.

Both of these informants espoused two main interlinked strategies: questioning and dialogue through various means; and encouraging the development of student self-evaluative expertise. In relation to the first, they tried to involve students in questioning and dialogue so that the students could learn how to think and work out answers for themselves. These strategies resonate with those carried out by Ali (see Chapters 6 and 11). With respect to the second, student self-evaluation is central to a number of their practices. For example, the Real Estate informant is intent on helping students to work things out for themselves. The Medicine informant attempts to train students to develop their own diagnoses. The link between feedback and self evaluative expertise is at the heart of dialogic and sustainable approaches to feedback.

The practices of these two informants also speak to other themes addressed in this chapter. They mainly focused on within-course feedback dialogues so that

Table 10.3 Examples of feedback strategies (Real Estate and Medicine)

Discipline	Signature feedback strategies	Other issues or suggestions
Real Estate and Construction	Dialogue and interactive discussions, in class or via email. Task design includes series of assessed oral presentations to promote improvement.	Dialogue aims to develop student thinking. Dialogue is related to disciplinary need to convince clients.
	Blog co-constructed by teachers and students and also involves practitioners from industry. Some blog topics are relevant to coursework assessment.	Blog is for sharing, does not count towards course assessment.
	When a student asks a question, often redirects it back to them to stimulate their thinking.	Acknowledges barriers to dialogic approach and some student complaints about asking students to try to answer their own questions.
	Some evidence of feedback at the self-regulation level.	'Students will treasure feedback if it addresses their needs and interests.'
Medicine	In-class dialogue and questioning based on problem-based learning.	Dialogue aims to promote deep engagement through interaction.
	Task design of three written assignments: short research essay (ungraded); longer research essay (10 per cent weighting); final research essay (90 per cent weighting).	Emphasises early feedback with less feedback on final task.
	Promotes student self-evaluation in relation to provisional medical diagnoses: feedback at the self-regulation level.	Prefers exploratory rather than directive feedback; talks of 'provocative feedback' to challenge student thinking. Notes tensions when students express preference for direct instruction.

the processes formed iterative cycles of guidance and feedback rather than comments coming at the end of a cycle. A particular means of facilitating student dialogue in the Real Estate case was through technology-enhanced interaction, using blogs; this was also a feature of Ali's practice. Some of the practices relate to conceptions of feedback opening up new perspectives (see McLean et al., 2014; and John's practices in Architecture in Chapters 9 and 11).

Implementing practices on the conventional–sustainable feedback continuum

Teachers and students are likely to be involved in a combination of practices along the conventional–sustainable feedback continuum. Those at the conventional end of the continuum are probably less challenging as they are familiar and within teachers' and students' comfort zones. More sustainable practices may require somewhat more complex pedagogic procedures, and may take participants outside their existing comfort zones. All four of the informants reported some struggles and challenges in implementing more sustainable practices. The informant from Arts used peer review with some success, but noted some challenges. The informant from Nursing experimented with student self-evaluation, but acknowledged that students found it difficult. The informants from Real Estate and Medicine identified challenges when students expressed a preference for more teacher-led, less demanding pedagogy. A way forward could be gradual increased emphasis on sustainable practices as a student moves through their undergraduate programme; this signals a need for persistency in encouraging learner independence. Such strategies are facilitated by trusting relationships between participants, including teachers' faith in students' willingness to engage and be challenged.

As I have emphasised throughout this book, it is useful to facilitate productive feedback processes through task design, and this was evident amongst all four of these teacher participants. Certain assessment tasks are more likely to stimulate productive opportunities for feedback dialogue than others. An iterative series of tasks is more likely to stimulate usable feedback than a single terminal assessment. In addition, certain tasks are specifically designed to produce dialogue around learning: for example, oral presentations or blogs. Productive peer review processes can also be integrated within task designs: for example, peer review of an oral presentation followed by a written report.

The evidence from the interviews summarised in Tables 10.2 and 10.3 also speak to other pertinent issues in the literature. The lack of consistency in teachers' handling of feedback resonates with points made in Price, Handley and Millar (2011) and suggests the need for programme-wide initiatives. Feedback from practitioners in the Real Estate blog is a further means of diversifying sources of feedback and reducing the burden on teachers as sole feedback providers (see Boud and Molloy, 2013b). Sustainable feedback involves students generating and utilising feedback from multiple sources in line with the emphasis on student self-regulation of their work. While the quality of the comments is important, the quality of the students' interaction with those comments is even more crucial (Nicol, 2010).

Finally, I bring together the main emphases in feedback processes in the old paradigm (analogous to conventional feedback) and the new paradigm (compatible with sustainable feedback) in the form of a Venn diagram (Figure 10.1). Feedback can place emphasis mainly on comments, such as when end-of-semester assignments are critiqued (the left-hand side of the figure); or it can involve dialogue in the form of peer feedback, internal feedback or teacher feedback (the right-hand side of the figure). When there is some combination of the two – the intersection of the two circles – comments lead to a degree of dialogic interaction.

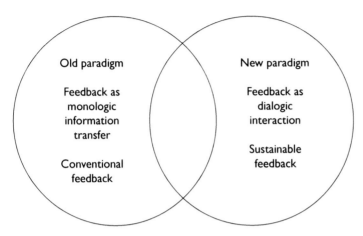

Figure 10.1 Interplay between feedback as information and as dialogue

Summary of chapter

In this chapter, I have discussed some different ways of conceptualising feedback, including an old paradigm of feedback as providing information on performance. I have reviewed some of the main challenges for effective feedback processes and set out the case for a new feedback paradigm focused on student self-regulation, internal feedback, peer review and dialogic teacher feedback. I have discussed some practices which I have classified on a continuum of conventional (old-paradigm) to sustainable (new-paradigm) feedback practices. In the next chapter, I present the feedback practices from the five case studies and relate them to these ideas.

Main implications for practice

- Teachers and students need to discuss the roles and purposes of feedback, and the student role in using feedback productively.
- A key role of feedback is to support students in self-regulating their work and learning strategies.
- New ways of thinking about feedback suggest its processes can be re-engineered to promote dialogue and self-regulation.
- Peers are a useful feedback resource with potential gains for both the provider and the receiver of the feedback.
- Technology-facilitated feedback should aim to promote dialogue around key issues.
- Feedback processes are facilitated by relational factors, such as empathy and trust.
- Sustainable feedback emphasises the student role in independently generating, processing and using feedback.

Chapter 11

Feedback processes in the cases

If students don't participate in feedback, it is sterile.

(Rick Glofcheski)

Scope of chapter

In this chapter, I explore how the five teachers manage feedback processes, and provide examples and commentaries from the cases. I discuss the Architecture case in some detail because feedback was a central element of the signature pedagogy of the crit. I also make some points about various forms of feedback in History, 'same-day feedback' in Law, group project feedback in Geology, and dialogic feedback in Business.

Feedback in the Architecture case

To reiterate some of the relevant processes of critical reviews from Chapter 9, in John's practice there were two main opportunities for dialogic feedback: first, regular one-to-one desk feedback on work in progress; and, second, the more formalised rituals of the series of public crits, where feedback was provided with other students observing. I mainly focus on feedback through the public means of the crit as it was a central element of the teaching and learning we observed. The social nature of the Architecture studio also facilitated peer feedback between students, but as that issue was discussed in Chapter 9 it is not revisited here except to reiterate that it was an important element in the dialogic feedback process.

From our observations, we inferred that the primary audience for the crit was the student presenter, and the secondary audience comprised the other students who had an opportunity to tune in to the architectural discourse. In other words, in addition to learning from the specific feedback on their own designs, students had the chance to develop some insights from the discussion of other students' designs. I term this 'public feedback' as it involves messages directed at the whole group.

To recap some of John's thinking, he sees the crit as allowing feedback to be focused on the students' intentions and what they are trying to achieve through their designs. This brings a personal nature to the feedback. In terms of being a provider of feedback, John saw himself taking on two different roles: as a coach and as a critic: 'In an individual review you are an adviser and then in the crit you try to distance yourself, take a more objective, detached stance and look at design work with a neutral stance from the outside.' He also made related distinctions between the micro and the macro in feedback. The micro is a more concrete, advisory kind of feedback in which the tutor makes suggestions about the student's design. The macro is a more abstract, more provocative kind of feedback in which the tutor raises wider issues, possibly of a generic nature.

John also reflected on some challenges and tensions in that some students express preferences for feedback which provides more concrete guidance: 'Sometimes the students are saying, "Tell me what I should do," and you have to resist that a little bit.' This resonates with the discussion near the end of Chapter 10, where teachers reported some student resistance to sustainable feedback practices. The skilful proponent of feedback for self-regulation often needs to resist the temptation to provide answers to students' questions that would increase their reliance on external feedback.

For John, a key teaching goal was to support students in learning how to critique and self-evaluate their own work. This is congruent with the argument articulated in Chapter 10 that a major purpose of feedback is to support students in self-regulating their work. Feedback at the process and self-regulation levels has the most potential for enhancing student learning (Hattie and Timperley, 2007).

Individualised feedback

I focus mainly on students' perceptions of feedback. We asked a number of students to comment on the usefulness of their individual desk or crit feedback. Yeung felt that the feedback he received consisted of two different aspects, both of which were useful:

> In the metaphysical aspect, John stated that design should make architecture professionals feel some freshness or surprise. I found this comment inspiring. In the concrete aspect, he suggested which walls should be made of transparent glass and which should be solid material.

Here, Yeung has expressed a similar conception to that of his teacher. He has articulated two levels of feedback: the metaphysical (or abstract, in John's terms) and the concrete.

When I asked him about the uptake of feedback, Yeung also made a distinction between feedback which promotes a minor adjustment of a design detail (e.g. making the walls transparent) and that which encourages a more fundamental change to the design. Ying also noted this distinction between micro and macro feedback: 'Some tutors are good at giving opinions on some specific details, such as what the windows should look like. John is good at giving suggestions at a macro level in terms of the holistic aspects of the design.' The fact that Ying was able to discern this difference in feedback style is indicative of an awareness of features of teacher feedback and its implications for her work – an aspect of student assessment literacy.

Laurence compared desk feedback with crits. He stated a preference for the regular, private feedback interaction with the tutor because 'This one-to-one feedback allows you to go into more depth and offers a chance to crystallise your views.' However, he also found the crit useful and commented on the feedback he received during it:

> As there are two critics, you are getting a fresh perspective. Your own tutor is already familiar with what you are working on, but the other one can give you a different viewpoint. Sometimes the two have similar views, particularly if there is a major problem . . . [but] they often have different thoughts.

From this, I infer that a potential advantage of the crit – over individual desk feedback – is that it exposes students to more than one view. However, students' perceptions were mixed on the benefits of receiving comments from two different tutors, and their reactions varied from case to case. Some students felt that, as 'the second tutor' was unfamiliar with their designs, their ability to provide useful feedback was limited. Others welcomed insights from an additional tutor because of the subjective nature of designs.

In the previous chapter, I emphasised the importance of acting on feedback. If students can articulate what they have learnt and how they are going to improve their work on the basis of the feedback, then that indicates engagement. Accordingly, I asked students what they had learnt and how they felt they could move forward from the feedback received during the crit. Laurence replied:

> What I learnt is the importance of reflecting critically. Sometimes you can't see the flaws and you need a third party to point them out. I had some tunnel vision and only considered certain aspects. The tutors pointed out, rightfully so, that I didn't consider other aspects. Now I will go and revise it.

I infer a number of points from this comment. First, the notion of reflecting critically reinforces the idea of the self-regulation function of feedback which I emphasised in Chapter 10. Second, as Laurence says he identified a flaw in his design as a direct result of the comments he received, he appears to have understood and acknowledged the value of the feedback he received. Third, he states his intention to act on the feedback in the process of building up his portfolio.

Both Ying and Yeung spoke of the complexity of acting on feedback.

> It is always good to know what the problems are in your design. However, I won't always do modifications accordingly because there will always be

some problems in your design, no matter how you modify it. If you fix one problem, then another more serious problem might arise, so you have to compromise.

(Ying)

A design has a close relationship with its context – i.e. the environment. Blind acceptance of the tutor's comments without relating to its context may cause problems.

(Yeung)

Ying appears to be developing her judgement over when to follow feedback and when to reject it, cognisant of the holistic nature of an architectural design in that a modification in one aspect often has implications for another. Yeung warns against accepting teachers' comments uncritically. Both of these students exhibit an ability to draw links between external feedback from the teacher and their own internal feedback to inform their work and progress.

These three students were all academically able and they seemed to use the tutor's comments to move their work forward in ways they found satisfying. They seemed to be striving to find their own path rather than just following the comments from the tutor. For example, Laurence talked of trying to achieve 'conceptual clarity' and Yeung wanted to 'work out a programme' by himself. Ying spoke of an awareness of when to follow feedback and when it might be wiser not to act on it in view of the holistic nature of the design. I inferred that a commonality amongst these three students was the development of their ability to judge their work and make sound architectural decisions which made sense to them.

Laurence also did not wish his autonomy and self-development to be constrained by grades. When I asked about his academic performance in the first semester, he commented on the relationship between grading, feedback and his beliefs:

The letter grade I got for the first semester is available to me but I have decided not to look at it. The process is the most important feedback; a letter grade is less helpful . . . I am looking for what I believe is right.

This comment surprised me as it contradicts the common belief that grades are a major focus of student interest. Laurence seems to be saying that feedback in the form of a grade may act as a distraction. There is some discussion of this in the literature: for example, Lipnevich and Smith (2009) found that the highest-performing group in an experimental study of college students was the one that received detailed feedback but no grade and no praise, and concluded that such feedback focuses students on the work rather than on themselves (see also Hattie and Timperley, 2007). Grades may reduce self-efficacy and induce negative affect in relation to a task, including positive grades, which may engender a sense of complacency.

Wider public feedback

A further aspect of crit feedback which I touched on in Chapter 9 is that the presence of other teachers and students introduces a public element so that it is not just a single student who has an opportunity to gain from the discussion. Of relevance to the theory and practice of feedback is the extent to which students may learn from public feedback comments or analysis which relate not to their work, but to that of their classmates. In Architecture, this takes the form of feedback on a particular student's work which is also intended to have collective relevance. In our interviews with students, we raised the issue of the extent to which the audience members could develop insight from public feedback. One student admitted:

> We find it difficult to understand the teachers' feedback sometimes because they may say things which are quite deep and we may only come to understand it one day in the future. It is still useful if we come to understand them gradually.

Some rich feedback may be of a complex nature that can be interpreted only at a later date. Student satisfaction surveys that assess feedback perceptions at a given point in time may not tap into this kind of slow, gradual, incremental learning. It may take longer for students to absorb deeper feedback. This is part of the invisibility of feedback, but that does not mean it has no value over the longer term.

Yeung commented on the group experience of listening to crits:

> I am interested in observing the other crits to see how the tutors evaluate designs. If one learns how to evaluate others' works, it is helpful for gaining clarity of thinking. Sometimes the tutors make useful general comments, such as one should not be too prescriptive in relation to design.

From this, I infer that Yeung sees value in the crit in terms of gaining access to the thoughts and analysis of the teacher. He actively observed the crits of many other students and told us that he sometimes formed his own view of the design being presented, and then compared and contrasted his critique with that of the jury.

Implications of the Architecture case

From my perspective as a first-time observer of the study of Architecture, it seemed that the students had abundant opportunities to receive feedback on work in progress. The open nature of the studio, with designs and drawings visible, and the frequent interactions between participants also seemed to facilitate dialogic forms of feedback, including spontaneous peer feedback.

A teacher has a small group of around a dozen students in a tutor group, so there is sufficient time and resources to provide feedback on draft designs. The disciplinary atmosphere of diligence and commitment also seems to encourage dialogic feedback, facilitated by the relationships of trust built up between tutors and students, and between the students themselves. These productive relationships seemed helpful in smoothing the feedback process and reducing potential anxiety in the crits.

John focused on the dialogic, dynamic nature of feedback, which should be guided by student interest. For him, effective feedback involves looking at a design process and seeing it differently, casting new light on a design project. In the previous chapter I stressed the importance of student uptake of feedback. Whilst holding to that principle, a further lesson I learnt from this case was that feedback can be more than the provision of advice that students should act upon when it opens up new ways of looking at things. This resonates with the work of McLean et al. (2014) in relation to a conception of feedback as opening up a different perspective. This could be provocative or even puzzling for students, creating potential anxiety in similar ways to what Barnett (2007a) calls venturing into new and strange places. Sometimes this might even contribute to student dissatisfaction with feedback in end-of-course surveys when they are challenged by the feedback but it does not meet their current psychological needs or preferences.

The dual private and public aspects of design crits imply that the processes should serve not only to provide individual feedback but also to raise generic issues which might induct students into the discourse of the discipline. As indicated by the students, one-to-one individual consultations tended to be more effective as direct advice, whereas the crit brought further issues into play: students gained experience in explaining and justifying their designs in public; they were exposed to pressure, anxiety, relief and satisfaction from presenting and receiving criticism; they had to handle their emotions; and they had the potential to gain insight from comments on other students' work. As discussed in Chapter 9, key generic messages from crits could be more explicitly signalled or summarised.

There are also other feedback possibilities. Students could be required to evaluate their own work in writing before and after the crit. This would allow them to identify how the crit feedback had informed their view and possibly mean they took even greater ownership of the process (Orr et al., 2007). Students could also be more actively involved in identifying the kinds of feedback they were seeking most (Parnell and Sara, 2007). This would bring an additional layer of dialogue into the crit in an analogous way to the strategy in a conventional written assignment of students stating what kind of feedback they would most like to receive.

The implications for other subjects of the processes in Architecture are to create opportunities for students to share work in progress, gain practice in presenting disciplinary ideas, and receive feedback from other participants. This seems relatively easy to envisage in applied subjects, such as Engineering and Business, but it could be encouraged in other disciplines, too. Raising students' estimations of their peers' expertise and their teachers' worth as professional role models is important when attempting to facilitate such processes (Schrand and Eliason, 2012).

More attention could be paid to strategies to promote iterative cycles of work which duplicate the uptake of feedback in Architecture. For example, students could submit their 'final' version of an assignment (worth, say, 80 per cent of the mark), receive feedback, and then revise and resubmit the assignment after taking the feedback into account (with this second submission worth, say, 20 per cent of the mark) (see Court, 2014). They could state in their revised submission how they interpreted the feedback and what they did to address it. Whilst such procedures would entail some additional workload, they might be useful in building students' commitment to engaging with feedback.

Feedback in the History case

I asked David what he saw as the principles of effective feedback: 'First of all, I think it should be timely feedback. As far as possible, I think proximity to the learning activity just being assessed is essential, because it's still fresh in students' minds.' As for the content of feedback, he continued:

> I really try to give them feedback which is comprehensible so that they pick up on what they need to do better. A lot of the time we see feedback saying 'This is good because you did this', but I think it is more valuable to show them how they could improve. So when I give feedback, I always try to address how they could achieve a better grade. That's a principle I apply across all my assessments.

In relation to dialogic forms of feedback, David used two main strategies. The first was the task design aspect of requiring a draft (with a weighting of 10 per cent) for the project so that there was some form of written and/or verbal interaction from the outset. He commented: 'The draft is an opportunity for students to showcase their understanding of the question and the intention to move in the right direction.' As they are first-years, he uses comments on the drafts as a means of guiding students in an appropriate direction and providing some suggestions on academic writing and presentation. He explained that the students submitted their drafts on Friday and he provided comments for all 110 of them by Sunday night. Clearly, then, he was acting on the principle of timeliness and demonstrating considerable commitment to providing prompt feedback.

His other strategy was to set up a Facebook group for the students. He encouraged them to post work in progress and provide peer feedback for one another. Some students were very active participants, whereas others were less enthusiastic. An advantage of Facebook, as opposed to Moodle, is that it is more attractive to students and something they are likely to access frequently. Its use in the course also positioned David as an up-to-date teacher and aligned with students' interests and lifestyles. Students also commented positively on his timely feedback and his promptness in replying to queries they posted on Facebook or sent by email.

David devised a simple feedback sheet using three headings, as shown in Box 11.1, with emphasis on the third component of how the student might improve. Dividing the comments under three separate headings seems helpful in signposting the main areas of commentary and easing student comprehension. This seems compatible with the point made by Willingham (1990) that feedback should be signposted and students should be able to see a hierarchy of importance in written comments.

Box 11.1 David's feedback sheet

- Comment – overall appraisal.
- Strengths – what is done well.
- For a higher grade you would have needed to . . .

With the third element of this feedback sheet, David is trying to explain how students could have performed better. In line with his pragmatic view that students tend to focus on grades, he phrases it in terms of what needs to be done to achieve a higher grade. However, it would be equally valid to focus on what students need to do to produce higher-quality work. And it might be even better to focus on generic issues that are applicable not just to this particular assignment but future ones. The third heading on the feedback sheet might then read: 'To achieve higher grades in future assignments, you might consider the following points'.

David's comments on how Shan's fieldwork report could have been improved are presented in Box 11.2.

These quite comprehensive comments are illustrative of David's diligence and professional commitment in providing feedback comments that will be helpful to students. They are also closely aligned with his stated expectations (see Box 8.3).

When asked to reflect on doing the fieldwork assignment and receiving feedback on it, Shan responded:

> Although I did not do particularly well in the museum report [62 per cent, B minus, which equates to lower second-class honours], I have some suggestions to improve it. First, photos of the museum could be included because pictures can sometimes elaborate better than words. Second, as he suggested, I could cite source materials like artefact numbers to support the argument and show the evidence. Thirdly, I could use subheadings to show a clearer structure and organisation.

Box 11.2 Sample feedback commentary

For a higher grade you would have needed to ...

- Demonstrate a more critical and less descriptive approach to the historical 'artefacts' examined. It is hard to get a sense that you visited the museum. Where are the references to what you observed? It is hard to discern a main argument, too narrative in its approach for a high grade.
- Demonstrate more effective use of evidence in support of your arguments: for example, you could have cited more clearly the specific artefacts (location, number, etc.) that provide evidence for your claims.
- Your analysis of the interconnections between past and present – how the museum space is organised (both its internal spaces and how it is set in its environment) – could have linked content more clearly to the issue of why the museum looks like it does.
- You might have explained more fully your views of what overall aim the museum curators might have had in putting the objects on display together, in the way that they did.

Shan's first two points relate to what Chetwynd and Dobbyn (2011) referred to as 'retrospective on content' comments, whereas his third is similar to 'future-altering on skills' comments, which in Chapter 10 I suggested are likely to be more useful. A further way to extend this feedback practice would be to require students to compose some kind of short response to David's feedback by restating how they would use it to inform future work. This strategy could play a role in closing the feedback loop and reinforcing the dialogic nature of the process.

My preconception prior to the research was that award-winning teachers might be inclined to be relatively generous in grading, and that this might contribute to their popularity. My general impression, however, was that David was not a particularly lenient marker: Shan, for example, seemed to be quite a good student, yet he was awarded only a B minus for the fieldwork. David charted some changes in his grading practices:

> I certainly don't see myself as a pushover, but I have reappraised my approach to using higher grades. Previously, A plus was something I would reserve for maybe one or two students, and I hesitated to award it to any first-year student. I had something of a relative interpretation. Now, if the work has convincingly demonstrated achievement of the outcomes, then why not award an A plus even to first-year students.

There seems to be a hint of moving away from an approach to grading based on normative lines to a more criterion- or standards-based approach and an increased willingness to offer grades at the top end of the scale.

Indeed, Juliet's project on time-travel fiction was awarded an A plus. She commented on David's appraisal of her draft as follows:

> He provided me with some useful critical advice, such as doing more comparison with other important historical time-travel novels. He suggested I look more into the historical background of their popularity and the social conditions of that time. The feedback is useful and I can remember it well because I built all his feedback into my final paper.

Clearly, this was a positive experience for the student and seemed to entail some productive dialogue between herself and David. Juliet revealed that her paper became very long and, with David's consent, she eventually wrote 6000 words rather than the guideline of 3000. There is some resonance here with the issue of fairness raised by Flint and Johnson (2011) and discussed in Chapter 1. Students in that study complained of a lack of fairness when word guidelines were not adhered to consistently by all students. In this case, it may not have occurred to all students, especially the less cue-conscious ones, that they could have negotiated an extended word limit if required.

Juliet also mentioned the feedback on her fieldwork report which suggested that she could have provided a more detailed description of her museum visit and more in-depth comments. She expressed the view that these comments were reasonable and congruent with her own reflections, and felt that the awarded grade of B plus was in line with her expectations. It was noticeable that she remembered the feedback clearly and seemed to have internalised its messages. The fact that she could quote the feedback almost verbatim on an assignment that had been marked six weeks earlier indicated strong engagement with its messages and perhaps Juliet's own high motivation. Previous studies have noted that high-achieving students are often well equipped to understand and act on feedback (see Orsmond and Merry, 2013).

We asked Juliet if the feedback she received from David could be applied to other courses. Her response was somewhat surprising:

> I never thought of applying a tutor's advice to other assignments. Thank you for reminding me of that possibility; I will consider that. I think sometimes it is possible, especially with those skills and requirements for academic research. I suppose they can be applied to other courses, but I have never tried that before.

So, although Juliet was skilful at using feedback to improve a specific assignment, she had not considered transferring feedback to other work. Whilst this is only a single response, it does resonate with some of the general challenges for feedback discussed in the previous chapter: the difficulty of using feedback on one course to inform work with another teacher on a different course; and students needing to have such processes modelled for them. Juliet is a diligent and high-achieving student, yet it had not occurred to her to generalise feedback from one course to another. Given that, it is hardly surprising that many students do not perceive end-of-semester tutor feedback to be particularly useful. Her comment also reinforces potential mismatches between tutor and student perceptions of feedback (see Adcroft, 2011), because one would assume that tutors hope students can absorb general messages from feedback for wider application across courses.

Turning from a high-achieving student to a low-achieving one, in Chapter 8 I described Geoff as cue-deaf. He earned a B minus for his museum report and showed us some of the comments he received. These are reproduced in Box 11.3.

Box 11.3 Extract from feedback comments

Demonstrate more effective use of evidence in support of your arguments . . .

You could have cited more clearly the specific artefacts . . . too narrative in its approach.

Geoff was confused by some of these comments: 'Actually, I don't understand the feedback. He said it is too narrative but he also seems to want more evidence or details, which I feel are quite conflicting.' Nevertheless, when it came to his project, Geoff tried to make it less narrative, in accordance with David's final comment. He also asked Connie, the teaching assistant, to have a look at his revised draft and told us that she thought it was okay. Hence, he was disappointed when he received a C grade. Having told us that David criticised the lack of details in his essay, Geoff said:

> If I had known that he wanted the details, I should have submitted the first draft . . . But I am confused about the criteria now. My first draft has many details but it's too narrative to be like an essay. I followed the advice to revise it and made it more like an essay, but the teacher said it lacked details! It's a paradox.

Geoff had difficulty interpreting the kind of cryptic academic discourse which was noted in the previous chapter as an inevitable feature of teacher-written comments on assignments. The external feedback he received did not help him to regulate his work. When a student is externally rather than internally regulated it is hard for them to apply teachers' comments as they find it difficult to judge the quality of their implementation of advice. Under these circumstances, feedback risks becoming frustrating and there is a danger that its interpretation might be counterproductive. Overall, the comments Geoff received did not connect with him or cater for his particular needs. As was mentioned above, he was initially disappointed with the C grade; but later, when he was awarded a D for another course (English for Academic Purposes), he revised his opinion somewhat.

David's comments to Shan and Geoff implied that their approaches were too narrative. If we revisit the guidance for this task presented in Box 8.3, it was emphasised that good performance should go beyond being a descriptive account and present critical analysis and engagement. It seems that some students found this challenging and may have needed more guidance or exemplification of this aspect of the task.

Nicole received a B minus for her museum report and a C for her project. She was rather disappointed with both. As far as the tutor feedback was concerned, she agreed with some points, was less convinced by others, and felt some were unclear. We asked her if she had sought clarification of the points she did not understand:

> I am not that kind of student; I don't really challenge the teachers. He gives me the feedback; I just receive it . . . I don't see where I am not satisfactory, so I need some detailed feedback on which parts are not so good. He said that the general points are not enough, but what is 'enough'? I don't know.

I infer that Nicole is unclear about the feedback but is not particularly driven to engage any further with it or initiate additional dialogue with the teacher. Her feelings of puzzlement resonate with those expressed by Geoff.

Implications of the History case

I was positive about David's feedback sheet (Box 11.1), in that organising comments under sub-themes seems helpful and he recognises students' pragmatism by providing suggestions as to how they might obtain higher grades. This kind of feedback is probably most effective when there are linkages between assignments so that students can build on comments from one assignment to the next; or when explicit generic elements are highlighted which could be relevant to later assignments (analogous to future-altering on skills comments). David's enthusiasm and commitment were also evident in his feedback practices and the effort he invested in providing timely and engaging comments. These practices are labour-intensive, which suggests a certain lack of sustainability, but this might be mitigated by further efforts at promoting peer collaboration and student self-evaluation.

A further inference from these data was that the weaker the student is, the less likely they are to be satisfied with feedback. Both Geoff and Nicole had difficulty interpreting the feedback, received relatively low grades, and so felt somewhat dissatisfied. They seemed to need more support to make a successful transition from school to university modes of working. Finding it hard to understand what the teacher means and receiving a low grade may challenge their sense of self-efficacy and lead to dissatisfaction or frustration. Perhaps this kind of scenario is a contributory factor to the low ratings feedback often receives in institutional surveys. Another possibility is that the old paradigm of feedback as comments is probably not particularly well suited to the needs of students who are less familiar with academic literacies and the conceptions of quality assumed by their tutors.

To what extent will the new paradigm of feedback as dialogic interaction prove more helpful? As I suggested in the previous chapter, drawing on Orsmond and Merry (2013), perhaps lower-achieving students might be aided by peer discussion around exemplars as well as systematic guidance and training in the development of self-assessment skills.

Feedback in the Law case

Rick believes that one of the main principles of feedback is that it is most powerful when the action on it carries some assessment weight. To my mind, this equates with there being real consequences and motivation for students to act on feedback. Rick expects his students to act on the feedback they have received on one task when they come to work on their next assessed problem.

His signature feedback strategy is 'same-day feedback' (which he also calls 'real-time feedback') – immediate follow-up to tutorial, test or examination questions. At the end of an exam or test, students are invited to remain on a voluntary basis to discuss the answers to the questions they have just attempted. This process is carried out either verbally or online due to pragmatic factors, such as whether students need to attend another class, or whether the room is still available. Rick prefers verbal discussion due to its interactive nature, but acknowledges that online discussion is often more feasible and can allow students to make more powerful, reasoned arguments. An early version of the same-day feedback strategy (Glofcheski, 2006) illustrates how Rick refines his learning-oriented assessment practices over time.

Rick explains the rationale as follows:

> In same-day feedback, the assessment question is the subject of class and/or online discussion immediately following the assessment. This allows students to engage in discussion of the assessment problem, clear up misconceptions and reinforce good learning when their focus is greatest. The immediacy of the feedback overcomes a major obstacle to learning, delayed typically ignored feedback, by providing feedback in a way and at a time when it can be absorbed and applied. A key principle is that the timing of feedback should be as close to the point of submission as possible.
>
> (Carless, 2014, p. 11)

This explains how Rick seeks to tackle the challenge of students failing to engage with conventional feedback, which often comes several weeks after a task has been submitted. The discussion which ensues also brings elements of dialogue into the feedback process. As a form of post-task feedback, the teacher commentary comes after the task has been completed but carries the potential to feed forward to a future task. For example, feedback on the mid-term test can benefit student learning and performance in the final examination.

Rick suggests a further rationale:

> The discussion often uncovers aspects of the question not considered in the marking rubric. This is not surprising, given that legal problems are by nature complex and open-ended. So students are expressly encouraged to critique the arguments and offer alternative ones which, if adequately supported by cogent legal analysis, will be included in the marking rubric.
>
> (Carless, 2014, p. 11)

He also talked of the co-construction of answers bringing a collaborative dimension to the assessment process:

> The collaboratively agreed solution is posted on the LMS so that students can continue to gauge their progress and build on their learning experience as they proceed to the next learning activity. This collaborative assessment gives students a sense of ownership, whilst also acknowledging the indeterminacy of legal enquiry and the creative possibilities of legal argument.

We wondered how Rick's students responded to same-day feedback. Two of them offered their opinions of the process:

> If you do the reflection immediately after the test or exam, then you will be able to understand and apply standards in the context, you know how they really work for this kind of question.
>
> I really appreciate it, and especially did when I was in the first year, because I didn't know how to write the answer for a Law exam. It is a rare and valuable chance for me to know more about the standards or the requirements.

Both of these students mention standards and suggest that the post-exam feedback clarifies them. For the first student, the discussion of the problem provides a context to apply and evaluate knowledge; and when the second student was a freshman, it provided valuable guidance in tailoring her answers to meet university standards.

Other students commented on the immediacy of the feedback:

> I like the immediate feedback, because the memory is fresh in my mind and I can remember all the details.

> Feedback sessions allow me to rectify my errors immediately before the wrong concept becomes rooted in my mind.
>
> This can really help us to clarify any misunderstanding or ambiguities while it is still fresh in our minds.

There were other benefits, too:

> I became aware of the depth of other students' answers; it is always good to know how other students think.
>
> It allows us to participate in developing the marking scheme. If some students have thought of some creative points that the tutors haven't thought of, if you can make a good case, you can help shape the marking scheme.

This final point is significant in terms of its potential for student empowerment in the assessment process and a related positive impact on motivation. Many students expressed appreciation of the possibility of contributing to the shaping or refinement of the marking scheme.

Overall, I infer that students are generally positive about the immediacy of the teacher feedback and its potential to inform the marking scheme. However, a few negative feelings were expressed:

> I felt awful because I missed a lot of points in my answers, but I really appreciate this kind of interactive learning.
>
> It feels a bit like a heart attack because you find out immediately about your answers.

These last two students highlight the potential emotional impact of hearing you have done badly. Some students admitted that they preferred not to attend the feedback sessions because they were worried about the additional stress of hearing precisely where they had gone wrong. As they were in the middle of an exam period, they were worried that this might affect their future performance. This re-emphasises the tension between the risk of critical feedback discouraging students and anodyne forms of feedback failing to challenge them sufficiently.

An unanticipated outcome of same-day feedback was that, due to its popularity with students, they requested other teachers in the Law Faculty to adopt similar strategies. In this way, the good practice of an award-winning teacher generated some pressure or momentum for other teachers to follow suit. Of course, some of Rick's colleagues may not have welcomed this pressure to adapt their own feedback strategies.

In sum, same-day feedback illustrates the possibilities of promoting student engagement with feedback through immediate, timely dialogue. A salient feature is the immediacy of the input, and this focus on timeliness resonates with David's approach. Even more significant is that students express the rationale for their answers and through dialogue with the teacher contribute to the potential reshaping of the marking scheme. This reinforces the point made by Torrance (2012) about the contingent nature of criteria and how they may be reappraised in light of how quality is evidenced in a particular case.

Some limitations of same-day feedback are also evident. Although some dialogue is built into the process, it is likely that the teacher's voice will dominate the verbal discussion due to time constraints and other factors. However, this is balanced by the extended opportunities for students to voice their views and present their arguments online. The immediacy is generally positive, although not all students are prepared for the potential emotional challenge of learning that they have not performed well within minutes of finishing a test.

Feedback in the Geology case

The main focus of the Geology case was in relation to assessment of a group project, as discussed in Chapter 6. The implications for feedback of this case were relatively limited, so this section is brief. However, it is included to illustrate a few salient points.

One of the enhancements to assessment practice in the implementation of the class we observed was to require students to submit a short draft of the topic, with the teachers then providing some brief feedback. Chan's rationale was to support the students in grasping the main purpose of the group project. He reported that a few groups had problems in focusing their projects appropriately, so he asked them to re-submit their outlines until he felt confident that they were developing in the right direction. From our interviews with students, it seemed that the feedback was most pertinent for them when they had been heading down the wrong track.

Two quotations from students exploring mass extinction illustrate the overall student response to the teachers' brief feedback on their outlines. Penny commented:

> The teacher just wrote a sentence which reminded us to integrate what we've learnt in this course in our project. It's succinct and useful. At the start, we approached the sixth mass extinction topic from a human activities or biological [perspective]. It was the teacher's feedback that reminded us to think from the perspective of geology. The feedback redirected us to the right track.

Wan also engaged with the feedback, but she expressed some difficulties in following it:

> I keep thinking about the suggestion to include geological content in the project. I wonder to what extent we can fulfil the requirement because the geology of the earth, such as the rock types, weathering, erosion processes, has very little impact on the mass extinction.

So the timely feedback seemed to be helpful in reminding the students that they were studying a Geology course, and that its concepts should be central to their work. From the limited evidence we collected, this was an indication of the usefulness of the minor change of introducing timely feedback into the process, and overall it seemed to be successful. Perhaps the conciseness, simplicity and clarity of the feedback were facilitating factors. Focusing feedback on the most important elements is also crucial (see Willingham, 1990).

Feedback, in the form of comments from professors and the teaching assistants, was also provided after the students' oral presentations. There was generally little time for interaction, but in one of the classes a teacher raised a number of critical comments about the presentations. Our perception was that these critiques were valuable and could be used to inform the students' subsequent written assignments. Although some students acknowledged that this was useful, several felt the challenging nature of the questions would make them nervous, so they did not welcome this type of feedback. This relates to the issue of student emotional response to assessment that was raised in Chapter 2. It may be that some students are more interested in saving face rather than receiving insightful critique. To some extent, this might be a universal issue; but it could be somewhat more significant in a Chinese context. Either way, issues relating to hard-hitting as opposed to more encouraging feedback merit further consideration in feedback research (see Molloy et al., 2013). I would speculate that more competent and confident students with greater intensity of grade-related desire will be more likely to welcome critical feedback.

Feedback in the Business case

In-class dialogic feedback was a particular feature of the Business case: instead of coming at the end of a cycle, feedback was firmly embedded within regular classroom interactions. Ali expected and demanded a high degree of student participation in his classes and this facilitated processes of dialogic feedback. For example, he used a variety of strategies during in-class interaction. He would sometimes praise students and encourage them to elaborate on an argument. On other occasions, he would interrupt students and ask them to get to the point or rephrase their ideas more concisely. Sometimes he would invite students to refocus their comments in different ways to address a particular issue. In these ways, he provided verbal feedback on multiple aspects of the course, including learning processes, the quality of ideas and thinking, and modes of communication. His practices resonate with a focus on the interrogative in that statements in academic life are invariably susceptible to questioning from other parties (Barnett, 2007b).

He also provided conventional feedback on assignment work in progress. So, in the Creativity and Business Innovation course, when students were generating socially innovative ideas, discussions with Ali sometimes led to a consensus that a concept was unfeasible. In such cases, students would go away and reformulate their proposal. Hence, timely comments prompted student action in ways that were analogous to the Geology case above.

Ali often focused on discussing learning strategies and learning to learn, which he believes is the essence of university education. He placed less emphasis on transmitting knowledge or teaching content, which he feels can be accessed easily online; and in the discipline of Business, many ideas become outdated relatively quickly. Most of his students appreciated this focus on learning how to learn, rather than on the delivery of content, although some questioned the balance between process and content.

A further means by which Ali promoted dialogue in his classes was through assessment design: 30–40 per cent of the grade for his classes arises from class-room participation. (A possible variation would be to provide interim feedback on their performance.) Peer feedback also arose through the collaboration around oral presentations and written interaction through the course blog.

Ali also explicitly sought to develop student self-evaluative capacities. One of the ways he does this (discussed in Carless, 2013a) is through videoing student oral presentations, replaying short extracts immediately afterwards, then inviting students to self-evaluate and reflect on how their presentations could be improved. After the student has self-evaluated their performance, Ali engineers a further reflective discussion in order to illuminate the characteristics of good business presentations. This kind of activity is facilitated by the development of an open classroom climate and trusting relationships between participants (see Carless, 2013b).

Another way of engineering productive feedback processes was through more conventional organisation of written reports to follow oral presentations. Ali explained: 'After the oral presentation, they have one more week to submit the project in written form. I want them to improve after the feedback by thinking back to the questions raised about their presentation.'

Dialogue in Ali's teaching was central to bringing students' voices into the classroom and prompting engagement with feedback messages. Students were welcome to voice their own thoughts and challenge the teacher's ideas. I conclude this brief discussion with one student's view, which encapsulates several key aspects of Ali's feedback practices:

> Sometimes his feedback is like a catalyst to promote the process, to direct the discussion from one student to another. Often he was challenging people to think more. He will ask the same student many 'why' questions. It is feedback showing that the teacher is interested in your answer and wants to explore your answer more.
>
> (Carless, 2013b, p. 97)

Implicit in this comment are relational issues in terms of the teacher showing genuine interest in the thoughts of students and commitment to entering into dialogic interaction.

Concluding implications

The teaching in Architecture is structured to encourage the uptake of feedback, whereas in the other cases the teaching processes often need some restructuring to facilitate promising feedback processes. John shifted along the continuum between conventional forms of feedback (when acting as a coach and commenting on students' work) and potentially more sustainable processes (when he acted as a critic). When he was more like a critic, he often raised issues at the macro level for students to reflect on and self-evaluate their progress over time. The essence of this form of feedback was to involve students in questioning and dialogue focused on developing their sense of quality in architectural design. To some extent, this relates to disciplinary norms of interaction; other aspects were the small class size and the intensive interaction between participants.

Ali similarly exploited the small class sizes to generate feedback processes with a sustainable emphasis. In his teaching, questioning, dialogue and the development of student self-evaluative capacities took centre-stage. The Business case was significant in showcasing a way of thinking that resonates with the new paradigm of feedback discussed in Chapter 10. Feedback was embedded within classroom activities; it was interactive and interrogative in nature; it sought to clarify expectations for quality work; and it was an element of task design, including the assessment of participation.

The History, Law and Geology cases all featured useful feedback practices which I place near the conventional end of the feedback continuum in that explicit efforts to develop student self-regulation were less evident. David, in History, enthusiastically provided prompt, detailed comments with a particular focus on advising students what they needed to do to achieve a higher grade. Similarly, in Law, Rick focused on timeliness, a key issue in feedback, according to our student informants. His same-day feedback was probably the most innovative practice as it turned around the traditional summative event of an examination to develop timely dialogue. This form of immediate response may be particularly attractive to the internet generation of students, who expect immediacy and interactivity (see Scott, 2014). Chan added a useful feedback layer in the early stages of the Geology group project so that students could receive timely feedback to facilitate a sound basis for their work.

Peer feedback was apparent in various forms in most of the cases. There was peer collaboration in the open-plan studio in Architecture, and peer feedback facilitated by sharing on Facebook in History. In Geology and Business, peer learning mainly focused on the processes of working in teams towards assessed group tasks. There was also a modest amount of technology-enhanced feedback. Notable elements were Ali's use of video to promote self-reflection on oral presentations, his use of an assessed blog to promote dialogue, and David's use of Facebook for peer collaboration and dialogue. The potential and challenges of using Facebook for educational rather than social purposes is generating considerable research interest (e.g. Hew, 2011).

In sum, these five cases have provided some concrete examples of how students can be stimulated to engage with feedback in different subjects. It might also be useful to explore feedback across disciplines further: is there the potential for more interdisciplinary cross-fertilisation of feedback ideas and practices?

Summary of chapter

This chapter has explored the feedback practices of the five case-study teachers. It has focused primarily on the Architecture case because dialogic feedback around architectural design issues was a fundamental part of the pedagogy in that course. The History, Law and Geology cases all showcased different aspects of timeliness in feedback. Finally, the Business case illustrates some possibilities for dialogic and sustainable feedback strategies.

Main implications for practice

- The development of student self-evaluative capacities is at the heart of good feedback practice.
- Feedback should be embedded within classroom processes and considered as an aspect of assessment task design.
- Dialogic feedback can be effective at clarifying student expectations of quality work.
- Interactive and timely feedback is most likely to engage students.

Chapter 12

Conclusions and ways forward for learning-oriented assessment

One of the traps in arguing for a shift in assessment practice is to propose an unrealistic ideal that can never be attained.

(Boud, 2000, p. 159)

Scope of chapter

In this final chapter, I sum up some key messages by reviewing some of the main implications for learning-oriented assessment in the cases. Some of the challenges and competing priorities from Chapter 1 are revisited and some possible ways forward are suggested. I discuss some possible strategies for implementing assessment change effectively, sum up the vision of excellence in assessment, and conclude with a consolidated list of main implications for practice.

Key messages for learning-oriented assessment

First, I discuss in some detail the implications of the cases for assessment task design – the key, overarching element of the learning-oriented assessment framework.

Assessment task design and implementation

A major contribution of this book has been to provide in-depth analysis of learning-oriented assessment practices in the context of different disciplines. What has emerged from the cases is that there are subject-specific differences and norms which impact on how assessment is carried out. There is also evidence that assessment often does not seem to follow a disciplinary signature, which suggests that there is plenty of scope for cross-fertilisation across cases and disciplines.

Modes of assessment

The main modes of assessment in the cases are presented in Table 12.1. A common assessment mode was an extended written piece of work in the form of an essay, case report or project report. This featured in four of the cases. With the

Table 12.1 Modes of assessment in the cases

	Business	History	Geology	Architecture	Law
Essay/report	Yes	Yes	Yes	No	Yes
Examination	No	No	Yes	No	Yes
Group project	Yes	No (although it is an option)	Yes	No	No (although it is an option)
Assessed participation	Yes	Yes	No	To some extent (implicitly)	No
Oral presentation	Yes	No	Yes	Yes (implicitly)	Tort Law, No; Labour Law, Yes
Portfolio	No	No	No	Yes	Yes (RMD)
Other		Fieldwork report	Lab work		Photo essay

exception of Chan (who teaches a hard-science discipline), the teachers seemed largely negative about exams, which featured in just two subjects, and reluctantly so in Rick's (Law) case. Group projects were emphasised in Business and Geology, and were a minor option in History and Law. There was also a focus on oral modes of communication by means of a participation grade (Business and History) and assessed oral presentations (Business, Geology and – implicitly – Architecture). There was an assessed oral presentation in Labour Law but not in Tort Law (due to the large class size). Portfolio-like assessment was a feature of Architecture and in the two Law courses (through RMD).

Given that the teachers were award-winners and popular with their students, it was not unexpected that these modes of assessment practice generally met with approval. With respect to the six main methods of assessment highlighted in Table 12.1, only examinations engendered more critical than positive comment, generally because they were seen as failing to lead to productive learning experiences. The students had mixed feelings about group projects, while the other four assessment methods were generally viewed positively.

As Table 12.1 indicates, students were exposed to a variety of assessment tasks and modes of performance. Our data suggested that students were positively inclined towards variety in that it permitted them to showcase different abilities and was more interesting than repeatedly doing similar kinds of task, such as examinations, that had dominated their school lives. The advantage of variety lies in its potential to cater for different strengths of students, with respect to written and verbal communication, individual and more collaborative skills, and use of technology. A potential disadvantage of variety is that students take time to understand the requirements of different tasks and so some students may be better served by familiarising themselves with a smaller number of modes of assessment (see Gibbs and Dunbar-Goddet, 2009). A clear picture did not emerge from the data but my view is that, for the less cue-conscious students, variety of assessment could result in difficulties in understanding and implementing what is required.

The tasks were well designed, meaningful and the main trend was three interlinked tasks for the module assessment, with the exception of the Architecture case, which was a cumulative portfolio. Multiple relatively small tasks facilitate regular student effort and involvement over the whole period of a course, may support students in managing their workload steadily, and permit variety, as discussed above. Is there a danger of multiple small tasks becoming bitty and piecemeal? Is there a risk of over-assessment? Small tasks seem most beneficial when they link in some way or when they build on each other. These important issues of integration and coherence are discussed further in the next section.

Features of assessment task design

Table 12.2 depicts key features of assessment task design, building on the discussion in Chapter 3, in relation to the case studies. I make further comments about the five features on the left-hand side of the table in what follows.

There was plenty of evidence from the cases that the teachers were promoting ways of thinking and practising which mirrored real-life uses of the discipline: for example, the museum visit in History; and the designs for a Chinese village house in Architecture. Although the concept of authentic assessment is useful, I remain unconvinced about the appropriateness of the term itself in that few forms of assessment are genuinely authentic because students would rarely do them in the

Table 12.2 Features of assessment in the cases

	Business	History	Geology	Architecture	Law
Real-life participation in discipline	Yes	Yes	Yes, to some extent	Yes	Yes
Effort spread evenly	Yes	Yes	Yes	Yes	Yes
Student choice and personal investment	Yes	Yes	Yes, to some extent	Yes	Yes
Integrated and coherent	Yes, to some extent	Yes, to some extent	Yes, to some extent	Yes	Yes, to some extent
Dialogic feedback	Yes	To some extent	To some extent	Yes	To some extent

same format if they were not being assessed for certification purposes. Accordingly, I prefer to use the term 'assessment mirroring real-life uses of the discipline'.

Students engaged with particular disciplinary forms of discourse, values or ways of acting congruent with the WTP described by McCune and Hounsell (2005). Business and Architecture students used persuasive strategies to present the merits of their product ideas or design work in progress. History students discussed how the past is presented and its implications for the present. The evidence from the cases suggests that, in addition to more conventional written forms, authentic achievement of disciplinary understanding can emerge from verbal expression, such as oral presentations in Business and Geology, or even (to some extent) through shorter pieces of writing, such as OSR in History or blog contributions in Business. Whilst these shorter written contributions may not fully provide opportunities for extended disciplinary communication, in view of the shortened attention span of students in the digital age the value of concise written communication may be increasing.

The second feature of the cases from Table 12.2 was that student effort was spread evenly over the semester. For example, in Business there was continuous assessment of class participation; in Geology, there was regular lab work, a group project and a final examination which built on the lab work. Multiple relatively small tasks facilitated regular intellectual participation in activities which required students to express their views. All of this seems more than what Gibbs (2006) described as 'distributing effort' in that producing consistent intellectual engagement through various forms of disciplinary participation was both required and rewarded. In other words, the evidence from the cases extends the notion of spreading effort to indicate something of what that effort entails.

Student choice was also a feature of the cases and manifested itself in different ways. These included the assessment task itself; topics to select for a project; the mode of presentation of work; and the members of one's group. Choice can be a way of providing students with options to cater for their preferences or, perhaps more fundamentally, a means of generating some student ownership of the assessment process and encouraging agency in academic work. There are also some potential disadvantages of choice, however. When permitted to choose, students may opt for something relatively easy to achieve; or something similar to what they have done in the past. A further downside of choice would be if it allows students to sample only a small part of course content or if their choice does not relate well to the intended learning outcomes. Then again, students may develop powerful emergent learning outcomes and may perform better when they are encouraged to select a focus for their work. Choice and flexibility seemed to be largely positive in all of the cases, and especially in History. In the Law case, there was also some student choice over the weighting of the various assessment tasks, a novel feature that has not been widely discussed in the literature. It merits further consideration.

The fourth feature from Table 12.2 – integration and coherence – is probably the most difficult to achieve. I felt the Architecture portfolio was the most fully integrated task in that it brought together learning and work in a unified way over an extended period. In that case, there was coherence between the portfolio assessment task and the interplay between student self-evaluation and dialogic feedback stimulated by the processes of critical reviews of students' designs. In the other four cases, the teachers clearly had integration in mind when they conceptualised and designed the tasks. The lab tasks in Geology, for example, bore relationships with similar tasks in the examinations. RMD in Law involved the analysis of real-life cases from local newspapers, a skill that was also required in the exam. Similarly, in History, short written analyses in the fieldwork and OSR developed the skills needed for the longer written project.

This rehearsal and reiteration of skills carries the potential to promote linkages and student progress over time in analogous ways to the nested tasks proposed by Molloy and Boud (2013). From the point of view of some of the less competent students, however, assessments might appear to be discrete tasks assessing different competencies, rather than coherent and interlinked tasks. An implication is that it is important for teachers to communicate with students frequently about the rationale, sequencing and integration of tasks. Further research might explore potentially differing teacher and student perceptions of integration and coherence of assessment tasks.

The final feature of Table 12.2 – dialogic feedback – suggests that engineering student engagement with feedback is partly a task design issue. I discuss this further in the section on feedback below.

Assessing participation

One final issue in relation to modes of assessment is that a prominent feature of both the Business and History cases was the assessment of participation comprising 30–40 per cent of the overall course grade. Before collecting data for the study, I was somewhat dismissive of the assessment of participation because of the challenges inherent in awarding a fair and reliable grade: at its worst, assessing participation could be a reward merely for attendance or an attempt to control students and their behaviours. However, my observation of the Business and History cases evidenced a number of positive elements of assessing participation: students were actively involved; they were more likely to prepare before coming to class; they learnt to articulate their own views; and they participated in disciplinary dialogue with the teacher and their peers. From the History case, I infer that 'one-sentence response' is a strategy that is well suited to eliciting regular student participation within a large class and merits further exploration. From the two Business courses, I view some combination of in-class and online participation as representing a useful combination that caters for both oral and written modes of expression.

It is probably fair to say that research into the assessment of participation is not advancing rapidly or being afforded much attention. Grading participation is a contentious issue and it is a reasonable position to reject it outright on the grounds of its imprecision and the associated difficulties of achieving reliability that can be demonstrated and audited. Clearly, from a quality assurance perspective, assessing participation appears risky and/or untrustworthy. However, by returning to the competing priorities and the arguments for learning-oriented assessment presented at the outset of the book, a different position may emerge. Learning-oriented assessment is predicated on the development of processes which encourage student learning. A key inference from the cases is that assessing participation encourages student engagement and active learning methods. My overall judgement is that as long as it involves clearly defined contributions evaluated by well-designed criteria, the assessment of participation can form a useful part of an overall assessment design.

Recommendations for assessment task design

To sum up, the evidence from the cases suggests that good assessment tasks:

- involve students in WTP through mirroring real-life uses of the discipline;
- encourage student engagement and promote deep approaches to learning;
- spread effort evenly throughout the module through a series of tasks or a portfolio and/or by assessing participation;
- permit some degree of student choice and personal investment so that students can develop some ownership of learning;
- provide some degree of integration and coherence so that students can build on the skills they are developing; and
- engineer regular in-class feedback opportunities in relation to tasks and work in progress.

The development of evaluative expertise

For students to be able to produce good performance on assessment tasks, they need a developing sense of what good academic work looks like. This aspect of evaluative expertise manifested itself in different ways in the cases. It comes out particularly strongly in the Architecture case (Chapter 9) in that the signature pedagogy of crits acted as both a forum for understanding the nature of quality work and as a means of feedback on student work in progress. Through these processes, students seemed to learn how to be self-critical and to self-evaluate their work.

When students are able to use and apply insights from clear, concise and task-specific criteria, this might also support the development of their evaluative expertise. The evidence from the student data seemed to point to several reasons why students tended to have limited engagement with criteria: they often found them vague and similar to other sets of criteria they had seen; they sometimes inferred there were 'hidden criteria' supplementing the published ones; and, in any case, teachers interpreted criteria in different ways. A related inference is that students with greater intensity of grade-related desire are more likely to engage actively with criteria. There was little evidence of student involvement in generating criteria. This represents a missed opportunity.

Students in Law, Architecture and Business generally seemed better able to gauge cues and be on the same wavelength as their tutors than those in Geology and History. This may relate to various factors, including calibre of the students and their motivation, class size and the nature of classroom interaction, and other relational and interpersonal issues. Student informants suggested that samples of previous work helped them to understand expectations and the nature of good performance, and they were more useful than lists of criteria. Thoughtful application of insights from studying exemplars could enhance student evaluative expertise. I argued in Chapter 7 that dialogic use of exemplars is a particularly useful way of prompting student engagement with quality in the discipline.

The evidence from the cases illustrated various uses of exemplars. In History, David showed a student sample to try to clarify his expectations for the project, but student engagement was limited for various reasons (see Chapter 4). In Law, Rick posted exemplars on the LMS and students welcomed the opportunity to see them, but there was no classroom follow-up (see Chapter 5). My judgement is that these are not optimal modes of implementation. More fruitful, in my view, was the practice in Business, where oral presentations were videoed and analysed so that they became exemplars of performance (Chapter 6). Classroom discussion facilitated dialogue around the nature of good business presentations, and although this was relatively time-consuming, it allowed ideas on the nature of quality presentations to be aired.

Both oral presentations and crits are examples of 'on-display assignments' (Hounsell, 2003), in which work is openly evident to peers rather than just privately submitted to tutors. These provide opportunities for student appreciation of quality and associated development of evaluative expertise. In the Architecture case, the public display of architectural designs allowed students to engage with, discuss and learn from other students' work. Although there was little peer input during the formal, teacher-led crit sessions, peer interaction was particularly evident in the informal discussions around the displays during the final review process. These processes resonate with the notion of spontaneous collaborative learning (Tang, 1993). The extent to which peer feedback needs to be facilitated by the teacher within classroom time or arises spontaneously amongst students may vary across disciplines and even across classes. The balance between engineered and spontaneous peer feedback merits further exploration in relation to its potential to contribute to student development of evaluative expertise.

To sum up, good practice in the development of student evaluative expertise involves:

- promoting engagement with quality through students generating, analysing and applying criteria;

- providing opportunities for students to analyse and discuss exemplars;
- showcasing on-display assignments which provide fruitful opportunities for dialogue around quality;
- promoting different forms of peer dialogue and collaboration; and
- encouraging student responsibility in self-evaluating work in progress.

Student engagement with feedback

The nature, sequence and cumulativeness of tasks can open up opportunities for dialogic forms of feedback and promote the intertwining of feedback and instruction. When assessment task design involves the integration of nested tasks or revisiting work in progress, feedback is more engaging and interactive than when it comes after the completion of an assignment. This is particularly so when it is integrated with classroom activities. Viewing feedback as an element of task design reinforces the integrated nature of the learning-oriented assessment framework in terms of the interconnections between feedback, task design and evaluative expertise.

The Architecture case was a prime example of the integration of these three elements of learning-oriented assessment. The cumulative portfolio task encouraged engagement with feedback and the associated development of student evaluative expertise. Students were involved in iterative cycles of drafting and redrafting their designs, self-evaluation of their work in progress, and both individual desk feedback and public discussion through crits. These processes supported the students in engaging with the nature of quality in architectural design.

The new feedback paradigm was also evident in Business. In-class interactive questioning and dialogic feedback were firmly embedded within classroom processes and supplemented by online participation in the course blog. The assessment task design feature of assessed participation also indicated expectations and reward for involvement in dialogues around business issues. Oral presentations were a further feature of task design which promoted peer feedback and self-reflections relating to the nature of quality business presentations. The explicit focus on learning how to learn, including the development of student self-evaluative expertise, suggests that those forms of feedback which most encourage learner independence and autonomy carry most potential for sustainability.

In the large classes, there was also a variety of feedback strategies. Some of these were valuable conventional feedback strategies, such as the timely and detailed responses to History students, although these were highly labour-intensive. David also promoted iterative cycles of feedback and revision through awarding part of the grade for the first draft of the project work. This was the only case with an explicit grade allocation for drafts, although the development of work over time was implicit in the way students in the Architecture case reworked their designs over time, in the group project processes in Business and Geology, and in RMD in Law.

There were some other useful feedback practices: future-altering on skills feedback and scaffolding aimed at enhancing students' abilities to self-regulate their learning. Timeliness of feedback was notable in the way Rick engineered a reflective discussion immediately at the end of a conventional summative Law examination. This was also the main example of a technique which one could describe as innovative.

If used skilfully, technology carries considerable potential for encouraging dialogic and sustainable forms of feedback. Technology-enhanced feedback was probably under-exploited in the case studies. The main highlights were David's use of Facebook for peer collaboration and Ali's use of an assessed blog to encourage students to express their thoughts effectively.

Double feedback duty did not seem to present a problem because teachers were firmly focused on supporting student learning processes without being distracted by extraneous factors, such as quality assurance, external examiners or fear of student complaint. There were, of course, examples when comments did not connect with students. This suggests a need for: further support in the transition from secondary to tertiary education; associated development of student feedback literacy; facilitating opportunities for peer collaboration; dialogue around on-display assignments and exemplars; and further development of student self-evaluative expertise.

To sum up, good practice in promoting student engagement with feedback involves:

- carefully designed cumulative assessment tasks which promote the integration of feedback and student development of evaluative expertise;
- timely dialogues around student work, including in-class, online or peer feedback;
- the use of technology-facilitated forms of communication to enhance dialogic interaction; and
- emphasis on the development of student self-regulation and learner independence as core aims of sustainable feedback processes.

Resolving competing priorities

In Chapter 1, I discussed the challenge of competing priorities in assessment and Boud's concept of double duty. One of the challenges is the uneasy interplay between summative and formative assessment, and there was evidence in the cases of these being effectively intertwined. The Architecture case blurred the boundaries between formative and summative assessment in the way that the process of developing designs through crits, presentations and feedback was integrated into a final portfolio. The project draft in History provided formative feedback that could be used for the final submission of the project. Through same-day feedback, Rick provided Law students with commentary and analysis on a summative task immediately after its conclusion, which fed forward to future assessed tasks.

It is worth reiterating that the large class sizes in the Geology, History and Tort Law cases were not insurmountable barriers to the implementation of varied, productive modes of assessment. A critical factor appeared to be the teachers' determination to overcome challenges in the interests of furthering the student experience. (Perhaps this is a significant characteristic of award-winners.) The teachers attended carefully to their students' learning and seemed to be implementing a conceptual change student-focused teaching approach in ways analogous to those discussed by Prosser and Trigwell (1999) (see Chapter 2).

Those teachers with more sophisticated assessment thinking can implement assessment flexibly and for different purposes (Offerdahl and Tomanek, 2011). By 'flexibly', I mean allowing assignment guidelines to be adapted to student needs and preferences so that they can develop some ownership of assessment tasks. This notion was exemplified in the History and Law cases, where the teachers strove to resolve challenges by allowing flexibility in relation to student choice of task and how it could be carried out. These options included the mode of presentation in History and the weighting of assignments in Law. The overriding principle seemed to be a responsiveness to students' needs and interests. I suggest that teachers with a flexible approach to assessment are well placed to find appropriate ways to tackle the challenges of double duty and competing priorities.

The evidence from the case studies suggested that the teachers often prioritised learning functions of assessment over grading functions. However, they also referred to grading elements of assessment. Chan talked about normative grading – the need to spread marks out and differentiate between students. John referred to the process of standardising grades for the design portfolio and ranking student performance. The Business and Geology teachers attended to fairness in relation to processes of group work. Rick was aware of the difficulties of grading his Law students' photo essays reliably. Overall, however, the teachers' discourses around assessment tended to focus mainly on the learning processes and outcomes they wished to promote.

Another aspect of double duty relates to potential tensions between quality assurance and learning-oriented assessment practices. The evidence suggested that these award-winning teachers' self-confidence encouraged them to do what they thought was right for their students, without being overly concerned about potential audit or quality assurance challenges. For example, Ali awarded marks for participation without concerning himself too much about an audit trail; and History students were relatively comfortable being assessed on participation because they had faith in David and his teaching assistant. Students generally appeared to accept the assessment judgements as fair, mainly because they trusted their teachers.

Developing assessment innovation

There were several innovative elements in the practices of the five teachers. Most notable were the OSR tasks in History; RMD and same-day feedback in Law;

and the videoing and self-evaluation of oral presentations in Business. A certain amount of innovation is necessary if universities are to move forward in developing quality learning-oriented assessment practice. In this section, I address four interrelated aspects of assessment change: incentives; trust and risk; sites for change; and workload issues.

Incentives for assessment change

People need incentives to change, and this applies to both teachers and students. There are various ways in which a university could develop institutional incentives for assessment change. In the same way as teaching award schemes seek to raise the status and recognition of teaching, it would be possible to develop awards for good assessment practices. There are various possible awards for good assessment practice which could act as both recognition and a means of dissemination, for instance: best presentation at an annual university symposium on teaching, learning and assessment; best assessment innovation; or best assessment-related publication. Such awards could raise the status of assessment practice and provide recognition of good practice.

As Rick observed in Chapter 5 in the context of Law, students often prefer familiar assessment tasks in which they have succeeded in the past. There is a need to communicate with students what they can gain from an assessment innovation in terms of learning skills, learning outcomes or intrinsic motivation. A further supporting element would be to show how an innovation works in practice, including through the use of exemplars. It may be most feasible to start assessment innovation in the first year, when students are adapting to university norms and should be relatively open to new practices.

Trust and risk

Innovative assessment thrives most in the context of a positive atmosphere which encourages risk-taking facilitated by trusting relationships between different stakeholders: management, staff and students. A facilitating factor for bold assessment practice in the case studies was the teachers' willingness to take risks and the trust they received from colleagues and at the institutional level. Students in the cases invariably responded positively to the innovative forms of assessment to which they were exposed. One of the main reasons was that they had faith in the teachers, and a characteristic of award-winning teachers is that they are usually trusted by their students. In turn, as these teachers did, staff need to believe that students want to learn; that they can be willingly engaged in challenging assessment tasks; and that they are eager to enter into dialogic feedback (see Sambell et al., 2013).

There are many aspects of teaching, learning and assessment on which trust and risk impinge. Building on an earlier study (Carless, 2009), I raise some issues which relate to the three elements of learning-oriented assessment. In relation to task design, what kinds of assessment tasks are more and less trusted? If group assessment is often considered unfair, what are the main ways of strengthening its processes (see Chapter 6)? With respect to evaluative expertise, how are classroom atmospheres developed in which students have faith in their classmates to provide useful peer feedback? Without trust, students may be unwilling to involve themselves fully in learning activities which reveal their vulnerabilities: for example, when they open themselves to peer feedback or critique (Carless, 2013b). To what extent do students trust teachers to implement useful feedback processes which can help them enhance their grades and develop positive learning outcomes? Trust is a fundamentally relational issue which is built on engaging learning experiences for students.

Sites for change

The cases discussed in this book are mainly at an individual level or involve small groups of colleagues, as in the Geology case. Whilst individuals are often well placed to make changes to their own practice, the cumulative impact from individual change can be relatively small. Rick, for example, had taken some measures to disseminate his practice and encourage assessment for learning reform in Law, but without proactive support from management or senior colleagues in his department, it was unlikely that more wide-ranging change would take place.

As I noted in Chapter 1, programme-wide approaches to assessment are a potential way forward. This could be particularly well applied to learning-oriented assessment issues. A programme approach to assessment task design could facilitate an appropriate variety of tasks to encourage a diverse range of learning outcomes; involve cumulative series of tasks so that students are progressively challenged; and develop coherence and integration in assessment design. Student evaluative expertise is developed more effectively when it is embedded in regular programme-wide activities, including generating and using criteria in relation to exemplars of student work or on-display assignments. Feedback processes would also benefit from a coherent and consistent approach in which students are encouraged to take ownership of feedback and build from one course to another on a path towards sustainability. Programme-wide approaches are also a useful site for embedded professional development of teachers in that they involve a range of colleagues discussing practice in context.

Workload and resources

A key issue in assessment change is that the costs of time and workload need to be balanced with anticipated benefits in terms of effectiveness and efficiency. The incentives for change can be relatively small and the additional workload can act as a discouragement. In Chapter 5, Rick proposed an important principle that an assessment innovation should not lead to more staff workload than the approach

Table 12.3 Possible shifts in priorities for feedback processes

Increase	Decrease
In-class dialogic feedback within module time	Unidirectional comments after completion of a module
Written feedback comments on the first assessment task of a module	Written feedback comments on the final task of a module
Feedback for first-year students	Feedback for final-year students

it replaces. RMD was teacher-workload friendly in that it placed the onus on students to collect, track and analyse media coverage of tort law issues. I also noted in Chapter 6 that Ali implemented the use of a blog in a way which maximised student autonomy and minimised his own workload. There are often tensions between what might be fully desirable and what is pragmatically feasible.

Staff resources are limited so need to be focused on tasks where they can have maximum impact on student learning processes. To illustrate the point in relation to feedback innovation, some possible shifts in resourcing are suggested in Table 12.3.

Prospects for developing assessment and feedback literacy

In Chapter 1, I introduced the important issue of assessment literacy. Here, in light of the case studies, I discuss the interrelated issues of assessment literacy and feedback literacy.

Assessment literacy

The learning-oriented assessment framework suggests that teachers need to have a reasonably sophisticated conception of assessment task design; possess a range of strategies for developing student evaluative expertise; and be aware of methods to promote student engagement with feedback. Teacher assessment literacy was not an implicit focus of our interviews but something which emerged indirectly. It was clear that all five award-winning teachers were very aware of the impact of assessment on the student experience and had given careful thought to the design of assessment tasks, supporting students' understanding of expectations and the nature of quality, and were striving to provide useful feedback. In this sense they possessed pedagogic assessment literacy without – except for Rick – engaging much with theory and literature on assessment.

Teacher assessment literacy is a facilitating factor for the development of student assessment literacy. One of the findings from the student data was the varying degree of assessment literacy amongst students. For example, some of them clearly understood what they were supposed to be doing in their assessment tasks and why, whereas others misunderstood aspects of assessment tasks. Some students were developing a feel for quality and an ability to absorb the essence of the task criteria, whereas others were finding the transition from school to university difficult and had only a limited understanding of what was expected of them. A minority of students displayed elements of cue-deafness, such as being unaware of assessment requirements. Invariably, the students with better understandings of assessment processes obtained higher grades.

Students develop assessment literacy when they communicate about and debate assessment issues, such as differing and conflicting purposes of assessment, the nature of criteria and standards, and the marking of sample work. They also need to develop feedback literacy, to which I turn next.

Feedback literacy

Feedback literacy is an important aspect of the broader notion of assessment literacy. It is probably fair to say that all stakeholders need a stronger appreciation of both the complexity of feedback and its key role in supporting the development of learning. The evidence of the teacher practices in Chapter 11 was that there was some awareness of relevant issues, such as the importance of in-class dialogues and providing timely comments which students could use to improve their ongoing work. With the exception of Ali, who placed particular emphasis on learning to learn, our observations did not reveal much communication around issues to do with the nature and purposes of feedback. When teachers are able to communicate with students about feedback processes and model suitable dialogic interaction there are prospects for student development of feedback literacy.

From the student perspective, there was varied evidence of their understandings of purposes and processes of feedback. The students in the Architecture case were probably the most sophisticated consumers of feedback because it was built into the signature pedagogies of the discipline. Feedback literacy for students requires understanding of standards and experience in making judgements; an ability to interpret teacher judgements and comments; an awareness of the different purposes of feedback; and the capacity to act on feedback as part of self-regulation of one's own work. It is likely that the more students are able to understand the purposes of feedback and their active role as consumers and users of it, the more skilled they will be in using it to advance their learning. A further aspect of feedback literacy is for students to develop a willingness or initiative to enter into dialogue around work, with both peers and teachers. Creating trusting course climates in which high standards are expected and attained can support such processes.

Areas for further research

As the book nears its conclusion, I propose four areas for further exploration. First, this research is framed around a framework for learning-oriented assessment which I have argued presents a coherent and integrated way of showing the relationships between key components of assessment for learning in higher education. Like all models and frameworks, it risks being somewhat static and failing to account adequately for some of the tensions inhibiting agency in assessment (see James, 2014). It invites further critique and exploration: for example, given that four of the five case studies are in the soft and applied disciplines, it might be useful to explore further its suitability for the hard sciences, with their different epistemological assumptions.

Second, the use of exemplars remains comparatively under-explored. There seems to be plenty of evidence that students are positively disposed towards exemplars in various ways, but we know very little about why teachers choose to use them or not. How common is the use of exemplars across disciplines in higher education? What are the preferred modes of exemplar use amongst teachers? What are the main concerns of teachers who do not use exemplars of student work as part of their teaching repertoire? What are the main disciplinary differences in the use of exemplars? Studies of this nature have the potential to make valuable contributions to the extension of research on exemplars. This research strand is particularly pertinent to learning-oriented assessment because the dialogic use of exemplars is one of the most effective ways of prompting students to engage with criteria and quality.

Third, the discussion in Chapter 10 does not fully resolve a number of questions about dialogic feedback. What are its assumptions and deeper theoretical underpinnings (see Anderson, 2014; McArthur and Huxham, 2013)? How feasible is it on a wide scale or with large classes (see Draper and Nicol, 2013)? What is its relationship with sustainable feedback (see Carless et al., 2011)? How might it be effective with less motivated or lower-achieving learners (see Orsmond and Merry, 2013)? A further strand of research would be to carry out longitudinal studies of how students perceive, understand and engage with feedback. How does students' engagement with feedback processes change over time in light of their accumulated experiences of assessment and feedback (cf. Handley, Price and Millar, 2011)? Such research might also uncover some of the invisibility I referred to in Chapter 10 in terms of understanding the processes of what students do with feedback.

Fourth, as I discussed in Chapter 2, there is a small but steadily growing literature on award-winning teachers. There has hitherto been a dearth of material on their assessment practices. I have attempted to fill some of the gaps, but have focused on what these teachers are doing and why; I have not conducted a detailed exploration of their underlying beliefs. A study of the conceptions of assessment of exemplary and/or award-winning teachers might therefore be a useful supplement to this book. It would also be worthwhile to research a wider sample of teachers who, in the same way as Rick, have been particularly recognised for their assessment practice.

Conclusion to book and chapter

The major themes of the book have been: assessment is central to the student learning experience; there is a need to focus more explicitly on the generation of appropriate student learning processes in relation to assessment; and the competing priorities of assessment represent a challenge that needs to be tackled in order to advance learning-oriented assessment.

It is probably fair to say that there has been substantial progress over the last few decades in relation to the three strands of the learning-oriented assessment framework. First, in terms of assessment task design, students are now exposed to more meaningful tasks and a wider variety of modes of assessment than ever before. Second, there is increased clarity and transparency about assessment requirements and standards, and greater use of criterion-referenced or standards-referenced forms of assessment. Third, whilst feedback remains a perennial source of discontent, there has been a major growth in research on ways to improve feedback processes, and some promising dialogic or sustainable practices have been developed.

Assessment practices must continue to develop so that students can see assessment not just as a tool to measure and grade them, but as an opportunity to carry out meaningful tasks, engage with quality in the discipline, and involve themselves in dialogue about their work and that of others. We need to move beyond pockets of good practice at individual levels to more sustained high-quality practice. This may include innovation in assessment at programme, departmental or institutional level. Innovation needs to be more than experiments in which something new is tried, and then perhaps forgotten or abandoned. We need a cumulative sense of moving forward in assessment, which is one of the main rationales for the reviews and syntheses of literature which are features of this book. Although a final paragraph is inadequate to sum up the complexities of the undertaking, I conclude with some key elements of a vision of quality assessment.

A primary aim of assessment should be to resolve competing priorities by focusing on the promotion of student learning. Assessment should be rigorous but not cowed by quality assurance, and use resources wisely so that it is not excessively time-consuming. Quality assessment encourages deep approaches to learning in which students develop new meanings rather than just reproduce knowledge with a goal of achieving higher-order learning outcomes. These may emanate from sustained engagement with tasks which mirror real-life applications of the discipline. Well-designed assessment permits flexibility and student choice so that students can engage with topics and issues which they find important and stimulating. Integrated and coherent assessment tasks progressively build capacity to achieve complex learning outcomes. Good assessment practices encourage dialogues between learners and their teachers and amongst themselves. Teachers need to engineer student engagement with criteria so as to develop their evaluative expertise and understanding of quality in the discipline. Dialogic use of exemplars is one of the most effective ways of enhancing student capacities to engage with criteria and quality work. Feedback needs to engage with students, their needs and interests. Its goal should be to support students in enhancing their capacities to self-regulate their own learning. In-class feedback dialogues during the process of working on assignments are often more useful than end-loaded unidirectional comments. The integration of task design, student development of evaluative expertise and engagement with feedback lies at the heart of good learning-oriented assessment.

Summary main implications for practice

- The development of effective student learning processes should be a primary focus of all assessment.
- Assessment should stimulate student engagement by encouraging deep approaches to learning.
- The design of assessments should promote contextualised ways of thinking and practising in forms which mirror real-life uses of the discipline.
- Tasks should be designed to provide students with opportunities to demonstrate higher-order learning outcomes.
- Students need to be involved in generating, applying or engaging with quality criteria.
- Dialogue around exemplars is an effective means of promoting student engagement with quality.
- Assessment task design and implementation should encourage the development of student evaluative expertise and engagement with feedback.
- A key role of feedback is to support students in self-regulating their work and learning strategies.
- Dialogic feedback can be embedded within classroom teaching and learning processes.
- Assessment and feedback innovation might be particularly focused at programme levels.
- The interlinked development of teacher and student assessment literacy represents a potential way forward for learning-oriented assessment.

References

Adcroft, A. (2011). The mythology of feedback. *Higher Education Research and Development*, 30(4), 405–419.

Akalin, A. and Sezal, I. (2009). The importance of conceptual and concrete modelling in architectural design education. *International Journal of Art and Design Education*, 28(1), 14–24.

Anderson, C. (2014). Only connect? Communicating meaning through feedback. In C. Kreber, C. Anderson, N. Entwistle and J. McArthur (eds), *Advances and Innovations in University Assessment and Feedback* (pp. 131–151). Edinburgh: Edinburgh University Press.

Anderson, C. and Hounsell, D. (2007). Knowledge practices: 'Doing the subject' in undergraduate courses. *The Curriculum Journal*, 18(4), 463–478.

Armstrong, M. and Boud, D. (1983). Assessing participation in discussion: An exploration of the issues. *Studies in Higher Education*, 8(1), 33–44.

Ashworth P., Bannister, P. and Thorne, P. (1997). Guilty in whose eyes? University students' perceptions of cheating and plagiarism in academic work and assessment. *Studies in Higher Education*, 22(2), 187–203.

Askew, S. and Lodge, C. (2000). Gifts, ping-pong and loops: Linking feedback and learning. In S. Askew (ed.), *Feedback for Learning* (pp. 1–17). London: Routledge.

Atkinson, D. and Lim, S. (2013). Improving assessment process in higher education: Student and teacher perceptions of the effectiveness of a rubric embedded in an LMS. *Australasian Journal of Educational Technology*, 29(5), 651–666.

Atkinson, R., Derry, S., Renkl, A. and Wortham, D. (2000). Learning from examples: Instructional principles from the worked examples research. *Review of Educational Research*, 70(2), 181–214.

Australian Council for Educational Research (ACER). (2010). *Doing More for Learning: Enhancing Engagement and Outcomes: Australasian Student Engagement Report*. Camberwell, Victoria: Australian Council for Educational Research.

Baartman, L., Bastiaens, T., Kirschner, P. and van der Vleuten, C. (2007). Evaluating assessment quality in competence-based education: A qualitative comparison of two frameworks. *Educational Research Review*, 2(2), 114–129.

Baeten, M., Dochy, F. and Struyven, K. (2008). Students' approaches to learning and assessment preferences in a portfolio-based learning environment. *Instructional Science*, 36(5–6), 359–374.

Bailey, R. and Garner, M. (2010). Is the feedback in higher education assessment worth the paper it is written on? Teachers' reflections on their practices. *Teaching in Higher Education*, 15(2), 187–198.

Bain, K. (2004). *What the Best College Teachers Do*. Cambridge, MA: Harvard University Press.

Ballantyne, R., Bain, J. and Packer, J. (1999). Researching university teaching in Australia: Themes and issues in academics' reflections. *Studies in Higher Education*, 24(2), 237–257.

Ballantyne, R., Hughes, K. and Mylonas, A. (2002). Developing peer assessment procedures for implementing peer assessment in large classes using an action research process. *Assessment and Evaluation in Higher Education*, 27(5), 427–441.

Barker, M. and Pinard, M. (2014). Closing the feedback loop? Iterative feedback between tutor and student in coursework assessments. *Assessment and Evaluation in Higher Education*, 39(8), 899–915.

Barnett, R. (2007a). *A Will to Learn: Being a Student in an Age of Uncertainty*. Maidenhead: Society for Research into Higher Education and Open University Press.

Barnett, R. (2007b). Assessment in higher education: An impossible mission? In D. Boud and N. Falchikov (eds), *Rethinking Assessment in Higher Education* (pp. 29–40). London: Routledge.

Barrie, S. (2006). Understanding what we mean by the generic attributes of graduates. *Higher Education*, 51(2), 215–241.

Baume, D. (2001). A briefing on assessment of portfolios. *Higher Education Academy*. www.bioscience.heacademy.ac.uk/ftp/Resources/gc/assess06portfolios.pdf. Accessed 31 July 2013.

Bean, J. and Peterson, D. (1998). Grading classroom participation. *New Directions for Teaching and Learning*, 74, 33–40.

Beaumont, C., O'Doherty, M. and Shannon, L. (2011). Reconceptualising assessment feedback: A key to improving student learning? *Studies in Higher Education*, 36(6), 671–687.

Becher, T. (1989). *Academic Tribes and Territories*. Buckingham: Society for Research into Higher Education and Open University Press.

Becker, H., Geer, B. and Hughes, E. (1968). *Making the Grade: The Academic Side of College Life*. New York: John Wiley & Sons.

Bell, A., Mladenovic, R. and Price, M. (2013). Students' perceptions of the usefulness of marking guides, grade descriptors and annotated exemplars. *Assessment and Evaluation in Higher Education*, 38(7), 769–788.

Benson, R. and Brack, C. (2010). *Online Learning and Assessment in Higher Education: A Planning Guide*. Oxford: Chandos.

Bevitt, S. (2014). Assessment innovation and student experience: A new assessment challenge and call for a multi-perspective approach to assessment research. *Assessment and Evaluation in Higher Education*, DOI:10.1080/02602938.2014.890170.

Biggs, J. (1996a). Enhancing teaching through constructive alignment. *Higher Education*, 32(3), 347–364.

Biggs, J. (1996b). Western misperceptions of the Confucian-heritage learning culture. In D. Watkins and J. Biggs (eds), *The Chinese Learner: Cultural, Psychological and Contextual Influences* (pp. 45–68). Hong Kong: Comparative Education Research Centre and Australian Council for Educational Research.

Biggs, J. (1999). *Teaching for Quality Learning at University*. Buckingham: Society for Research into Higher Education and Open University Press.

Biggs, J. and Tang, C. (2011). *Teaching for Quality Learning at University* (4th edition). Maidenhead: Society for Research into Higher Education and Open University Press.

Biglan, A. (1973). The characteristics of subject matter in different academic areas. *Journal of Applied Psychology*, 57(3), 195–203.

Black, P. and Wiliam, D. (1998). Assessment and classroom learning. *Assessment in Education*, 5(1), 7–74.

Blair, B. (2006). 'At the end of a huge crit in the summer, it was "crap" – I'd worked really hard but all she said was "fine" and I was gutted'. *Art, Design and Communication in Higher Education*, 5(2), 83–95.

Bloxham, S. (2009). Marking and moderation in the UK: False assumptions and wasted resources. *Assessment and Evaluation in Higher Education*, 34(2), 209–220.

Bloxham, S. (2013). Building 'standards' frameworks': The role of guidance and feedback in supporting the achievement of learners. In S. Merry, M. Price, D. Carless and M. Taras (eds), *Reconceptualising Feedback in Higher Education: Developing Dialogue with Students* (pp. 64–74). London: Routledge.

Bloxham, S. and Boyd, P. (2007). *Developing Effective Assessment in Higher Education: A Practical Guide*. New York: McGraw Hill and Open University Press.

Bloxham, S., Boyd, P. and Orr, S. (2011). Mark my words: The role of assessment criteria in UK higher education grading practices. *Studies in Higher Education*, 36(6), 655–670.

Bloxham, S. and Campbell. L. (2010). Generating dialogue in assessment feedback: Exploring the use of interactive cover sheets. *Assessment and Evaluation in Higher Education*, 35(3), 291–300.

Bloxham, S. and West, A. (2004). Understanding the rules of the game: Marking peer assessment as a medium for developing students' conceptions of assessment. *Assessment and Evaluation in Higher Education*, 29(6), 721–733.

Booth, A. (2003). *Teaching History at University: Enhancing Learning and Understanding*. London: Routledge.

Boud, D. (1995). *Enhancing Learning through Self-assessment*. London: Kogan Page.

Boud, D. (2000). Sustainable assessment: Rethinking assessment for the learning society. *Studies in Continuing Education*, 22(2), 151–167.

Boud, D. (2014). Shifting views of assessment: From secret teachers' business to sustaining learning. In C. Kreber, C. Anderson, N. Entwistle and J. McArthur (eds), *Advances and Innovations in University Assessment and Feedback* (pp. 13–31). Edinburgh: Edinburgh University Press.

Boud, D. and associates (2010). Assessment 2020: Seven propositions for assessment reform in higher education. www.olt.gov.au/system/files/resources/Assessment%20 2020_final.pdf. Accessed 28 October 2014.

Boud, D. and Falchikov, N. (2007). Developing assessment for informing judgment. In D. Boud and N. Falchikov (eds), *Rethinking Assessment in Higher Education* (pp. 181–197). London: Routledge.

Boud, D. and Molloy, E. (2013a). Decision-making for feedback. In D. Boud and L. Molloy (eds), *Feedback in Higher and Professional Education* (pp. 202–218). London: Routledge.

Boud, D. and Molloy, E. (2013b). Rethinking models of feedback for learning: The challenge of design. *Assessment and Evaluation in Higher Education*, 38(6), 698–712.

Bourner, J., Hughes, M. and Bourner, T. (2001). First year undergraduate experiences of doing project work. *Assessment and Evaluation in Higher Education*, 26(1), 19–39.

Bridges, P., Cooper, A., Evanson, P., Haines, C., Jenkins, D., Scurry, D., Woolf, H. and Yorke, M. (2002). Coursework marks high, examination marks low: Discuss. *Assessment and Evaluation in Higher Education*, 27(1), 35–48.

Brooks, C. and Ammons, J. (2003). Free-riding in group projects and the effects of timing, frequency and specificity of criteria in peer assessments. *Journal of Education for Business*, 78(5), 268–272.

Brooks, V. (2012). Marking as judgment. *Research Papers in Education*, 27(1), 63–80.

Broughan, C. and Jewell, S. (2012). Conclusion. In L. Clouder, C. Broughan, S. Jewell and G. Steventon (eds), *Improving Student Engagement and Development through Assessment: Theory and Practice in Higher Education* (pp. 210–211). London: Routledge.

Brown, C. and McIlroy, K. (2011). Group work in healthcare students' education: What do we think we are doing? *Assessment and Evaluation in Higher Education*, 36(6), 687–699.

Brown, E. and Glover, C. (2006). Evaluating written feedback. In C. Bryan and K. Clegg (eds), *Innovative Assessment in Higher Education* (pp. 81–91). London: Routledge.

Brown, G. (1997). *Assessing Student Learning in Higher Education*. London: Routledge.

Brown, G.T.L. (2010). The validity of examination essays in higher education: Issues and responses. *Higher Education Quarterly*, 64(3), 276–291.

Bryan, C. (2006). Developing group learning through assessment. In C. Bryan and K. Clegg (eds), *Innovative Assessment in Higher Education* (pp. 150–157). London: Routledge.

Bryson, C. and Hand, L. (2007). The role of engagement in inspiring teaching and learning. *Innovations in Education and Teaching International*, 44(4), 349–362.

Butler, D. and Winne, P. (1995). Feedback and self-regulated learning: A theoretical synthesis. *Review of Educational Research*, 65(3), 245–274.

Cambridge, D. (2010). *ePortfolios for Lifelong Learning and Assessment*. San Francisco, CA: Jossey Bass.

Campbell, J., Smith, D. and Brooker, R. (1998). From conception to performance: How undergraduate students conceptualise and construct essays. *Higher Education*, 36(4), 449–469.

Carless, D. (2002). The 'mini-viva' as a tool to enhance assessment for learning. *Assessment and Evaluation in Higher Education*, 27(4), 353–363.

Carless, D. (2006). Differing perceptions in the feedback process. *Studies in Higher Education*, 31(2), 219–233.

Carless, D. (2007a). Conceptualizing pre-emptive formative assessment. *Assessment in Education*, 14(2), 171–184.

Carless, D. (2007b). Learning-oriented assessment: Conceptual basis and practical implications. *Innovations in Education and Teaching International*, 44(1), 57–66.

Carless, D. (2009). Trust, distrust and their impact on assessment reform. *Assessment and Evaluation in Higher Education*, 34(1), 79–89.

Carless, D. (2011). *From Testing to Productive Student Learning: Implementing Formative Assessment in Confucian-heritage Settings*. New York: Routledge.

Carless, D. (2013a). Sustainable feedback and the development of student self-evaluative capacities. In S. Merry, M. Price, D. Carless and M. Taras (eds), *Reconceptualising*

Feedback in Higher Education: Developing Dialogue with Students (pp. 113–122). London: Routledge.

Carless, D. (2013b). Trust and its role in facilitating dialogic feedback. In D. Boud and L. Molloy (eds), *Feedback in Higher and Professional Education* (pp. 90–103). London: Routledge.

Carless, D. (2014). Exploring learning-oriented assessment processes. *Higher Education*, DOI: 10.1007/s10734-014-9816-z.

Carless, D., Joughin, G., Liu, N. and associates. (2006). *How Assessment Supports Learning: Learning-oriented Assessment in Action*. Hong Kong: Hong Kong University Press.

Carless, D., Joughin, G. and Mok, M. (2006). Learning-oriented assessment: Principles and practice. *Assessment and Evaluation in Higher Education*, 31(4), 395–398.

Carless, D., Salter, D., Yang, M. and Lam, J. (2011). Developing sustainable feedback practices. *Studies in Higher Education*, 36(4), 395–407.

Cheng, W. and Warren, M. (2000). Making a difference: Using peers to assess individual students' contributions to a group project. *Teaching in Higher Education*, 5(2), 243–255.

Chetwynd, F. and Dobbyn, C. (2011). Assessment, feedback and marking guides in distance education. *Open Learning*, 26(1), 67–78.

Chiu, Y. (2009). Facilitating Asian students' critical thinking in online discussions. *British Journal of Educational Technology*, 40(1), 42–57.

Churchill, D. (2009). Educational applications of Web 2.0: Using blogs to support teaching and learning. *British Journal of Educational Technology*, 40(1), 179–183.

Colbeck, C., Campbell, S. and Bjorklund, S. (2000). Grouping in the dark: What college students learn from group projects. *Journal of Higher Education*, 71(1), 60–83.

Costa, A. and Kallick, B. (1995). Teams build assessment and assessment builds teams. In A. Costa and B. Kallick (eds), *Assessment in the Learning Organization: Shifting the Paradigm* (pp. 141–152). Alexandria, VA: Association for Supervision and Curriculum Development.

Court, K. (2014). Tutor feedback on draft essays: Developing students' academic writing and subject knowledge. *Journal of Further and Higher Education*, 38(3), 327–345.

Cramp, A., Lamond, C., Coleyshaw, L. and Beck, S. (2012). Empowering or disabling? Emotional reactions to assessment amongst part-time students. *Teaching in Higher Education*, 17(5), 509–521.

Crook, C., Gross, H. and Dymott, R. (2006). Assessment relationships in higher education: The tension of process and practice. *British Educational Research Journal*, 32(1), 95–114.

Crossman, J. (2007). The role of relationships and emotions in student perceptions of learning and assessment. *Higher Education Research and Development*, 26(3), 313–327.

Cumming, J. and Maxwell, G. (1999). Contextualising authentic assessment. *Assessment in Education*, 6(2), 177–194.

Cummings, R. and Maddux, C. (2010). The use of e-portfolios as a component of assessment and accreditation in higher education. In N. Buzzetto-More (ed.), *The ePortfolio Paradigm: Informing, Educating, Assessing and Managing with e-Portfolios* (pp. 207–223). Santa Rosa, CA: Informing Science Press.

Dancer, D. and Kamvounias, P. (2005). Student involvement in assessment: A project designed to assess class participation fairly and reliably. *Assessment and Evaluation in Higher Education*, 30(4), 445–454.

Davies, W. (2009). Groupwork as a form of assessment: Common problems and recommended solutions. *Higher Education*, 58, 563–584.

Deng, L. and Tavares, N. (2013). From Moodle to Facebook: Exploring students' motivation and experiences in online communities. *Computers and Education*, 68, 167–176.

Dochy, F., Segers, M., Gijbels, D. and Struyven, K. (2007). Assessment engineering: Breaking down barriers between teaching and learning, and assessment. In D. Boud and N. Falchikov (eds), *Rethinking Assessment in Higher Education* (pp. 87–100). London: Routledge.

Dochy, F., Segers, M. and Sluijsmans, D. (1999). The use of self-, peer and co-assessment in higher education: A review. *Studies in Higher Education*, 24(3), 331–350.

Doherty, C., Kettle, M., May, L. and Caukill, E. (2011). Talking the talk: Oracy demands in first year university assessment tasks. *Assessment in Education*, 18(1), 27–39.

Draper, S. and Nicol, D. (2013). Achieving transformational or sustainable educational change. In S. Merry, M. Price, D. Carless and M. Taras (eds), *Reconceptualising Feedback in Higher Education: Developing Dialogue with Students* (pp. 190–203). London: Routledge.

Dunkin, M. and Precians, R. (1992). Award-winning teachers' concepts of teaching. *Higher Education*, 24(4), 483–502.

Ecclestone, K. (2001). 'I know a 2-1 when I see it': Understanding criteria for degree classifications in franchised university programmes. *Journal of Further and Higher Education*, 25(3), 301–313.

Eisner, E. (1985). *The Art of Educational Evaluation: A Personal View*. London: Falmer Press.

Elton, L. and Laurillard, D. (1979). Trends in research on student learning. *Studies in Higher Education*, 4(1), 87–102.

Entwistle, N. (2009). *Teaching for Understanding at University*. Basingstoke: Palgrave Macmillan.

Entwistle, A. and Entwistle, N. (1992). Experiences of understanding in revising for degree examinations. *Learning and Instruction*, 2(1), 1–22.

Entwistle, N. and Entwistle, D. (2003). Preparing for examinations: The interplay of memorizing and understanding and the development of knowledge objects. *Higher Education Research and Development*, 22(1), 19–41.

Entwistle, N. and Karagiannopoulou, E. (2014). Perceptions of assessment and their influences on learning. In C. Kreber, C. Anderson, N. Entwistle and J. McArthur (eds), *Advances and Innovations in University Assessment and Feedback* (pp. 75–98). Edinburgh: Edinburgh University Press.

Entwistle, N., McCune, V. and Walker, P. (2001). Conceptions, styles and approaches within higher education: Analytic abstractions and everyday experience. In R. Sternberg and L. Zhang (eds), *Perspectives on Thinking, Learning and Cognitive Styles* (pp. 103–136). Mahwah, NJ: Lawrence Erlbaum.

Entwistle, N. and Ramsden, P. (1983). *Understanding Student Learning*. London: Croom Helm

Evans, C. (2013). Making sense of assessment feedback in higher education. *Review of Educational Research*, 83(1), 70–120.

Falchikov, N. (2005). *Improving Assessment through Student Involvement*. London: Routledge Falmer.

Falchikov, N. and Boud, D. (2007). Assessment and emotion: The impact of being assessed. In D. Boud and N. Falchikov (eds), *Rethinking Assessment in Higher Education* (pp. 144–156). London: Routledge.

Falchikov, N. and Thomson, K. (2008). Assessment: What drives innovation? *Journal of University Teaching and Learning practice*, 5(1). http://ro.uow.edu.au/jutlp/vol5/iss1/5. Accessed 28 October 2014.

Finger, G. and Jamieson-Proctor, R. (2009). Assessment issues and new technologies: ePortfolio possibilities. In C. Wyatt-Smith and J. Cumming (eds), *Educational Assessment in the 21st Century: Connecting Theory and Practice* (pp. 63–82). New York: Springer.

Flint, N. and Johnson, B. (2011). *Towards Fairer University Assessment: Recognizing the Concerns of Students*. London: Routledge.

Fredricks, J., Blumenfeld, P. and Paris, A. (2004). School engagement: Potential of the concept, state of the evidence. *Review of Educational Research*, 74(1), 59–109.

Frost, J., de Pont, G. and Brailsford, I. (2012). Expanding assessment methods and moments in history. *Assessment and Evaluation in Higher Education*, 37(3), 293–304.

Gibbs, G. (1999). Using assessment strategically to change the way students learn. In S. Brown and A. Glasner (eds), *Assessment Matters in Higher Education* (pp. 41–56). Maidenhead: Society for Research into Higher Education and Open University Press.

Gibbs, G. (2006). How assessment frames student learning. In C. Bryan and K. Clegg (eds), *Innovative Assessment in Higher Education* (pp. 23–36). London: Routledge.

Gibbs, G. (2008). Designing teaching award schemes. Report for Higher Education Academy, June. www.jisctechdis.ac.uk/assets/Documents/evidence_informed_practice/Gibbs_Final_Manual.pdf. Accessed October 21, 2014.

Gibbs, G. and Dunbar-Goddet, H. (2007). *The Effects of Programme Assessment Environments on Student Learning*. York: Higher Education Academy.

Gibbs, G. and Dunbar-Goddet, H. (2009). Characterising programme level assessment environments that support learning. *Assessment and Evaluation in Higher Education*, 34(4), 481–489.

Gibbs, G. and Simpson, C. (2004). Conditions under which assessment supports students' learning. *Learning and Teaching in Higher Education*, 1(1), 3–31.

Gijbels, D., Coertjens, L., Vanthournout, G., Struyf, E. and van Petegem, P. (2009). Changing students' approaches to learning: A two-year study within a university teacher training course. *Educational Studies*, 35(5), 503–513.

Gijbels, D., Segers, M. and Struyf, E. (2008). Constructivist learning environments and the (im)possibility to change students' perceptions of assessment demands and approaches to learning. *Instructional Science*, 36(5–6), 431–443.

Gipps, C. (1999). Socio-cultural aspects of assessment. *Review of Research in Education*, 24(1), 355–392.

Glendinning, I. (2014). Responses to student plagiarism in higher education across Europe. *International Journal for Educational Integrity*, 10(1), 4–20.

Glofcheski, R. (2006). Same day feedback and analysis of assessed coursework. In D. Carless, G. Joughin, N. Liu and associates, *How Assessment Supports Learning: Learning-oriented Assessment in Action* (pp. 39–42). Hong Kong: Hong Kong University Press.

Gosling, D. and Moon, J. (2002). *How to Use Learning Outcomes and Assessment Criteria* (3rd edition). London: Southern England Consortium for Credit Accumulation and Transfer (SEEC).

Gould, J. and Day, P. (2013). Hearing you loud and clear: Student perspectives of audio feedback in higher education. *Assessment and Evaluation in Higher Education*, 38(5), 554–566.

Gulbahar, Y. and Tinmaz, H. (2006). Implementing project-based learning and e-portfolio assessment in an undergraduate course. *Journal of Research on Technology in Education*, 38(3), 309–328.

Gulikers, J., Bastiaens, T. and Kirschner, P. (2004). A five dimensional framework for authentic assessment. *Educational Technology Research and Development*, 52(3), 67–86.

Gulikers, J., Bastiaens, T., Kirschner, P. and Kester, L. (2006). Relations between student perceptions of assessment authenticity, study approaches and learning outcome. *Studies in Educational Evaluation*, 32(4), 381–400.

Gullifer, J. and Tyson, G. (2014). Who has read the policy on plagiarism? Unpacking students' understanding of plagiarism. *Studies in Higher Education*, 39(7), 1202–1218.

Hager, P. and Butler, J. (1996). Two models of educational assessment. *Assessment and Evaluation in Higher Education*, 21(4), 367–378.

Haggis, T. (2003). Constructing images of ourselves? A critical investigation into 'Approaches to Learning' research in Higher Education. *British Educational Research Journal*, 29(1), 89–104.

Halse, C., Deane, E., Hobson, J. and Jones, G. (2007). The research–teaching nexus: What do national teaching awards tell us? *Studies in Higher Education*, 32(6), 727–746.

Hand, L. and Clewes, D. (2000). Marking the difference: An investigation of the criteria used for assessing undergraduate dissertations in a business school. *Assessment and Evaluation in Higher Education*, 25(1), 5–21.

Handley, K., Price, M. and Millar, J. (2011). Beyond 'doing time': Investigating the concept of student engagement with feedback. *Oxford Review of Education*, 37(4), 543–560.

Handley, K. and Williams, L. (2011). From copying to learning: Using exemplars to engage students with assessment criteria and feedback. *Assessment and Evaluation in Higher Education*, 36(1), 95–108.

Hartley, P. and Whitfield, R. (2011). The case for programme-focused assessment. *Educational Developments*, 12(4), 8–12.

Hattie, J. and Timperley, H. (2007). The power of feedback. *Review of Educational Research*, 77(1), 81–112.

Hendry, G. and Anderson, J. (2013). Helping students understand the standards of work expected in an essay: Using exemplars in mathematics pre-service education classes. *Assessment and Evaluation in Higher Education*, 38(6), 754–768.

Hendry, G., Armstrong, S. and Bromberger, N. (2012). Implementing standards-based assessment effectively: Incorporating discussion of exemplars into classroom teaching. *Assessment and Evaluation in Higher Education*, 37(2), 149–161.

Hendry, G., Bromberger, N. and Armstrong, S. (2011). Constructive guidance and feedback for learning: The usefulness of exemplars, marking sheets and different types of feedback in a first year law subject. *Assessment and Evaluation in Higher Education*, 36(1), 1–11.

Hendry, G. and Tomitsch, M. (2014). Implementing an exemplar-based approach in an interaction design subject: Enhancing students' awareness of the need to be creative. *International Journal of Technology and Design Education*, 24(3), 337–348.

Hennessy, C. and Forrester, G. (2014). Developing a framework for effective audio feedback: A case study. *Assessment and Evaluation in Higher Education*, 39(7), 777–789.

Hepplestone, S., Holden, G., Irwin, B., Parkin, H. and Thorpe, L. (2011). Using technology to encourage student engagement with feedback: A literature review. *Research in Learning Technology*, 19(2), 117–127.

Hew, K.F. (2011). Students' and teachers' use of Facebook. *Computers in Human Behavior*, 27(2), 662–676.

Higgins, R., Hartley, P. and Skelton, A. (2001). Getting the message across: The problem of communicating assessment feedback. *Teaching in Higher Education*, 6(2), 269–274.

Higher Education Funding Council for England (HEFCE) (2010). National student survey. www.hefce.ac.uk/pubs/hefce/2010/10_18/. Accessed 1 February 2011.

Higher Education Funding Council for England (HEFCE) (2014). National student survey. www.hefce.ac.uk/whatwedo/lt/publicinfo/nss/. Accessed 3 October 2014.

Hounsell, D. (1984). Learning and essay-writing. In F. Marton, D. Hounsell and N. Entwistle (eds), *The Experience of Learning* (pp. 103–123). Edinburgh: Scottish Academic Press.

Hounsell, D. (2003). Student feedback, learning and development. In M. Slowey and D. Watson (eds), *Higher Education and the Lifecourse* (pp. 67–78). Maidenhead: Society for Research into Higher Education.

Hounsell, D. (2007). Towards more sustainable feedback to students. In D. Boud and N. Falchikov (eds), *Rethinking Assessment in Higher Education* (pp. 101–113). London: Routledge.

Hounsell, D., Falchikov, N., Hounsell, J., Klampfleitner, M., Huxham, M., Thomson, K. and Blair, S. (2007). Innovative assessment across the disciplines: An analytical review of the literature. York: Higher Education Academy. www.heacademy.ac.uk/assets/documents/research/innovative_assessment_lr.pdf. Accessed 24 September 2013.

Hounsell, D., McCune, V., Hounsell, J. and Litjens. J. (2008). The quality of guidance and feedback to students. *Higher Education Research and Development*, 27(1), 55–67.

Hounsell, D., Xu, R. and Tai, C. (2007). Integrative assessment: Balancing assessment of and for learning. Guide No. 2. Gloucester: The Quality Assurance Agency for Higher Education.www.enhancementthemes.ac.uk/docs/publications/guide-no-2---balancing-assessment-of-and-assessment-for-learning.pdf?sfvrsn=16. Accessed 28 October 2014.

Howie, P. and Bagnall, R. (2013). A critique of the deep and surface approaches to learning model. *Teaching in Higher Education*, 18(4), 389–400.

Hughes, C. (2013). A case study of assessment of graduate learning outcomes at the programme, course and task level. *Assessment and Evaluation in Higher Education*, 38(4), 492–506.

Hussey, T. and Smith, P. (2003). The uses of learning outcomes. *Teaching in Higher Education*, 8(3), 357–368.

Hussey, T. and Smith, P. (2008). Learning outcomes: A conceptual analysis. *Teaching in Higher Education*, 13(1), 107–115.

Huxham, M. (2007). Fast and effective feedback: Are model answers the answer? *Assessment and Evaluation in Higher Education*, 32(6), 601–611.

Huxham, M., Campbell, F. and Westwood, J. (2012). Oral versus written assessments: A test of student performance and attitudes. *Assessment and Evaluation in Higher Education*, 37(1), 125–136.

Jacobs, L. and Chase, C. (1992). *Developing and Using Tests Effectively*. San Francisco, CA: Jossey Bass.

James, D. (2014). Investigating the curriculum through assessment practice in higher education: The value of a 'learning cultures' approach. *Higher Education*, 67(2), 155–169.

James, R. (2003). Academic standards and the assessment of student learning. *Tertiary Education and Management*, 9(3), 187–198.

Jessop, T., El Hakim, Y. and Gibbs, G. (2014). The whole is greater than the sum of its parts: A large-scale study of students' learning in response to different programme assessment patterns. *Assessment and Evaluation in Higher Education*, 39(1), 73–88.

Jessop, T., McNab, N. and Gubby, L. (2012). Mind the gap: An analysis of how quality assurance processes influence programme assessment patterns. *Active Learning in Higher Education*, 13(2), 143–154.

Jin, X.-H. (2012). A comparative study of effectiveness of peer assessment of individuals' contributions to group projects in undergraduate construction management core units. *Assessment and Evaluation in Higher Education*, 37(5), 577–589.

Johnston, B. (2004). Summative assessment of portfolios: An examination of different approaches to agreement over outcomes. *Studies in Higher Education*, 29(3), 395–412.

Jones, O. and Gorra, A. (2013). Assessment feedback only on demand: Supporting the few not supplying the many. *Active Learning in Higher Education*, 14(2), 149–161.

Joughin, G. (1998). Dimensions of oral assessment. *Assessment and Evaluation in Higher Education*, 23(4), 367–378.

Joughin, G. (2007). Student conceptions of oral presentations. *Studies in Higher Education*, 32(3), 323–336.

Joughin, G. (2010). The hidden curriculum revisited: A critical review of research into the influence of summative assessment on learning. *Assessment and Evaluation in Higher Education*, 35(3), 335–345.

Kahneman, D. (2011). *Thinking, Fast and Slow*. London: Penguin.

Kandlbinder, P. (2013). Signature concepts of key researchers in higher education teaching and learning. *Teaching in Higher Education*, 18(1), 1–12.

Kember, D. (1996). The intention to both memorise and understand: Another approach to learning? *Higher Education*, 31(3), 341–351.

Kember, D. (2000). Misconceptions about the learning approaches, motivation and study practices of Asian students. *Higher Education*, 40(1), 99–121.

Kember, D. (2007). *Enhancing University Teaching: Lessons from Research into Award-winning Teachers*. London: Routledge.

Kember, D. and Gow, L. (1990). Cultural specificity of approaches to study. *British Journal of Educational Psychology*, 60(3), 356–363.

Kerr, H. (1983). Motivation losses in small groups: A social dilemma analysis. *Journal of Personality and Social Psychology*, 45(4), 819–828.

King, S. and Robinson, C. (2009). 'Pretty Lights' and Maths! Increasing student engagement and enhancing learning through the use of electronic voting systems. *Computers and Education*, 53(1), 189–199.

Klenowski, V. (2002). *Developing Portfolios for Learning and Assessment*. London: Routledge.

Klenowski, V. (2010). Portfolio assessment. In B. McGaw, E. Baker and P. Peterson (eds), *International Encyclopedia of Education* (3rd edition) (pp. 236–242). Oxford: Elsevier.

Klenowski, V. and Wyatt-Smith, C. (2014). *Assessment for Education: Standards, Judgment and Moderation*. Thousand Oaks, CA: Sage.

Kluger, A. and DeNisi, A. (1996). The effects of feedback interventions on performance: A historical review, a meta-analysis, and a preliminary feedback intervention theory. *Psychological Bulletin*, 119(2), 254–284.

Knight, P. (2002a). *Being a Teacher in Higher Education*. Buckingham: Society for Research into Higher Education and Open University Press.

Knight, P. (2002b). Summative assessment in higher education: Practices in disarray. *Studies in Higher Education*, 27(3), 275–286.

Knight, P. and Yorke, M. (2003). *Assessment, Learning and Employability*. Maidenhead: Society for Research into Higher Education and Open University Press.

Krause, K. and Coates, H. (2008). Students' engagement in first-year university. *Assessment and Evaluation in Higher Education*, 33(5), 493–505.

Kuh, G. (2009). What student affairs professionals need to know about student engagement. *Journal of College Student Development*, 50(6), 683–706.

Lai, K. (2012). Assessing participation skills: Online discussion with peers. *Assessment and Evaluation in Higher Education*, 37(8), 933–947.

Laming, D. (2004). *Human Judgment: The Eye of the Beholder*. London: Thomson.

Leung, D., Ginns, P. and Kember, D. (2008). Examining the cultural specificity of approaches to learning in universities in Hong Kong and Sydney. *Journal of Cross-cultural Psychology*, 39(3), 251–266.

Li, J. and De Luca, R. (2012). Review of assessment feedback. *Studies in Higher Education*, 39(2), 378–393.

Li, M. and Campbell, J. (2008). Asian students' perceptions of group work and group assignments in a New Zealand tertiary institution. *Intercultural Education*, 19(3), 203–216.

Lipnevich, A. and Smith, J. (2009). Effects of differential feedback on students' examination performance. *Journal of Experimental Psychology: Applied*, 15(4), 319–333.

Liu, N. and Carless, D. (2006). Peer feedback: The learning element of peer assessment. *Teaching in Higher Education*, 11(3), 279–290.

Lizzio, A. and Wilson, K. (2013). First-year students' appraisal of assessment tasks: Implications for efficacy, engagement and performance. *Assessment and Evaluation in Higher Education*, 38(4), 389–406.

Lunt, T. and Curran, J. (2010). 'Are you listening please?' The advantages of electronic audio feedback compared to written feedback. *Assessment and Evaluation in Higher Education*, 35(7), 759–769.

Lyons, P. (1989). Assessing classroom participation. *College Teaching*, 37(1), 36–38.

Macdonald, J. (2002). 'Getting it together and being put on the spot': Synopsis, motivation and examination. *Studies in Higher Education*, 27(3), 329–338.

Macfarlane, B. (2015). *Freedom to Learn*. London: Routledge.

Maclellan, E. (2001). Assessment for learning: The differing perceptions of tutors and students. *Assessment and Evaluation in Higher Education*, 26(4), 307–318.

Maclellan, E. (2004a). Authenticity in assessment tasks: A heuristic exploration of academics' perceptions. *Higher Education Research and Development*, 23(1), 19–33.

Maclellan, E. (2004b). How convincing is alternative assessment for use in higher education? *Assessment and Evaluation in Higher Education*, 29(3), 311–321.

Magin, D. and Helmore, P. (2001). Peer and teacher assessments of oral presentation skills: How reliable are they? *Studies in Higher Education*, 26(3), 289–298.

Mann, S. (2001). Alternative perspectives on the student experience: Alienation and engagement. *Studies in Higher Education*, 26(1), 7–19.

Marton, F. and Säljö, R. (1976). On qualitative differences in learning. II: Outcome as a function of the learner's conception of the task. *British Journal of Educational Psychology*, 46(2), 115–127.

McArthur, J. and Huxham, M. (2013). Feedback unbound: From master to usher. In S. Merry, M. Price, D. Carless and M. Taras (eds), *Reconceptualising Feedback in Higher Education: Developing Dialogue with Students* (pp. 92–102). London: Routledge.

McCune, V. and Hounsell, D. (2005). The development of students' ways of thinking and practising in three final-year biology courses. *Higher Education*, 49(3), 255–289.

McDowell, L. and Brown, S. (2001). Assessing students: Cheating and plagiarism. http://78.158.56.101/archive/palatine/files/987.pdf. Accessed 27 September 2013.

McDowell, L. and Sambell, K. (1999). The experience of innovative assessment: Student perspectives. In S. Brown and A. Glasner (eds), *Assessment Matters in Higher Education* (pp. 71–82). Maidenhead: Society for Research into Higher Education and Open University Press.

McLean, A., Bond, C. and Nicholson, H. (2014). An anatomy of feedback: A phenomenographic investigation of undergraduate students' conceptions of feedback. *Studies in Higher Education*, DOI: 10.1080/03075079.2013.855718.

Messick, S. (1994). The interplay of evidence and consequences in the validation of performance assessment. *Educational Researcher*, 23(2), 13–23.

Miller, C. and M. Parlett. (1974). *Up to the Mark: A Study of the Examination Game*. London: Society for Research into Higher Education.

Mogey, N., Cowan, J., Paterson, J. and Purcell, M. (2012). Students' choices between typing and handwriting in examinations. *Active Learning in Higher Education*, 13(2), 117–128.

Molloy, E., Borrell-Carrio, F. and Epstein, R. (2013). The impact of emotions in feedback. In D. Boud and E. Molloy (eds), *Feedback in Higher and Professional Education* (pp. 50–71). London: Routledge.

Molloy, E. and Boud, D. (2013). Changing conceptions of feedback. In D. Boud and E. Molloy (eds), *Feedback in Higher and Professional Education* (pp. 11–33). London: Routledge.

Mostert, M. and Snowball, J. (2013). Where angels fear to tread: Online peer-assessment in a large first-year class. *Assessment and Evaluation in Higher Education*, 38(6), 674–686.

Neumann, R., Parry, S. and Becher, T. (2002). Teaching and learning in their disciplinary contexts: A conceptual analysis. *Studies in Higher Education*, 27(4), 405–417.

Newton, P. (2007). Clarifying the purposes of educational assessment. *Assessment in Education*, 14(2), 149–170.

Nicol, D. (2007). Laying a foundation for lifelong learning: Case studies of e-assessment in large 1st-year classes. *British Journal of Educational Technology*, 38(4), 668–678.

Nicol, D. (2009). Assessment for learner self-regulation: Enhancing achievement in the first year using learning technologies. *Assessment and Evaluation in Higher Education*, 34(3), 335–352.

Nicol, D. (2010). From monologue to dialogue: Improving written feedback processes in mass higher education. *Assessment and Evaluation in Higher Education*, 35(5), 501–517.

Nicol, D. and Draper, S. (2009). A blueprint for transformational organizational change in higher education: REAP as a case study. In T. Mayes, D. Morrison, H. Mellar, P. Bullen and M. Oliver (eds), *Transforming Higher Education through Technology-enhanced Learning* (pp. 191–207). York: Higher Education Academy.

Nicol, D. and Macfarlane-Dick, D. (2006). Formative assessment and self-regulated learning: A model and seven principles of good feedback practice. *Studies in Higher Education*, 31(2), 199–218.

Nicol, D., Thomson, A. and Breslin, C. (2014). Rethinking feedback practices in higher education: A peer review perspective. *Assessment and Evaluation in Higher Education*, 39(1), 102–122.

Norton, L. (2004). Using assessment criteria as learning criteria: A case study in psychology. *Assessment and Evaluation in Higher Education*, 29(6), 687–702.

Norton, L., Dickins, T. and McLaughlin Cook, A. (1996). Rules of the game in essay writing. *Psychology Teaching Review*, 5(1), 1–14.

Norton, L., Norton, B. and Shannon, L. (2013). Revitalising assessment design: What is holding new lecturers back? *Higher Education*, 66(2), 233–251.

Norton, L., Tilley, A., Newstead, S. and Franklyn-Stokes, A. (2001). The pressures of assessment in undergraduate courses and their effect on student behaviours. *Assessment and Evaluation in Higher Education*, 26(3), 269–284.

O'Donovan, B., Price, M. and Rust, C. (2001). The student experience of the introduction of a common criteria assessment grid across a department. *Innovations in Education and Teaching International*, 38(1), 74–85.

Offerdahl, E. and Tomanek, D. (2011). Changes in instructors' assessment thinking related to experimentation with new strategies. *Assessment and Evaluation in Higher Education*, 36(7), 781–795.

Orr, S. (2007). Assessment moderation: Constructing the marks and constructing the students. *Assessment and Evaluation in Higher Education*, 32(6), 645–656.

Orr, S. (2010a). Collaborating or fighting for the marks? Students' experiences of group work assessment in the creative arts. *Assessment and Evaluation in Higher Education*, 35(3), 301–313.

Orr, S. (2010b). 'We kind of try to merge our own experience with the objectivity of the criteria': The role of connoisseurship and tacit practice in undergraduate Fine Art assessment. *Art, Design and Communication in Higher Education*, 9(1), 5–19.

Orr, S. and Bloxham, S. (2012). Making judgments about students making work: Lecturers' assessment practices in art and design. *Arts and Humanities in Higher Education*, 12(2–3), 234–253.

Orr, S., Blythman, M. and Blair, B. (2007). Critiquing the crit. Higher Education Academy. www.adm.heacademy.ac.uk/library/files/adm-hea-projects/learning-and-teaching-projects/crit-staff-guide.pdf. Accessed 19 April 2013.

Orr, S., Yorke, M. and Blair, B. (2014). 'The answer is brought about from within you': A student-centred perspective on pedagogy in Art and Design. *International Journal of Art and Design Education*, 33(1), 32–45.

Orsmond, P. and Merry, S. (2013). The importance of self-assessment in students' use of tutors' feedback: A qualitative study of high and non-high achieving Biology undergraduates. *Assessment and Evaluation in Higher Education*, 38(6), 737–753.

Orsmond, P., Merry, S. and Reiling, K. (2002). The use of exemplars and formative feedback when using student derived marking criteria in peer and self-assessment. *Assessment and Evaluation in Higher Education*, 27(4), 309–323.

Orsmond, P., Merry, S. and Reiling, K. (2005). Biology students' utilization of tutors' formative feedback: A qualitative interview study. *Assessment and Evaluation in Higher Education*, 30(4), 369–386.

Panadero, E. and Jonsson, A. (2013). The use of scoring rubrics for formative assessment purposes revisited: A review. *Educational Research Review*, 9, 129–144.

Park, C. (2003). In other (people's) words: Plagiarism by university students – literature and lessons. *Assessment and Evaluation in Higher Education*, 28(5), 471–488.

Parkin, H., Hepplestone, S., Holden, G., Irwin, B. and Thorpe, L. (2012). A role for technology in enhancing students' engagement with feedback. *Assessment and Evaluation in Higher Education*, 37(8), 963–973.

Parnell, R. and Sara, R. (2007). *The Crit: An Architecture Student's Handbook*. Amsterdam: Architectural Press.

Patry, M. (2009). Clickers in large classes: From student perceptions towards an understanding of best practices. *International Journal for the Scholarship of Teaching and Learning*, 3(2). http://digitalcommons.georgiasouthern.edu/ij-sotl/vol3/iss2/17. Accessed 28 October 2014.

Patton, C. (2012). 'Some kind of weird, evil experiment': Student perceptions of peer assessment. *Assessment and Evaluation in Higher Education*, 37(6), 719–731.

Pauli, R., Mohiyeddini, C., Bray, D., Michie, F. and Street, B. (2008). Individual differences in negative group work experiences in collaborative student learning. *Educational Psychology*, 28(1), 47–58.

Payne, B., Monk-Turner, E., Smith, D. and Sumter, M. (2006). Improving group work: Voices of students. *Education*, 126(3), 441–448.

Payne, E. and Brown, G. (2011). Communication and practice with examination criteria: Does this influence performance in examinations? *Assessment and Evaluation in Higher Education*, 36(6), 619–626.

Pekrun, R., Goetz, T., Titz, W. and Perry, R. (2002). Academic emotions in students' self-regulated learning and achievement: A program of qualitative and quantitative research. *Educational Psychologist*, 37(2), 91–105.

Percy, C. (2004). Critical absence versus critical engagement: Problematics of the crit in design learning and teaching. *Art, Design and Communication in Higher Education*, 2(3), 143–154.

Pieterse, V. and Thompson, L. (2010). Academic alignment to reduce the presence of 'social loafers' and 'diligent isolates' in student teams. *Teaching in Higher Education*, 15(4), 355–367.

Polanyi, M. (1967). *The Tacit Dimension*. New York: Anchor Books.

Postareff, L., Virtanen, V., Katajavuori, N. and Lindblom-Ylanne, S. (2012). Academics' conceptions of assessment and their assessment practices. *Studies in Educational Evaluation*, 38(1), 84–92.

Poulos, A. and Mahony, M. (2008). Effectiveness of feedback: The students' perspective. *Assessment and Evaluation in Higher Education*, 33(2), 143–154.

Price, M. (2005). Assessment standards: The role of communities of practice and the scholarship of assessment. *Assessment and Evaluation in Higher Education*, 30(3), 215–230.

Price, M. (2013). Fostering institutional change: Overview. In S. Merry, M. Price, D. Carless and M. Taras (eds), *Reconceptualising Feedback in Higher Education: Developing Dialogue with Students* (pp. 145–146). London: Routledge.

Price, M., Carroll, J., O'Donovan, B. and Rust, C. (2011). If I was going there I wouldn't start from here: A critical commentary on current assessment practice. *Assessment and Evaluation in Higher Education*, 36(4), 479–492.

Price, M., Handley, K. and Millar, J. (2011). Feedback: Focusing attention on engagement. *Studies in Higher Education*, 36(8), 879–896.

Price, M., Handley, K., Millar, J. and O'Donovan, B. (2010). Feedback: All that effort, but what is the effect? *Assessment and Evaluation in Higher Education*, 35(3), 277–289.

Price, M. and Rust, C. (1999). The experience of introducing a common criteria assessment grid across an academic department. *Quality in Higher Education*, 5(2), 133–144.

Price, M., Rust, C., O'Donovan, B. and Handley, K. (2012). *Assessment Literacy: The Foundation for Improving Student Learning*. Oxford: Oxford Centre for Staff and Learning Development.

Prosser, M. (2013a). Quality teaching, quality learning. In D. Salter (ed.), *Cases on Quality Teaching Practices in Higher Education* (pp. 26–37). Hershey, PA: Information Science.

Prosser, M. (2013b). The four-year degree in Hong Kong: An opportunity for quality enhancement. In R. Land and G. Gordon (eds), *Enhancing Quality in Higher Education: International Perspectives* (pp. 201–212). London: Routledge.

Prosser, M., Martin, E., Trigwell, K., Ramsden, P. and Lueckenhausen, G. (2005). Academics' experiences of understanding of their subject matter and the relationship of this to their experiences of teaching and learning. *Instructional Science*, 33(2), 137–157.

Prosser, M. and Trigwell. K. (1999). *Understanding Learning and Teaching: The Experience in Higher Education*. Philadelphia, PA: Open University Press.

Quality Assurance Agency for Higher Education in England (QAA) (2009). *Thematic Enquiries into Concerns about Academic Quality and Standards in Higher Education in England*. www.qaa.ac.uk/Publications/InformationAndGuidance/Documents/Final ReportApril09.pdf. Accessed 8 April 2013.

Ramsden, P. (1992). *Learning to Teach in Higher Education*. London: Routledge.

Ramsden, P. (2003). *Learning to Teach in Higher Education* (2nd edition). London: Routledge Falmer.

Reddy, Y. and Andrade, H. (2010). A review of rubric use in higher education. *Assessment and Evaluation in Higher Education*, 35(4), 435–448.

Richardson, J. (2014). Coursework versus examinations in end-of-module assessment: A literature review. *Assessment and Evaluation in Higher Education*, DOI: 10.1080/02602938.2014.919628.

Rocca, K. (2010). Student participation in the college classroom: An extended multidisciplinary review. *Communication Education*, 59(2), 185–213.

Rogers, S. (2013). Calling the question: Do college instructors actually grade participation? *College Teaching*, 61(1), 11–22.

Roxa, T. and Martensson, K. (2009). Significant conversations and significant networks. *Studies in Higher Education*, 34(5), 547–559.

Roxa, T., Martensson, K. and Alveteg, M. (2011). Understanding and influencing teaching and learning cultures at university: A network approach. *Higher Education*, 62(1), 99–111.

Russell, M., Bygate, D. and Barefoot, H. (2013). Making learning-oriented assessment the experience of all our students: Supporting institutional change. In S. Merry, M. Price, D. Carless and M. Taras (eds), *Reconceptualising Feedback in Higher Education: Developing Dialogue with Students* (pp. 172–189). London: Routledge.

Rust, C., O'Donovan, B. and Price, M. (2005). A social constructivist assessment process model: How the research literature shows us this could be best practice. *Assessment and Evaluation in Higher Education*, 30(3), 231–240.

Rust, C., Price, M. and O'Donovan, B. (2003). Improving students' learning by developing their understanding of assessment criteria and processes. *Assessment and Evaluation in Higher Education*, 28(2), 147–164.

Sadler, D.R. (1987). Specifying and promulgating achievement standards. *Oxford Review of Education*, 13(2), 191–209.

Sadler, D.R. (1989). Formative assessment and the design of instructional systems. *Instructional Science*, 18(2), 119–144.

Sadler, D.R. (2002). Ah! . . . So that's 'quality'. In P. Schwartz and G. Webb (eds), *Assessment: Case Studies, Experience and Practice from Higher Education* (pp. 130–136). London: Kogan Page.

Sadler, D.R. (2005). Interpretations of criteria based assessment and grading in higher education. *Assessment and Evaluation in Higher Education*, 30(2), 175–194.

Sadler, D.R. (2009a). Grade integrity and the representation of academic achievement. *Studies in Higher Education*, 34(7), 807–826.

Sadler, D.R. (2009b). Indeterminacy in the use of preset criteria for assessment and grading. *Assessment and Evaluation in Higher Education*, 34(2), 159–179.

Sadler, D.R. (2009c). Transforming holistic assessment and grading into a vehicle for complex learning. In G. Joughin (ed.), *Assessment, Learning and Judgment in Higher Education* (pp. 45–63). Dordrecht: Springer.

Sadler, D.R. (2010a). Beyond feedback: Developing student capability in complex appraisal. *Assessment and Evaluation in Higher Education*, 35(5), 535–550.

Sadler, D.R. (2010b). Fidelity as a precondition for integrity in grading academic achievement. *Assessment and Evaluation in Higher Education*, 35(6), 727–743.

Sadler, D.R. (2013a). Assuring academic achievement standards: From moderation to calibration. *Assessment in Education*, 20(1), 5–19.

Sadler, D.R. (2013b). Opening up feedback: Teaching learners to see. In S. Merry, M. Price, D. Carless and M. Taras (eds), *Reconceptualising Feedback in Higher Education: Developing Dialogue with Students* (pp. 54–63). London: Routledge.

Sambell, K. (2013). Involving students in the scholarship of assessment: Student voices on the feedback agenda for change. In S. Merry, M. Price, D. Carless and M. Taras (eds), *Reconceptualising Feedback in Higher Education: Developing Dialogue with Students* (pp. 80–91). London: Routledge.

Sambell, K. and McDowell, L. (1998). The construction of the hidden curriculum: Messages and meanings in the assessment of student learning. *Assessment and Evaluation in Higher Education*, 23(4), 391–402.

Sambell, K., McDowell, L. and Brown, S. (1997). 'But is it fair?' An exploratory study of student perceptions of the consequential validity of assessment. *Studies in Educational Evaluation*, 23(4), 349–371.

Sambell, K., McDowell, L. and Montgomery, C. (2013). *Assessment for Learning in Higher Education*. London: Routledge.

Samuelowicz, K. and Bain, J. (2002). Identifying academics' orientations to assessment practice. *Higher Education*, 43(2), 173–201.

Savin-Baden, M. (2010). The sound of feedback in higher education. *Learning, Media and Technology*, 35(1), 53–64.

Schrand, T. and Eliason, J. (2012). Feedback practices and signature pedagogies: What can liberal arts learn from the design critique? *Teaching in Higher Education*, 17(1), 51–62.

Scoles, J., Huxham, M. and McArthur, J. (2013). No longer exempt from good practice: Using exemplars to close the feedback gap in exams. *Assessment and Evaluation in Higher Education*, 38(6), 631–645.

Scott, S. (2014). Practising what we preach: Towards a student-centred definition of feedback. *Teaching in Higher Education*, 19(1), 49–57.

Scouller, K. (1998). The influence of assessment method on students' learning approaches: Multiple choice question examination versus assignment essay. *Higher Education*, 35(4), 453–472.

Shay, S. (2005). The assessment of complex tasks: A double reading. *Studies in Higher Education*, 30(6), 663–679.

Shay, S. (2008). Beyond social constructivist perspectives on assessment: The centring of knowledge. *Teaching in Higher Education*, 13(5), 595–605.

Shreeve, A., Sims, E. and Trowler, P. (2010). 'A kind of exchange': Learning from art and design teaching. *Higher Education Research and Development*, 29(2), 125–138.

Shulman, L. (2005). Signature pedagogies in the professions. *Daedalus*, 134(3), 52–59.

Shute, V. (2008). Focus on formative feedback. *Review of Educational Research*, 78(1), 153–189.

Sin, C. (2013). Lost in translation: The meaning of learning outcomes across national and institutional policy contexts. *Studies in Higher Education*, 39(10), 1823–1837.

Skelton, A. (2005). *Understanding Teaching Excellence in Higher Education: Towards a Critical Approach*. London: Routledge.

Smith, C., Worsfold, K., Davies, L., Fisher, R. and McPhail, R. (2013). Assessment literacy and student learning: The case for explicitly developing students' 'assessment literacy'. *Assessment and Evaluation in Higher Education*, 38(1), 44–60.

Smith, K. and Tillema, H. (2008). The challenge of assessing portfolios: In search of criteria. In A. Havnes and L. McDowell (eds), *Balancing Dilemmas in Assessment and Learning in Contemporary Education* (pp. 183–195). New York: Routledge.

Snyder, B. (1971). *The Hidden Curriculum*. New York: Knopf.

Stefani, L., Mason, R. and Pegler, C. (2007). *The Educational Potential of ePortfolios: Supporting Personal Development and Reflective Learning*. London: Routledge.

Stowell, M. (2004). Equity, justice and standards: Assessment decision-making in higher education. *Assessment and Evaluation in Higher Education*, 29(4), 495–510.

Sutton, P. (2012). Conceptualizing feedback literacy: Knowing, being and acting. *Innovations in Education and Teaching International*, 49(1), 31–40.

Swaray, R. (2012). An evaluation of a group project designed to reduce free-riding and promote active learning. *Assessment and Evaluation in Higher Education*, 37(3), 285–292.

Tang, C. (1993). Spontaneous collaborative learning: A new dimension in student learning experience? *Higher Education Research and Development*, 12(2), 115–130.

Taras, M. (2006). Do unto others or not: Equity in feedback for undergraduates. *Assessment and Evaluation in Higher Education*, 31(3), 365–377.

Thomson, R. (2013). Implementation of criteria and standards-based assessment: An analysis of first-year learning guides. *Higher Education Research and Development*, 32(2), 272–286.

Tiwari, A. and Tang, C. (2003). From process to outcome: The effect of portfolio assessment on student learning. *Nurse Education Today*, 23(4), 269–277.

Torrance, H. (2007). Assessment as learning? How the use of explicit learning objectives, assessment criteria and feedback in post-secondary education and training can come to dominate learning. *Assessment in Education*, 14(3), 281–294.

Torrance, H. (2012). Formative assessment at the crossroads: Conformative, deformative and transformative assessment. *Oxford Review of Education*, 38(3), 323–342.

Torrance, M., Thomas, G. and Robinson, E. (2000). Individual differences in undergraduate essay-writing strategies: A longitudinal study. *Higher Education*, 39(2), 181–200.

Trevitt, C., Macduff, A. and Steed, A. (2014). (e)Portfolios for learning *and* as evidence of achievement: Scoping the academic practice development agenda ahead. *Internet and Higher Education*, 20, 69–78.

Trigwell, K. and Prosser, M. (1991). Relating learning approaches, perceptions of context and learning outcomes. *Higher Education*, 22(3), 251–266.

Trowler, P. and Knight, P. (2002). Exploring the implementation gap: Theory and practices in change interventions. In P. Trowler (ed.), *Higher Education Policy and Institutional Change* (pp. 142–163). Buckingham: Society for Research into Higher Education and Open University Press.

Tuck, J. (2012). Feedback-giving as social practice: Teachers' perspectives on feedback as institutional requirement, work and dialogue. *Teaching in Higher Education*, 17(2), 209–221.

Vardi, I. (2013). Effectively feeding forward from one written assessment task to the next. *Assessment and Evaluation in Higher Education*, 38(5), 599–610.

Värlander, S. (2008). The role of students' emotions in formal feedback situations. *Teaching in Higher Education*, 13(2), 145–156.

Voelkel, S. and Bennett, D. (2013). New uses for a familiar technology: Introducing mobile phone polling in large classes. *Innovations in Education and Teaching International*, 51(1), 46–58.

Volet, S. and Mansfield, C. (2006). Group work at university: Significance of personal goals in the regulation strategies of students with positive and negative appraisals. *Higher Education Research and Development*, 25(4), 341–356.

Walker, J. (2010). Measuring plagiarism: Researching what students do, not what they say they do. *Studies in Higher Education*, 35(1), 41–59.

Walker, M. (2009). An investigation into written comments on assignments: Do students find them usable? *Assessment and Evaluation in Higher Education*, 34(1), 67–78.

Watkins, D., Dahlin, B. and Ekholm, A. (2005). Awareness of the backwash effect of assessment: A phenomenographic study of the views of Hong Kong and Swedish lecturers. *Instructional Science*, 33(4), 283–309.

Weaver, M. (2006). Do students value feedback? Students perceptions of tutors' written responses. *Assessment and Evaluation in Higher Education*, 31(3), 379–394.

Webster, H. (2006). Power, freedom and resistance: Excavating the design jury. *International Journal of Art and Design Education*, 25(3), 286–296.

White, R. (2000). The student-led 'crit' as a learning device. In D. Nicol and S. Pilling (eds), *Changing Architectural Education: Towards a New Professionalism* (pp. 211–220). London: Taylor & Francis.

Wiggins, G. (1993). Assessment: Authenticity, context and validity. *Phi Delta Kappan*, 75(3), 200–214.

Williams, J. and Kane, D. (2008). Exploring the national student survey: Assessment and feedback issues. www.heacademy.ac.uk/assets/documents/nss/NSS_Assessment_and_Feedback_FullReport_06.05.08.pdf. Accessed 23 September 2013.

Willingham, D. (1990). Effective feedback on written assignments. *Teaching of Psychology*, 17(1), 10–13.

Wimshurst, K. and Manning, M. (2013). Feed-forward assessment, exemplars and peer marking: Evidence of efficacy. *Assessment and Evaluation in Higher Education*, 38(4), 451–465.

Wingate, U. (2010). The impact of formative feedback on the development of academic writing. *Assessment and Evaluation in Higher Education*, 35(5), 519–533.

Wingate, U. (2012). 'Argument!' helping students understand what essay writing is about. *Journal of English for Academic Purposes*, 11(2), 145–154.

Wolf, A. (1995). *Competence-based Assessment*. Buckingham: Open University Press.

Woolf, H. (2004). Assessment criteria: Reflections on current practices. *Assessment and Evaluation in Higher Education*, 29(4), 479–493.

Yang, M. and Carless, D. (2013). The feedback triangle and the enhancement of dialogic feedback processes. *Teaching in Higher Education*, 18(3), 285–297.

Yorke, M. (2008). *Grading Student Achievement in Higher Education: Signals and Shortcomings*. London: Routledge.

Yorke, M. (2011). Summative assessment: Dealing with the measurement fallacy. *Studies in Higher Education*, 36(3), 251–273.

Yorke, M. (2013). Surveys of 'the student experience' and the politics of feedback. In S. Merry, M. Price, D. Carless and M. Taras (eds), *Reconceptualising Feedback in Higher Education: Developing Dialogue with Students* (pp. 6–18). London: Routledge.

Youmans, R. (2011). Does the adoption of plagiarism-detection software in higher education reduce plagiarism? *Studies in Higher Education*, 36(7), 749–761.

Yucel, R., Bird, F., Young, J. and Blanksby, T. (2014). The road to self-assessment: Exemplar marking before peer review develops first year students' capacity to judge the quality of a scientific report. *Assessment and Evaluation in Higher Education*, 39(8), 971–986.

Author index

Subject index